9/2017

D0392272

WITHDRAWN

Unprepared

Unprepared

GLOBAL HEALTH IN A TIME
OF EMERGENCY

Andrew Lakoff

UNIVERSITY OF CALIFORNIA PRESS

University of California Press, one of the most distinguished university presses in the United States, enriches lives around the world by advancing scholarship in the humanities, social sciences, and natural sciences. Its activities are supported by the UC Press Foundation and by philanthropic contributions from individuals and institutions. For more information, visit www.ucpress.edu.

University of California Press
Oakland, California

Library of Congress Cataloging-in-Publication Data

Names: Lakoff, Andrew, 1970- author.
Title: Unprepared : global health in a time of emergency / Andrew Lakoff.
Description: Oakland, California : University of California Press, [2017] | Includes bibliographical references and index.
Identifiers: LCCN 2017005494 (print) | LCCN 2017009193 (ebook) | ISBN 9780520295766 (alk. paper) | ISBN 9780520295759 (cloth : alk. paper) | ISBN 9780520968417 (ebook)
Subjects: LCSH: World health. | Bioterrorism—Prevention. | Emergency management—United States. | Biopolitics. | Public health—United States.
Classification: LCC RA441 .L35 2017 (print) | LCC RA441 (ebook) | DDC 363.325/3—dc23
LC record available at https://lccn.loc.gov/2017005494

Manufactured in the United States of America

26 25 24 23 22 21 20 19 18 17
10 9 8 7 6 5 4 3 2 1

For Daniela

Contents

Introduction

In late 2015, health officials in Brazil reported the appearance and rapid spread of a mosquito-borne pathogen, the Zika virus. The spread of the virus was tentatively linked to an apparent epidemic of a rare and devastating birth defect, microcephaly, and to an upsurge in the number of cases of the neurological disorder Guillain-Barré. Although Zika was not a novel virus, it had never before been linked to such severe outcomes. By February 2016, the virus had infected more than a million Brazilians, and several thousand cases of infant microcephaly had been reported. Infectious disease experts hypothesized that the virus had traveled with tourists to Brazil from French Polynesia two years earlier and feared that the upcoming summer Olympics in Rio de Janeiro would be a likely setting for further global circulation. As the virus was detected in other Latin American countries, some public health officials recommended that women of childbearing age delay pregnancy during the outbreak. The U.S. Centers for Disease Control and Prevention (CDC) issued an advisory suggesting that pregnant women avoid travel to affected areas.

Researchers from North America and Europe hurried to the region of the epidemic to investigate its characteristics. How many cases were there? Could Zika be definitively linked to the cases of microcephaly? The prevention of further transmission would be a challenge, authorities warned. It would be difficult to extinguish the virus through control of its host because the species of mosquito that carried it thrived in crowded urban settings with poor infrastructures of water provision and drainage. And it would be at least a year before researchers could test a potential vaccine against the virus. As the North American summer approached, U.S. health officials became increasingly concerned that the disease would affect populations in southern regions of the country. In the face of mounting worries, the U.S. Food and Drug Administration approved experimental trials of a genetically modified mosquito in Florida, and the CDC released funds to state and local health agencies to support Zika preparedness efforts.

Global health authorities also moved to intervene. On February 1, the Director-General of the World Health Organization (WHO) declared the Zika outbreak a "public health emergency of international concern" (PHEIC). With this announcement, the organization sought to galvanize "a coordinated international response to minimize the threat in affected countries and reduce the risk of further international spread."[1] The act of classifying the situation as a global health emergency indicated both the potential for disaster and the urgency of immediate response.[2] But the official declaration of emergency also did something else: it brought the Zika virus into a technical and administrative relationship with a range of other public health threats. The category of PHEIC, according to WHO, not only encompassed infectious disease outbreaks but could also include incidents of food contamination, toxic chemical releases, or nuclear accidents.[3] Although unique in many respects, the Zika virus now also conformed to a class of event that had come to prominence among scientists, health authorities, and security officials over the prior decade.

The emergency declaration was a way of assimilating the specific event into a more general form, making it comprehensible and potentially manageable.[4] Through the act of classification, Zika was brought into a preexisting governance framework, the International Health Regulations (IHR), which provided health authorities with guideposts for technical and administrative action. The first such action was the establishment of an Emergency Committee comprising infectious disease experts whose task was to advise the WHO director-general on how to manage the outbreak.

The committee's initial recommendations included enhanced surveillance for cases of microcephaly in areas of Zika transmission, precautionary measures to prevent infection, increased research into the etiology of microcephaly, and ongoing discussions with the drug industry and regulatory agencies on vaccine development.

The declaration of a global health emergency, then, did not point to an extralegal state of exception but was rather a technocratic classification designed to integrate the outbreak of a novel disease into a preexisting regulatory framework.[5] The IHR framework envisioned a dangerous new world of potentially catastrophic outbreaks and bound its signatories to provisions for detecting and intervening in such outbreaks. However, although the regulations served as the ligature for the strategy WHO called "global public health security in the 21st century," their actual operation rested on a twentieth-century paradigm of international health in which nation-states remained the site of authority and responsibility while WHO played a role of administrative coordination and technical norm-making.[6] As we will see, the ability of the framework to govern the actions of states in the name of a global space of public health security was highly constrained.

It is with the declaration of a "public health emergency of international concern" that the regulatory capacity of the IHR framework is put to the test. Although the regulations provide criteria for determining whether a specific event should be considered a global health emergency, the effort to galvanize intensive global response through the declaration of a PHEIC has proven politically fraught. Tensions have arisen around questions such as the following: which diseases should be prioritized as potential emergencies? What obligations do wealthy countries have to poor ones at the advent of an emergency? And to what extent does the declaration of an emergency authorize international health officials to regulate the actions of nation-states? In April 2009, WHO made the very first such emergency declaration shortly after the appearance of a novel strain of influenza with the potential to cause a pandemic. When the pandemic strain proved milder than initially feared, the organization faced sharp criticism from some quarters for its proactive response. Five years later, the question of when to declare a health emergency was at the center of another controversy, as the Ebola epidemic raged out of control in West

Africa: in this case, WHO was widely accused of having failed to react in time to the severe threat posed by the outbreak.

With this backdrop in mind, the members of the newly established Emergency Committee charged with Zika response contributed a commentary in *The Lancet* early in 2016 to address the question, "Why is this situation a PHEIC?" The commentary began by listing the legal criteria that a given situation must meet to be considered an official global health emergency: it must constitute a health risk to other countries through international spread; it must require a coordinated response because it is unexpected, serious, or unusual; and it must have implications beyond the affected country that require immediate action.[7] But this list of criteria did not quite address the question that had been posed: what exactly made the situation an emergency? The committee members noted that they had been asked how their decision to declare the Zika epidemic a global health emergency related to deliberations by a different Emergency Committee, two years earlier, over the classification of the outbreak of Ebola in West Africa. "The answer to us is clear," they wrote. The 2014 Ebola epidemic had been classified as a PHEIC "because of what science knew about the Ebola from many years of research during outbreaks in the past." In contrast, the current PHEIC had been declared "because of what is not known about the current increase in reported clusters of microcephaly and other disorders, and how this might relate to concurrent Zika outbreaks." In the first case, the emergency declaration was a result of knowledge; in the second case, it was due to ignorance. Given the state of non-knowledge concerning Zika, the emergency declaration was a call for an intensive scientific mobilization, in particular to understand the relation between the spread of the mosquito-borne pathogen and the upsurge in reported cases of microcephaly.

The explicit goal of the International Health Regulations is to minimize the global spread of an infectious disease and at the same time to discourage countries from imposing unnecessary trade and travel restrictions in response to outbreaks. The regulations were revised in 2005 in response to a newly articulated problem: an apparent surge in the appearance of "emerging diseases" such as hemorrhagic fevers, West Nile virus, pandemic influenza, and extensively drug-resistant tuberculosis (XDR-TB). In the wake of the 2002 SARS (severe acute respiratory syndrome) outbreak, a number of health authorities argued that the existing international health regulations were insufficient to manage this new kind of threat. Emerging diseases had several features in common: they were caused either by previously unknown pathogens or by novel mutations of existing pathogens; their emergence and spread was difficult to predict or prevent; they were difficult or impossible to contain or to treat; and their appearance carried the portent of global catastrophe if not quickly contained.

Another feature shared by these diseases was the explanation of why they were emerging: specialists argued that the increasingly frequent appearance of novel pathogens was the result of radical transformations in the relationship between humans and their environments. These changes included the disturbance of previously isolated ecosystems, increasing population density in urban slums, the rapid global circulation of people, the industrialization of food and agricultural production systems, and the overuse of antibiotics in clinics and livestock facilities. More generally, according to this diagnosis, intensifying modernization processes had generated novel threats that traditional public health measures, from sanitation engineering to mass vaccination, were incapable of managing. As infectious disease specialists and public health authorities looked toward a future horizon of ever-emergent pathogenic threats, they saw a fragile world characterized by interdependence and vulnerability.

If the category of emerging disease seemed self-evident by early 2016, it is important to underline its relatively recent invention. Beginning in the late 1980s and early 1990s, in the midst of the HIV/AIDS pandemic—which unsettled the mid-twentieth-century assumption that infectious disease was on the decline—a group of microbiologists and infectious disease epidemiologists argued that AIDS was a harbinger of many more, as-yet-unknown diseases to come. By the time of the appearance and spread of Zika virus two and a half decades later, international health authorities had sketched, and begun to implement, a diagram for the governance of such diseases, known as "global public health security."[8] This diagram brought together a number of techniques of surveillance and response, such as: internet based disease reporting tools that transcended national systems of case reporting, regional laboratories capable of rapidly analyzing biological samples, stockpiles of vaccines and antimicrobial drugs, incentives to develop new medical countermeasures, and emergency operations centers to coordinate response among disparate agencies. The diagram also included political and administrative measures such as decision tools to guide authorities in selecting which events constitute a global health emergency and injunctions against the imposition of economically damaging travel and trade restrictions.

The objective of global health security is to detect and contain the outbreak of a novel pathogen before it can spread to become a global catastrophe. But the various technical and administrative measures gathered together as part of this diagram should not be understood simply as direct responses to a growing number of emerging disease outbreaks; rather, these measures function to constitute a given situation as an emergency, one that requires an urgent and rapid collective response. In other words, it is not the inherent characteristics of a given disease outbreak but rather the classificatory schema as it combines with the techniques and politics of global health security that makes the event a candidate to become an official emergency. As a result, there is often a lack of fit between the characteristics of a disease event and the systems that are mobilized to respond to it. This is well illustrated by the international response to the early stages of the 2014 Ebola epidemic—or rather, the initial lack of such response. Crucially, for several months as the epidemic spread in West Africa, the event was not officially classified as a PHEIC and was, more broadly, ignored by the international community, with the exception of medical humanitarian organizations. The reasons for this delay remain a topic of debate, but arguably, at its early stages the outbreak did not fit international health officials' administrative criteria for the declaration of an emergency. At the time, many infectious disease specialists considered Ebola to be a highly dangerous but locally manageable disease and one that was unlikely to lead to a catastrophic and widespread epidemic.

As this dire failure of response demonstrates, global health security is better seen as a schema or a plan than as a set of effectively functioning mechanisms that can successfully manage any outbreak of emerging disease. Indeed, the rapid declaration by WHO of a global health emergency in the case of Zika can be understood at least in part as a reaction to widespread denunciation of the organization for its slow response to the Ebola epidemic. And in turn, the slow response to Ebola was likely related to criticism for an overly intensive response to swine flu in 2009. With each outbreak of a dangerous new pathogen, then, gaps in the putative global health security system become apparent and calls for reform gain purchase.

This book tells the story of how the fragile and still-uncertain machinery of global health security was cobbled together over a two-decade period, beginning in the early 1990s. It is neither a heroic account of visionary planning by enlightened health authorities, nor a sinister story of the securitization of disease by an ever-expansive governmental apparatus. Rather, it is a story of the assemblage of disparate elements—adapted from fields such as civil defense, emergency management, and international public health—by well-meaning experts and officials and of response failures that have typically led, in turn, to reforms that seek to strengthen or refocus the apparatus.[9] The analysis centers on the ways that authorities—whether public health officials, national security experts, life scientists, or other privileged observers—conceptualize and act on an encroaching future of disease emergence. This uncertain future can be taken up and made into an object of present intervention according to multiple rationalities: as an object of probabilistic calculation, as a specter that must be avoided through precautionary intervention, or as a potential catastrophe that cannot be evaded but can only be prepared for.[10] In the chapters that follow, we see how these various logics come into tension or combine in response to actual and anticipated disease emergencies.

The book builds conceptually on work in the field of historical ontology, which asks how taken-for-granted objects of existence—whether the economy, the psyche, or the population—are brought into being through contingent and often-overlooked historical processes. Such entities, as Ian Hacking argues, "do not exist in any recognizable form until they are objects of scientific study."[11] Expert knowledge not only describes its objects of interest, then; it also helps to constitute them. In this case, the technical and administrative category of global health emergency is a product not only of the forms of human-ecological interaction through which new pathogens emerge, but also of the scientific frameworks and governmental practices that seek to know and manage these pathogens. From this perspective, the invention of a concept, such as "emerging infectious disease," is a significant event not because it marks the discovery of what had hitherto been unknown, but because it helps bring a new kind of entity into being.

This book tracks the unstable consolidation of global health security through a series of recent episodes and follows the controversies and criticisms these episodes have provoked. Such disputes are productive sites for inquiry into the tacit assumptions that guide the everyday work of experts in fields like epidemiology, virology, and public health policy.[12] It is not, then, a story about a generalized cultural discourse or social imaginary. Rather, it tracks the "serious speech acts" made by authorities in settings of contestation; these statements may come from published articles, official inquiries, public testimony, or journalistic reports.[13] The cases illustrate distinctions in the tacit regimes of knowledge and intervention that experts bring to bear to address situations of urgency and uncertainty, distinctions that become most apparent at moments of public disagreement.

Chapter 1 serves as a prelude to the investigation of global health emergencies, looking into the history of preparedness as a style of reasoning and a set of governmental techniques for approaching uncertain threats. The chapter introduces a key distinction between two ways of thinking about and intervening into a dangerous future. A potential threat can be taken up first as a regularly occurring event whose probability can be calculated based on known patterns of historical incidence and that can be managed through the distribution of risk. Alternatively, it can be understood and managed as an unprecedented but potentially catastrophic event whose consequences can only be managed by using methods of imaginative enactment that enable planners to mitigate vulnerabilities.

The chapter draws on the argument made by historians of statistics that, in the nineteenth century, the accumulation of detailed knowledge about European populations by government bureaucracies made it possible to envision the probable future using new calculative techniques.[14] It asks, in turn: how do contemporary authorities seek to manage potential future dangers, such as an ecological catastrophe or a devastating pandemic, whose probability cannot be statistically calculated and whose potential consequences outstrip the capacities of existing prevention and mitigation measures? To address this question, the chapter turns to the history of civil defense and emergency management. Beginning in the 1960s, the new field of emergency management adapted a number of techniques that had been invented to prepare for nuclear attack, such as scenario-based planning, early warning systems, and medical supply stockpiling, and repurposed them to address a range of other potential emergencies such as natural disasters, ecological accidents, and terrorist attacks. In recent years, the techniques and the thought-style of emergency management have been incorporated into significant policy framework documents such as the *National Preparedness Guidance* and the *National Critical Infrastructure Protection Plan*, and they have structured governmental response to a range of events from Hurricane Katrina to the 2009 swine flu pandemic.

Chapter 2 investigates how these techniques of emergency management were assimilated into the field of public health in the United States, beginning with approaches to the threat of bioterrorism in the 1990s. This process involved the composition of a new object of knowledge and intervention for public health: no longer, or not only, the population but also the infrastructure that underpins response to health emergencies; this includes disease surveillance, stockpiles of countermeasures and methods of rapid distribution, hospital surge capacity, and crisis communications systems. This story is framed through the historical juxtaposition of two responses to the onset of a potential influenza pandemic: first, the 1976 swine flu outbreak; second, the specter of avian influenza in 2005. Whereas in 1976, government officials understood and managed a potential pandemic mainly in terms of the available public health framework of prevention, three decades later, a new regime of public health preparedness had been put in place to address the avian influenza threat.

This shift was the result of a broader transformation: health authorities now conceptualized a future outbreak of a new or reemerging infectious disease as a potentially catastrophic event whose consequences could be mapped in advance using techniques of imaginative enactment such as the scenario-based exercise. This approach was adopted as part of U.S. health and security policy beginning in the mid-1990s, as the specter of emerging disease merged with post–Cold War concerns about bioterrorism to become a generic biological threat. Through the analysis of a 2001 exercise that simulated a smallpox attack, the chapter shows how public health and security were brought together in response to this newly constituted threat.

Chapter 3 examines how public health preparedness was extended as a global strategy in relation to the threat of emerging disease, beginning in the early 2000s. It focuses on the development of the revised International Health Regulations, adopted in 2005 as part of the WHO strategy of "global public health security." The chapter develops an analytic distinction between two regimes for governing global health problems: global health security and humanitarian biomedicine. If global health security focuses on protecting nation-states, especially in the advanced industrial world, from the social and economic threat posed by emerging diseases, humanitarian biomedicine emphasizes the need to save all lives, regardless of political boundaries, from treatable but deadly maladies such as malaria, tuberculosis, and HIV/AIDS.

To illustrate this distinction, the chapter examines tensions that arose as the WHO sought to operationalize its global disease surveillance and response capacity to manage the threat of an avian influenza pandemic. Beginning in 2007, Indonesian health officials refused to share samples of highly pathogenic avian influenza H5N1 with WHO's global influenza surveillance network on the grounds of equity in access to the benefits of virus sharing. Specifically, they sought guarantees that the population would have access to vaccines that had been developed using virus strains found in Indonesian flu patients. Critics of this position argued that in claiming sovereignty over these influenza strains and excluding them from the global surveillance network, the Indonesian government was threatening global health security.

Chapter 4 explores the problem of how to sustain vigilance, among officials and the public, for an event that may or may not occur. It looks in particular at the decision instruments that guide emergency intervention at the outset of an epidemic. Such instruments are designed to focus global attention on the appearance of a novel biological threat, but at the same time they raise new questions: what is a global health emergency? Who is charged with governing such events, and what does such governance imply? These questions were at the center of a 2009 controversy in Europe over the WHO's decision to declare H1N1 swine flu to be a full-blown pandemic, which set in motion mass vaccination campaigns in western Europe and North America.

The chapter introduces the concept of the "sentinel device" to examine the alert system that is at the heart of global health security. Sentinel devices are designed to detect the onset of an otherwise invisible or imperceptible threat; but to trigger intervention, they must be linked to larger systems of response. Although the controversy around the H1N1 pandemic was cast in terms of an ethical debate over possible conflicts of interest within WHO's emergency committee, the chapter shows that it is better understood as a conflict between two distinct ways of understanding and managing public health threats—an approach that must justify action through the statistical calculation of risk versus one that requires vigilant attention to the ongoing possibility of surprise.

Chapter 5 examines the tension between risk assessment as a standard tool for regulatory decision on the one hand, and the demand for preparedness for a catastrophic disease outbreak on the other. It focuses on an unintended consequence of government support for basic virology research as part of pandemic preparedness: the laboratory creation of the very threat that such support is designed to address. The chapter looks at the 2012 controversy over scientists' use of genetic manipulation techniques to create a humanly transmissible strain of H5N1 avian influenza. This research was supported by the National Institutes of Health and was carried out by university-based influenza virologists as part of the U.S. government's pandemic preparedness initiative.

The debate among scientists and regulators over how and whether to regulate such "gain-of-function" experiments demonstrates the problems involved in seeking to quantitatively assess the risk posed by an emerging disease: whereas the regulatory guidelines developed to govern scientific research on pathogenic threats are based on the framework of technical risk assessment, the threat of the emergence of a humanly transmissible strain of H5N1 eludes such calculation. The chapter shows how actors on each side of the debate justify their claims using the idiom of risk assessment and how each group insists on the validity of its calculation. In the end, the debate escapes resolution precisely because of the difficulty of assimilating the risk of either a deadly mutation in nature or a catastrophic accident in a laboratory within the technical framework of risk assessment.

In the final chapter, the book investigates the intense public criticism faced by WHO in the aftermath of the 2014 Ebola epidemic. These denunciations focused in particular on the organization's late declaration of a global health emergency. The chapter suggests that the slow international response to the early stages of the epidemic was at least partly the result of a transformation in the meaning of Ebola. From the perspective of global health governance, the significance of the disease shifted between the late 1980s, when the problem of emerging infectious disease was first articulated, and early 2014, when the epidemic in West Africa began. Whereas in the earlier period, Ebola was paradigmatic of the potentially catastrophic outbreak of a novel pathogen, by 2014 many experts saw the disease as a dangerous but relatively manageable affliction that typically struck marginal, rural populations. In other words, it had become a disease that could be contained through the organizations and techniques of humanitarian biomedicine rather than those of global health security.

This contrast between two visions of the same disease helps explain why, at the initial stages of the 2014 Ebola epidemic, WHO and other public health authorities did not expect the outbreak to turn into a global health catastrophe—and thus did not invoke the decision instrument designed to galvanize intensive global response. The failure of global health security to manage the Ebola crisis led to widespread criticism and calls for reform. The demand was for more and better preparedness, in anticipation of the next emergency. As we can see from these various instances, preparedness has come to be a taken for granted norm of government. Indeed, a failure to be prepared for a foreseeable event—if the event occurs—can prove to be politically disastrous, as the aftermath of Hurricane Katrina demonstrated.

Gradually, over the course of two and a half decades, a new assemblage for understanding and intervening in global health problems has been cobbled together. This book explores the condition of its formation, as well as its possibilities and limitations as new disease emergencies continue to arise. The book seeks neither to warn its readers that we must become more prepared for future health disasters nor to criticize governments and health authorities for anticipating the wrong things. Rather, it asks: how did we come to be "unprepared" for future disease emergencies? By this question, I do not mean to suggest that we were once well prepared and are now less so, but instead to pose the question: how did the norm of preparedness come to structure expert thought and action concerning the future of infectious disease?

1 A Continuous State of Readiness

One evening the week after Hurricane Katrina struck the Gulf Coast in August 2005, the television news anchor Anderson Cooper was interviewed by talk show host Charlie Rose. Cooper was still on the scene in New Orleans, with the inundated city in the background and a look of harried concern on his face. Cooper had been among the first reporters to challenge official accounts that hurricane relief operations were functioning smoothly, based on the stark contradiction between disturbing images on the ground and governmental claims of a competent response effort. He was shocked and dismayed by what he was finding in New Orleans, but also seemed moved, even transformed, by his role as a chronicler of domestic catastrophe. He had covered disasters in Somalia, Sri Lanka, and elsewhere, he said, but never expected to see images like these in the United States: hungry refugees, widespread looting, corpses left on the street to decompose. Toward the end of the interview, Rose asked him what he had learned from covering the event. Cooper paused, reflected for a moment, and then answered: "We are not as ready as we can be."

There were a number of possible lessons that could have been drawn from the hurricane and its aftermath: concerning the role of urban poverty in increasing vulnerability to disaster, the social isolation of the elderly, the deterioration of flood protection infrastructure, and so on. But Cooper's intuitive, if inchoate, interpretation of the hurricane's meaning—in terms of a state of collective "readiness"—was common among authorized observers of the event, from journalists to public officials. Notably, this shared interpretation was prospective and generic, alluding to a range of potential future disasters rather than focusing on the hurricane itself.

In the aftermath of Katrina, it was common to see comparisons made between the federal government's failed response to the hurricane and its ostensibly more successful response to the terrorist attacks of September 11, 2001. To an observer a decade earlier, it might have been surprising that a natural disaster and a terrorist attack would be considered part of a shared problem space. And the image, three weeks after Katrina struck, of President George W. Bush flying to the headquarters of USNORTHCOM, a military installation designated for use in national security crises, to monitor the progress of Hurricane Rita as it hurtled toward Texas would have been equally perplexing. The failed governmental response to Katrina also pointed toward the onset of other possible emergencies, such as the outbreak of a novel and deadly infectious disease. "The danger of a major hurricane hitting the Gulf Coast was ignored until it was too late," declared Senator Ted Kennedy in early October. "We must not make the same mistake with pandemic flu. Other nations have taken effective steps to prepare, and America cannot afford to continue to lag behind."[1]

Six months after the hurricane, the White House released its official assessment of the "lessons learned" from the federal government's response to the event. What Cooper's response and the White House report had in common was their understanding of the occurrence of a catastrophic event in terms of the failure of a preparedness system. Preparedness, noted the report, was essential not only in anticipation of natural disasters but also for managing intentional acts of malice: the task of the White House report was to help the nation to become "better prepared for any challenge of nature or act of evil men that could threaten our people." The report interpreted the hurricane, in retrospect, as a test of the nation's preparedness system. It sought to assess "the key failures during the Federal response to Hurricane Katrina," not to affix blame but rather "to identify systemic gaps and improve our preparedness for the next disaster—natural or man-made."

According to the report, "four critical flaws in our national preparedness became evident" in the government's response to the hurricane.[2] Each of these flaws concerned the political administration of emergency: the unified management of the national response, command and control structures, knowledge of preparedness plans, and regional planning and coordination. In sum, the report outlined a schema of governmental preparedness designed to serve as the basis for corrective action.

This chapter describes the historical emergence and gradual consolidation of "national preparedness" as a governmental approach to managing perceived threats. As a normative rationality coupled to a set of administrative techniques, national preparedness provides authorities with tools for grasping uncertain future events and bringing them into a space of present intervention. This analysis helps to explain an otherwise puzzling aspect of contemporary governmental practice: how a range of seemingly disparate potential threats—including terrorist attacks, natural disasters, and pandemics—have been brought into a common framework of collective security. It also points forward to the broader theme of the book: how the norm of preparedness came to be applied to the category of "emerging disease" at a global scale.

Preparedness marks out a limited but generally agreed-on terrain for the management of threats to collective life, making it possible to gather together a range of possible events under a common rubric. Its techniques operate to bring these potential events into the present as potential future disasters that expose current vulnerabilities. In making future disasters into objects of present reflection and action, preparedness also generates responsibility: the fact that one might have prepared means that, if the anticipated disaster does occur and response is insufficient, one should in retrospect have been better prepared. The techniques of preparedness, then, are a response to the political demand posed by the contemporary category of emergency.[3] The chapter begins with a schematic contrast between two styles of reasoning about potential future threats: risk and preparedness. It argues that preparedness is an especially salient approach to events that seem to exceed the capacities of the tools of risk assessment—threats whose likelihood is difficult to calculate using statistical means but whose consequences could be catastrophic.

THE LIMITS OF RISK ASSESSMENT

In its technical sense, the term "risk" does not signify a danger or peril per se, but rather a "specific mode of treatment of certain events capable of happening to a group of individuals," as the historian François Ewald writes.[4] In the field of private insurance, where tools of risk assessment were invented, these events might include accidents, illnesses, or unemployment. Risk as a "mode of treatment" of such events involves, first, tracking the historical incidence of such events over time within a given population and then, based on this data, calculating the anticipated rate of occurrence of such events in the future. As Ewald notes, the assessment of risk is a way of reordering reality: what was previously understood as a singular event that disrupted the normal order comes to be seen as a normal, relatively predictable occurrence. Knowledge of this rate of incidence, gathered through actuarial tables, has enabled insurers to rationally distribute risk across a population.

The assessment of risk has also been central to governmental efforts to know and improve the welfare of national populations, beginning in the nineteenth century when European governments began to adopt the actuarial tools that were initially developed in the context of private insurance. Such efforts have focused in particular on phenomena occurring with regularity over a population such as disease, poverty, and industrial accidents.[5] Through programs such as public health and social insurance, modern governments have sought to manage the risks faced by national populations.

This chapter takes up the history of governmental risk management at a novel conjuncture, in the second half of the twentieth century. As social theorists such as Ulrich Beck and Anthony Giddens have argued, this period saw the appearance of a new problem for the government of risk: how to approach threats whose probability was difficult or impossible to calculate but whose consequences could be catastrophic.[6] In the decades after World War II, experts and policy-makers became increasingly concerned with the challenge posed by such catastrophic threats—from nuclear accidents, to mass casualty terrorism, to anthropogenic climate change. These dangers, Beck writes, "shape a perception that uncontrollable risk is now irredeemable and deeply engineered into all the processes that sustain life in advanced societies."[7] For such observers, the existing knowledge practices and institutions of risk governance were inadequate for understanding and managing the new catastrophic threats. Indeed, some of the very technological systems that had been designed to improve collective well-being were now identified as sources of vulnerability.

In recent years, a number of analysts have pursued the question of how governments and the public should assess and manage the risk posed by catastrophic threats.[8] Much of this work has focused on the limits of calculative rationality in approaching the threat of occurrences that are either uncertain—because knowledge about their frequency or harm is lacking—or that would be so devastating in their consequences that the usual calculus of cost and benefit cannot be applied. This has led to questions such as the following: Can formal techniques of risk assessment be applied to uncertain or potentially catastrophic threats? And what mechanisms of risk governance might be relevant where formal risk assessment reaches a limit?

For one line of scholarship on risk and rationality, which arose from social anthropology, psychology, and economics in the 1970s, the central issue concerns the divide between expert and lay evaluations of risk and the implications of this divide for public policy. Classic studies sought to explain why individuals and social groups either over- or undervalued certain risks, through the examination of collective values, common cognitive heuristics, or structures of bounded rationality.[9] Such approaches often share an assumption, whether implicit or explicit, that lay "misperceptions" of risk can be contrasted with neutral expert understandings. The role of government, in this view, is to use objective methods of risk assessment to shape rational public policy, even in the face of highly uncertain or potentially catastrophic threats.[10]

Scholars in the social studies of science have cast doubt on any assumption that there is an objective and secure position of expert knowledge about risk that can be reliably used to correct public misperceptions. Observing disagreement among experts on issues such as drug safety or the regulation of environmental toxins, and broad uncertainties in areas like emerging pathogens and terrorism, they have argued that any framework of risk governance must acknowledge the limits of technical risk assessment. Moreover, these scholars have also pointed out that certain members of the public—or "lay experts"—may have important insights into the nature of risk that authorized experts miss, given their narrow framings of cost and benefit.[11] The limits of expert risk assessment, they argue, point toward a new politics of precaution in the face of catastrophic threats, or toward a democratization of risk governance.[12]

In what follows, I build on this work on the role of expert knowledge in governing catastrophic risk but pose a different set of questions. My analysis builds from the observation that, over the past several decades and in multiple arenas of scientific and governmental activity, experts have invented an array of technical practices that are designed to assess and manage uncertain and potentially catastrophic threats. Here I consider risk assessment and preparedness as distinctive "styles of reasoning" about potential threats, following Ian Hacking's analysis of the plurality of ways of making truth claims in the sciences.[13] In other words, there is not a singular or unified method for technically and politically approaching security problems. Rather, there are different ways of understanding and managing threats that may be incommensurable with one another and that may be associated with particular institutional settings, forms of professional training, or political stances. In looking at the practices of experts charged with managing catastrophic risk, the task for the critical observer is not to judge which approach to future threats is most valid, but rather to explain how a given style of reasoning has emerged in a specific context and then extended into new arenas.

FROM PRECAUTION TO PREPAREDNESS

The framework of risk assessment does not assume that the future will necessarily turn out as calculated. Rather, having performed a risk assessment provides a technically defensible rationale for a given decision so that future blame can be avoided. Niklas Luhmann describes the vantage point of risk assessment as one of "provisional foresight": the present, he writes, can calculate a future that "can always turn out otherwise." So long as one has calculated correctly, one cannot be blamed later for having made the wrong decision. However, Luhmann notes, this approach to the uncertain future is potentially undermined by the prospect of the incalculable but catastrophic threat. Such an event "is the occurrence that no one wants and for which neither probability calculations nor expert opinions are acceptable."[14] One alternative is the principle of precaution, which claims that in the face of uncertainty, one must act to prevent the occurrence of a catastrophic outcome. From the perspective of precaution, having made a risk assessment does not insulate the decision-maker from future blame. According to this logic, in approaching the uncertain future, one must take into account not what is probable or improbable but what is most feared. "I must, out of precaution, imagine the worst possible," writes Ewald.[15]

The principle of precaution has been an influential response to certain hazards, especially the threat of ecological disaster posed by industrial and technological developments such as nuclear power and agricultural biotechnology. Although it operates at the limit point of risk assessment, the principle of precaution is addressed to the same question: whether the potential benefits of a given action outweigh its potential harms. Precaution answers by saying that because we cannot determine the likelihood of the catastrophic event or because its potential consequences are so dire that they cannot be mitigated, we must take action to avoid its occurrence.[16] As we will see, the framework of preparedness poses the question differently. Like precaution, it is applied to threats that "as measured by the existing institutional yardsticks—are neither calculable nor controllable," as Beck puts it.[17] In contrast to precaution, however, preparedness does not prescribe avoidance of the threatening event. Rather, preparedness assumes that the occurrence of the event may not be avoidable and so generates knowledge about its potential consequences through imaginative practices like simulation and scenario planning. Such practices make it possible to gauge vulnerabilities in the present, which can then be the target of anticipatory intervention.

Risk assessment and preparedness are both ways of making the uncertain future available to present intervention, but they require different types of expert knowledge, and they generate different kinds of response (see Table 1.1). From the perspective of preparedness, it may not be possible to evade the onset of a disastrous event. Although the likelihood of its occurrence is not known, one must act as though it were going to happen. The task for preparedness planners, then, is to mitigate present vulnerabilities and to put in place response measures that will prevent the disastrous event from spiraling into a catastrophe. As a governmental strategy,

Table 1.1.   Managing an Uncertain Future

	Risk Assessment	Preparedness
Type of event to be addressed	Regularly occurring, of limited scale	Unpredictable but potentially catastrophic
Foresight	One can predict how often it will occur but not to whom	One cannot predict its likelihood but can envision its consequences
Knowledge required	Archival-historical record	Imaginative enactment
How to manage the threat	Distribute risk over the population	Mitigate vulnerabilities; build response capacities
Temporal orientation	Continuity between past and future	Vigilant alertness for the onset of surprise
Initial site of development	Seventeenth-century maritime trade	Cold War specter of nuclear war
Extension to new sites	Property, illness and mortality, accidents	Natural disaster, terrorism, pandemics

preparedness organizes a set of techniques meant to sustain order and preserve life in a future time of emergency. These techniques include early warning systems, scenario-based exercises, stockpiling of essential supplies, and the capacity for crisis communications. The duration of intensive response by a preparedness apparatus is limited to the immediate onset and aftermath of crisis, but the requirement of vigilant attention to the prospect of catastrophe is ongoing.

As illustrated by the case of Hurricane Katrina, governmental preparedness measures face a number of challenges. First, there is the question of how to prioritize among disparate threats, given a wide range of potential disasters and a limited amount of resources available to address them: should a public health agency, for example, focus on the possibility of a smallpox attack, an influenza pandemic or an outbreak of drug-resistant tuberculosis? Second, there is the problem of how to sustain a condition of ongoing vigilance, over an indefinite period of time, for an event that may or may not occur: how to avoid the fatigue of sustained anticipation, especially as the anticipated event continually fails to appear? Third, there is the question of who is in charge of preparedness in a system of dispersed sovereignty: what are the respective responsibilities of federal, state, and local officials, what authority does the military have, and what is the role of nongovernmental organizations? Given these challenges, governmental preparedness efforts often remain in unstable and highly fragmentary form; however, this condition of "unpreparedness" typically becomes apparent only in the wake of the potential event's actual occurrence and a failure of the response apparatus.

MOBILIZATION OF THE POPULATION

Many of the capacities as well as the limitations of governmental preparedness can be traced to the context of its historical emergence. The techniques of preparedness that are now applied to a wide range of potential disasters were initially assembled in the United States during the early years of the Cold War. In this context, the condition of preparedness referred to military and civilian readiness, in peacetime, for an anticipated future war. Cold War mobilization and civil defense plans were developed in response to the rise of new forms of warfare in the mid-twentieth century: first, air attacks on civilian population centers; second, the prospect of nuclear attack. As World War II came to an end, military strategists argued that the nation should not demobilize as it had after the First World War. To meet the threat posed by its new enemy, they argued, the United States would have to remain in a state of permanent mobilization for total war. What historian Michael Sherry describes as "an ideology of preparedness" thus arose, among national security thinkers, even before the end of World War II.[18]

Civilian defense was one dimension of mobilization preparedness. Based on an assessment of the effects of allied air attacks during World War II, the *United States Strategic Bombing Survey* (1946) recommended the development of domestic shelter and evacuation programs "to minimize the destructiveness of such attacks, and so organize the economic and administrative life of the Nation so that no single or small group of attacks can paralyze the national organism."[19] The report also argued for the dispersion of critical industrial facilities outside of vulnerable urban areas and for measures to ensure the continuity of essential government functions in the wake of an attack.[20] More generally, the *Strategic Bombing Survey* enjoined national security thinkers to envision the United States in terms of its key sites of vulnerability—that is, to understand the national territory and population as a set of potential targets whose destruction would cripple its industrial and military capabilities.[21]

Given these concerns about American susceptibility to a sudden and devastating attack, Cold War national security strategists sought to ensure that the nation could rapidly put into motion an efficient military production apparatus in the midst of a future emergency. "If an attack were to come without warning," writes Sherry, "the war machine had to be ever ready." As part of the 1947 National Security Act, the National Security Resources Board (NSRB) was established to centralize and coordinate defense mobilization efforts. The NSRB organized its programs assuming the need for ongoing anticipation of an enemy attack: "The national security requires continuous mobilization planning and, to maximum feasible degree, a continuous state of readiness."[22] Such a state of readiness included, among other measures, the development of civil defense plans.

An early study of this problem defined civil defense as "the mobilization of the entire population for the preservation of civilian life and property from the results of enemy attacks, and with the rapid restoration of normal conditions in any area that has been attacked."[23] With the passage of the Federal Civil Defense Act of 1950, Congress distributed operational responsibility for this function to states and localities, assigning a more limited role of planning and coordination to federal civil defense officials. Cold War civil defense programs included the development of evacuation plans, stockpiling essential medical supplies, holding training exercises, and mounting public awareness campaigns. Despite elaborate planning efforts at both the federal and local levels during the 1950s, ambitious civil defense measures such as a national shelter program were for the most part stymied over the course of the Cold War, due to in part to congressional recalcitrance to allocate sufficient funds and more broadly to skepticism, both among national security strategists and within the general population, about the efficacy of civil protection measures when faced with the devastating prospect of nuclear attack. Nevertheless, the normative rationality underlying civil defense—the injunction to continually prepare for a catastrophic threat that might or might not arrive—along with many of the techniques it fostered, would eventually serve as the basis for a more general approach to health and security threats.

IMAGINATIVE ENACTMENT

The problem addressed by Cold War defense mobilization and civil defense planners was how to maintain the nation's military and economic capacities even in the aftermath of a catastrophic enemy attack. For civilian security experts such as Herman Kahn of the RAND Corporation, this issue was imperative given U.S. military doctrine: the strategy of deterrence depended on convincing the enemy that the United States was prepared to engage in a full-scale nuclear war and had therefore made plans for both conducting such a war and recovering in its aftermath. Kahn criticized military planners for failing to envision how a future nuclear war would unfold. Given their strategic posture, he argued, it was irresponsible not to think in detail about the consequences of such a war: what civil defense measures might lead to the loss of only fifty million rather than a hundred million lives? What would collective life be like after a nuclear war? How could one plan for postwar reconstruction in a radiation-contaminated environment? Prewar preparation was essential to ensure continued postwar existence.

In the quest to be adequately prepared for the eventuality of thermonuclear war, Kahn counseled in the late 1950s and early 1960s, no expense should be spared: "With sufficient preparation," he wrote, "we actually will be able to survive and recuperate if deterrence fails."[24] Kahn avidly promoted a method for "thinking about the unthinkable" that would make such planning possible: scenario development. Kahn did not invent this method but rather drew on existing governmental practices: civilian exercises based on scenarios of enemy attack had been part of defense mobilization and civil defense planning efforts since the early 1950s.[25] For Kahn, developing scenarios of a future nuclear war served two related purposes. One was to assist in designing role-playing games in which decision-makers would enact the lead-up to war with the Soviet Union. In the absence of the actual experience of nuclear standoff, such exercises could provide government officials and strategic planners with something akin to the sense of urgency and uncertainty that such a crisis would bring.[26] The second use of such scenarios was to force both officials and members of the public to face the prospect of nuclear catastrophe as a potential future event that must be planned for in all of its grotesque detail.

Through the development of scenarios, Kahn envisioned a range of postwar conditions whose scale of devastation was a function of prewar preparations, especially civil defense efforts. The imaginative enactment of these scenarios produced knowledge about current vulnerabilities and pointed to practical measures to mitigate them. For example, in the wake of nuclear war, a radioactive environment could hamper postwar reconstruction unless there was a way to determine individual levels of exposure. For this reason, Kahn recommended a program to distribute radioactivity dosimeters to the entire population in advance of war so that postwar survivors could gauge their exposure levels and act accordingly.

Scenarios were not predictions or forecasts but opportunities for exercising an agile response capability. They trained leaders to deal with the unanticipated. "Imagination," Kahn wrote, "has always been one of the principal means for dealing in various ways with the future, and the scenario is simply one of the many devices useful in stimulating and disciplining the imagination."[27] In the wake of Kahn's promotion of the technique, scenario planning radiated outside of the field of nuclear preparedness and began a prolific career in other fields concerned with anticipating an uncertain future, ranging from corporate strategy to environmental management.

Another iteration of this practice of imaginative enactment was the development of "political exercises." These exercises were carefully scripted activities in which decision-makers were presented with the details of a crisis situation, took action in response, and then studied the results of their decisions. For the exercises to be realistic, they had to generate a sense of urgency among participants. Early developers of these scenario-based exercises reflected on the problem of how to foster this sense of urgency, despite participants' awareness that they were engaged in a simulation. One method was to create an atmosphere of "controlled contingency," in which participants experienced a charged combination of uncertainty about the outcome of a given decision alongside responsibility for its consequences.

Two members of the social science division of the RAND Corporation, Herbert Goldhamer and Hans Speier, experimented with this type of exercise beginning in the early 1960s. The focus of their exercises was on public officials' decision-making processes in crisis situations: specifically, the challenge of understanding the motivations and anticipating the likely behavior of the enemy. Goldhamer and Speier emphasized the importance of incorporating qualitative social science into their exercise design. They were skeptical of the ability of formal models of behavior, as used in game-theoretic approaches, to provide insight into the complex realities of political decision.[28] Rather than simplifying the international situation as a formal model would require, the RAND political exercise made it possible "to simulate as faithfully as possible much of its complexity." As opposed to game theorists' abstract simulations of nuclear confrontation, the political exercise used concrete political and historical knowledge and thereby sought to replicate the chance and contingency characteristic of real-life political crises.

The events depicted in the RAND political exercises were typically diplomatic crises in which a blue team representing the United States and its allies faced off against a red team representing the Soviet Union. Goldhamer and Speier pointed to the need for players to emotionally invest themselves in the exercise for the experience of participation to generate the affect of anxious uncertainty that would characterize an actual crisis situation. Insofar as the exercise provided players with "new insight into the pressures, the uncertainties, and the moral and intellectual difficulties under which foreign policy decisions are made," they argued, this was "a tribute to the earnestness and sense of responsibility with which the participants played their roles, since otherwise these pressures and perplexities would not have made themselves felt."

How, then, to ensure that participants played their roles earnestly and thereby took responsibility for the consequences of their actions? A key requirement of the exercise's success in generating a sense of realism was the "simulation of contingent factors"—what Goldhamer and Speier termed "Nature."[29] Unplanned events had to be designed into the exercise. Designated referees played the role of Nature during the exercise, evaluating and intervening in the "state of affairs" that had been reached at a given point in the game. The referees exercised control over the players' ostensibly contingent experiences through the introduction of unanticipated developments from the outside world: "the referees could introduce such evaluations in the form of press roundups, trade union resolutions, intelligence reports, speeches made in the United Nations, etc." Interventions coming from "Nature" pointed to limitations on the players' capacity to shape the course of events. As Goldhamer and Speier put it, "the role of 'Nature' was to provide for events of the type that happen in the real world but are not under the control of any government: certain technological developments, the death of important people, non-governmental political action, famines, popular disturbances, etc." By generating a reality effect, the hidden interventions of the referee during the staged exercise fostered participants' experience of responsibility for their actions.[30]

THE GENERIC EMERGENCY

Although costly civil defense measures in anticipation of nuclear attack such as a national fallout shelter system were never successfully implemented, the state and local offices spawned by the Federal Civil Defense Act served as a springboard for the extension of the rationality of preparedness to new problem areas. Beginning in the early Cold War era, and with increasing momentum over the next decades, an alternate variant of preparedness arose in parallel to the federal government's efforts to protect the national population against atomic war. State and local offices drew on federal civil defense resources to prepare localities for natural disasters such as hurricanes, floods, and earthquakes. As E. L. Quarantelli, a leading figure in the establishment of the field of emergency management, later recalled: "At the national level, a civil defense system developed earlier than any comparable disaster planning or emergency management system. However, at the local level, the prime concern after World War II became to prepare for and respond to disasters."[31] Although it was oriented to a different kind of threat, the new field of emergency management was structured by the underlying logic of civil defense: anticipatory mobilization for a disaster that might or might not arrive.

Some governmental measures for alleviating the damage caused by natural disasters, especially floods and wildfires, were already in place.[32] But beginning in the mid-1950s, state and local officials took up a number of the techniques associated with nuclear attack preparedness and applied them to natural disaster planning. Such techniques included early detection and alert systems, evacuation plans, and the use of scenario-based exercises to train emergency responders. These two forms of preparedness did not always easily coexist. There were debates over prioritization: should emergency managers focus their attention on likely natural disasters or on the prospect of a nuclear attack? And there were questions concerning the chain of command: while federal civil defense planners tended to assume a hierarchical organization, local emergency managers sought a distributed, decentralized structure.[33]

Despite such differences in mission and organization, civil defense and emergency management shared a similar field of intervention—future disasters—making many of their techniques potentially transferable. Moreover, complementary interests were at play in the migration of elements of federal civil defense to local emergency management. For local officials federal civil defense funds provided an opportunity to support disaster preparedness. From the federal perspective, local disaster planning honed capabilities that would prove useful for nuclear preparedness. As the Director of the Office of Defense Mobilization put it in 1957, "natural disasters bear a close affinity, in what they do to us and what we do about them, to the unnatural disasters caused by man in modern warfare."[34] The practice of using civil defense resources to address peacetime disasters was officially sanctioned by a 1976 amendment to the 1950 Federal Civil Defense Act. In the following years, the kind of disaster that could be addressed through emergency management expanded further to include environmental catastrophes, such as Love Canal and Three Mile Island, and humanitarian emergencies such as the 1980 Cuban refugee crisis.

When the Federal Emergency Management Agency (FEMA) was established in 1979, the new agency consolidated civil defense and disaster management functions under the rubric of "all-hazards planning." All-hazards planning assumed that, for the purposes of emergency management, a disparate set of potential events could be treated in the same way: earthquakes, floods, nuclear reactor accidents, and terrorist attacks were

brought into a common operational space, given certain shared characteristics. As Quarantelli commented, "It is being more and more accepted
that civil protection should take a generic rather than agent specific
approach to disasters."[35] The need for capabilities such as early warning,
the coordination of response among multiple agencies, public communication to minimize panic, and the rapid provision of relief was shared
across these various forms of disaster. Thus, all-hazards planning focused
not on assessing specific threats, but on building generic capabilities that
functioned across multiple domains of threat. In 1983, for example, FEMA
implemented the Integrated Emergency Management System (IEMS).
Initially developed in the context of wildfire management in the American
West, IEMS elaborated a set of standards for command, control and coordination across disparate agencies, making possible a "broader, functional,
and multi-hazard method of emergency management."[36]

THE NONSPECIFIC ADVERSARY

Beginning in the 1990s, authorities perceived increasing affinities between
developments in the field of emergency management and transformations
in the national security environment. After the dissolution of the Soviet
Union, one aspect of Cold War national security that retrospectively stood
out was the relative stability of the threat it sought to mitigate. For defense
strategists, the Soviet threat seemed to be knowable through formal techniques such as game theory and manageable through policies such as deterrence. With the end of the Cold War, national security thinkers were almost
nostalgic for a time when, however dire the threat of nuclear catastrophe
might have been, it was at least clear what danger they were supposed to
protect against. As Chairman of the Joint Chiefs of Staff General Colin
Powell said in 1991, "We no longer have the luxury of having a threat to plan
for."[37] In the years that followed, new security formations consolidated
around this question: what is the threat for which we must now plan?

According to experts and officials, there was no longer a rational enemy
whose likely actions could be anticipated and managed. The key change in
the nature of the national security threat was from the stable enemy to the
nonspecific adversary.[38] This shift became more palpable after the terrorist

attacks of September 11, 2001. In a 2002 speech to the Council on Foreign Relations, Secretary of Defense Donald Rumsfeld counseled that the United States must vigilantly prepare for the unexpected: "September 11 taught us that the future holds many unknown dangers, and that we fail to prepare for them at our peril." He elaborated, using the language of the anticipation of surprise familiar from scenario planning: "The Cold War is gone and with it the familiar security environment. The challenges of the new century are not predictable. We will probably be surprised again by new adversaries who may strike in unexpected ways. The challenge is to defend our nation against the unknown, the uncertain, the unseen, the unexpected."[39]

Rumsfeld described the U.S. military's strategic shift, after the Cold War, from a threat-based strategy to a "capabilities-based" approach. This new strategy focused less on *who* might threaten the United States and more on *how* the United States might be threatened. Instead of building its armed forces around a plan to fight this or that particular enemy, Rumsfeld argued, the United States must examine its own vulnerabilities. Such an approach would make it possible for the military to plan for multiple, nonspecific forms of threat. It also resonated with the "all-hazards" approach that had developed in the field of emergency management, so that, as we will see, after the Department of Homeland Security was established in late 2002, there was an easy transferability between planning for a terrorist attack and planning for a natural disaster.

TOWARD NATIONAL PREPAREDNESS

The demand for a coherent domestic emergency management system that could consolidate multiple governmental systems of preparedness and response crystalized, after the attacks of September 11, 2001, and the anthrax letters that followed, in the formation of the Department of Homeland Security in late 2002. The new agency assembled security functions from a number of previously distinct areas of government: civil defense, disaster management, border security, intelligence, and transportation security. Although DHS was widely seen as a counter-terrorism agency, the Department characterized its overall mission in broader terms familiar from the field of emergency management. As its first director,

Michael Chertoff, said in unveiling the department's *National Preparedness Guidance* in 2005: "The Department of Homeland Security has sometimes been viewed as a terrorist-fighting entity, but of course, we're an all-hazards Department. Our responsibilities include not only fighting the forces of terrorism, but also fighting the forces of natural disasters."[40]

The *National Preparedness Guidance* elaborated a set of administrative mechanisms for making governmental preparedness a measurable condition. The *Guidance* was a plan for administrative decision and organizational self-assessment across multiple governmental and nongovernmental entities concerned with problems of risk and disaster. It sought to bring disparate forms of threat into a common security field, articulating a number of techniques that had been honed over the prior five decades of planning for emergency—including early warning systems, scenario-based exercises, coordinated response plans, and metrics for assessment of the nation's current state of readiness.[41]

The goal of DHS preparedness planning was to "attain the optimal state of preparedness."[42] What was a state of preparedness, according to the Department? As another planning document, the *National Preparedness Goal*, defined it, "preparedness is a continuous process involving efforts at all levels of government and between government and private-sector and nongovernmental organizations to identify threats, determine vulnerabilities, and identify required resources."[43] In other words, preparedness was the relation of capabilities to vulnerabilities, given a selected range of threats. The integration of task lists, exercises, and assessment metrics together formed a system of critical rectification through which the nation's state of preparedness could continually be measured and refined.

National preparedness sought to mitigate vulnerabilities in the nation's "critical infrastructure."[44] This latter term referred to the sociotechnical systems necessary to sustain economic and social life. The *National Infrastructure Protection Plan* compiled a list of assets in infrastructural sectors including agriculture and food, public health, drinking water and wastewater treatment, energy, banking and finance, telecommunications, and transportation. This compendium of the nation's vital and vulnerable systems hearkened back to the resource management activities of Cold War nuclear preparedness agencies such as the National Security Resources Board and the Office of Defense Mobilization.[45] From the perspective of national preparedness, collective dependence on these systems was an ongoing source of vulnerability. Threats to the sustained operation of vital systems could come from a number of sources, including hostile actors, natural disasters, and infectious diseases. Given the range of hazards for which the department was required to plan, it approached such threats through an emphasis on capabilities that ranged across multiple types of event. "Capabilities-based planning" was based on Department of Defense methods developed at the end of the Cold War, as mentioned earlier, but was also coherent with a central premise of all-hazards planning: that one should focus not on specific threats but rather on developing a portfolio of response capabilities that could be applied across a range of potential events.[46]

The department did not claim to be able to protect against all potential dangers. As Chertoff commented, "There's risk everywhere; risk is a part of life. I think one thing I've tried to be clear in saying is we will not eliminate every risk."[47] Given a proliferation of threats and finite resources to address them, the department would "concentrate first and foremost, most relentlessly, on addressing threats that pose catastrophic consequences."[48] Among the many dire possibilities, what were the criteria for selecting the most salient threats? A process called "risk-based" prioritization would in principle guide the allocation of federal resources for improving preparedness. This meant distributing funds according to the relative likelihood and catastrophic potential of a given attack or disaster in a given place. However, exactly how to make such an assessment given the uncertain occurrence of the most significant threats remained both a technical and a political challenge.[49]

CONCLUSION

For government planners, the achievement of optimal preparedness did not require knowledge about the norms of living beings; unlike measures to secure the well-being of the population, national preparedness did not target its interventions based on epidemiological or demographic calculation. Rather, efforts to assess and improve current preparedness required methods to generate knowledge about infrastructural vulnerabilities in relation to available response capacities. Here the technique of scenario development proved useful. As we have seen, scenarios do not claim to be predictions or forecasts of what is likely to happen; rather, they are tools for discovering gaps in present readiness. As part of its preparedness planning process, DHS selected fifteen disaster scenarios as "the foundation for a risk-based approach."[50] The potential events included in the portfolio—including an anthrax attack, an influenza pandemic, a nuclear bomb detonation, and a major earthquake—were chosen on the basis of their plausibility and their catastrophic scale.

The scenarios were useful in generating knowledge about current system vulnerabilities and the capabilities that were necessary to mitigate them. As homeland security expert David Heyman of the Center for Strategic and International Security (CSIS) commented, "We have a great sense of vulnerability, but no sense of what it takes to be prepared. These scenarios provide us with an opportunity to address that."[51] On the basis of the scenarios in its portfolio, DHS preparedness planners developed a menu of the "critical tasks" that would have to be performed in various kinds of major disasters. In turn, the department assigned responsibility for performing each of these tasks to a range of governmental and nongovernmental agencies.[52]

The DHS planning scenarios did not require definitive agreement about which threats were most salient; rather, the portfolio was to be regularly evaluated and, if necessary, transformed. As the preparedness guidance document explained, "DHS will maintain a National Planning Scenario portfolio and will update it periodically based on changes in the homeland security strategic environment."[53] The plan envisioned a process of ongoing reflexive self-transformation in relation to an evolving ecology of threats. "Our enemy constantly changes and adapts, so we as a department must be nimble and decisive," explained Chertoff.[54] National preparedness had to continually pose the question to itself: are we preparing for the right threats?

While an examination of these homeland security documents helps in understanding the style of reasoning that guided national preparedness planning in the early 2000s, its actual operation was far from stabilized. In its first years, DHS was fraught with bureaucratic infighting, budgetary struggles, and cronyism, leading to a widespread perception that it had failed to achieve its mission, especially in the wake of Hurricane Katrina.[55] It is worth underlining, however, that such criticism assumed the normative rationality of preparedness: the intense criticism of the federal response to Katrina was premised on an agreement that government was responsible for imagining and planning for future disasters.

Technical Reform

Scenario 10 of the DHS planning scenarios, released in 2004, was entitled "Natural Disaster–Major Hurricane."[56] As the federal response to Hurricane Katrina the following year demonstrated, the existence of a planning scenario did not guarantee a condition of preparedness—far from it. In any case, the massively failed response to the actual hurricane did not undermine the presumed utility of all-hazards planning. Rather, from the perspective of thinkers of preparedness, the failure pointed to problems such as the competent implementation of disaster management plans and the distribution of responsibility in a federal system. What followed the catastrophe was the redirection and intensification of already-developed preparedness techniques rather than a basic rethinking of security questions.

Reform proposals after Hurricane Katrina were primarily technical and administrative: in the context of the Gulf Coast, rebuild the flood protection infrastructure, improve urban evacuation plans, ensure that there are coherent systems in place for communication and coordination in crisis. More generally, as the White House Report on the federal response to Hurricane Katrina argued, it would be necessary to scrutinize the relationships among federal, state, local, private sector, and philanthropic responsibilities for dealing with various aspects of emergency management.[57] Meanwhile, given the shared rubric of preparedness, it was difficult to pose questions concerning the social basis of vulnerability. This difficulty points to the issue of what kind of governmental techniques are most salient for looking after the well-being of citizens, and what the goals of knowledge and intervention in the name of collective security should be.

Here we can point to some of the differences between the objects and aims of governmental efforts to ensure population security on the one hand, and those of national preparedness on the other. If population security emphasizes tasks such as the development of public health infrastructure and the provision of social assistance, national preparedness is oriented to crisis situations and to localized sites of disruption. These latter events are typically of short duration and are seen to require urgent and acute response.[58] The possibility of the event's occurrence in a given setting demands a condition of vigilant readiness, as opposed to a long-term work of sustained attention to collective well-being. The object to be known and managed also differs: for preparedness, the key site of vulnerability is not population health but rather the critical infrastructure that guarantees the continuity of political and economic order. If population security efforts involve the development and management of critical infrastructures, national preparedness catalogs these infrastructures and mitigates their vulnerabilities. Finally, although preparedness measures emphasize saving the lives of victims in moments of duress, they do not seek to intervene in the living conditions of human beings as members of a social collectivity.

To consider Hurricane Katrina and its aftermath a problem of preparedness rather than one of population security was to focus political questions concerning the failure around a fairly circumscribed set of issues. For the purposes of national preparedness, the poverty rate in New Orleans and the number of citizens lacking health insurance were not salient indicators of readiness or response capability. Rather, preparedness emphasized questions such as hospital surge capacity, the efficiency of evacuation plans, and the resilience of the electrical grid. In contrasting these two frameworks I do not mean to argue that they are incommensurable. On the contrary, I want to suggest that the success of preparedness measures may depend on the existence of effective mechanisms of population security. This is a theme to which we return in the coming chapters.

2 The Generic Biological Threat

In early 1976, federal health officials warned the Ford administration that a virulent new strain of influenza had appeared in the United States and threatened to become a deadly pandemic. A soldier had died at Fort Dix in New Jersey, and others at the base were infected with the virus. Infectious disease experts gathered and quickly recommended a plan of action to the president: an urgent, intensive program to immunize the entire U.S. population before the next flu season, at an estimated cost of $135 million. Such a program had never been tried before—indeed, it had only recently become technically feasible. But given the perceived scale of the swine flu threat and the new possibility of intervention, public health experts were nearly unanimous about the most responsible course of action: mass vaccination. "If we believe in preventive medicine," as one well-regarded expert said, "we have no choice."[1]

Three decades later, in the fall of 2005, the U.S. government again focused its attention on the threat of pandemic influenza. This time the threat had not arrived suddenly—public health officials had been warning of the danger of an avian influenza pandemic with increasing urgency since the appearance of a highly pathogenic strain of the virus in Hong Kong in 1997. But it seemed that now a major initiative was possible—in part because of an increasing perception among health authorities of the seriousness of the threat, as the virus spread globally through poultry stocks and migratory birds, and in part as a result of fallout from the administration's widely perceived failure to respond adequately to Hurricane Katrina. President George W. Bush described the combination of urgency and uncertainty posed by threat of pandemic influenza: "Scientists and doctors cannot tell us where or when the next pandemic will strike, or how severe it will be, but most agree: at some point, we are likely to face another pandemic."[2] Or, as a concerned U.S. senator put it, echoing the admonitions of health officials: "Experts no longer ask if such a pandemic could occur, rather they question when it will occur."[3]

In November 2005, the Bush administration unveiled a $7.1 billion pandemic preparedness strategy described by the Secretary of Health and Human Services as "the most robust proposal ever made for public health at one time."[4] The plan included funds for disease surveillance, stockpiling antiviral medication, and research into new methods of vaccine production. It was initially criticized in the public health world for focusing too much on pharmaceutical intervention and not enough on the needs of state and local health agencies. But among various commentators, there was impressive agreement on several points. First, that pandemic planning was a matter of urgent and immediate concern; second, that the nation was currently far from adequately prepared for a pandemic; and third, that whether or not a pandemic in fact occurred, the process of preparing for it would strengthen readiness for other potential threats. As the senator put it, "Even if we are spared from a flu pandemic, the work that we do today will serve us all well in the event of any national emergency."[5]

Governmental anticipation of a pandemic had become a vehicle for a more general form of planning, one oriented to a range of potential threats. In testimony before Congress, the Assistant Secretary of Health argued, "preparedness for a pandemic makes us a nation better prepared for any and all hazards, manmade or natural."[6] But, he warned, such a condition would not arrive quickly or easily: "Preparedness is a journey, not a destination. It's a journey that must be nationwide, involve federal, state and local leaders in partnership, and include every sector of society." The condition of national preparedness could be improved upon but never perfected, as the secretary of health testified: "We're overdue and we're not as well prepared as we need to be. We're better prepared than we were yesterday. We'll be better prepared tomorrow than we are today. It's a continuum of preparedness."[7] A leading state health official echoed this sense of a journey without end: "Are we fully prepared? Absolutely not. We are more prepared than we were several years ago but not prepared enough."[8]

In juxtaposing the 1976 and 2005 cases, we can see that over the course of three decades, a new way of thinking about and acting on disease threat had taken hold: it was no longer only a question of prevention, but also— and perhaps even more—one of preparedness. How did this shift happen? How did the U.S. public health and national security establishments come to see the nation as unprepared for a future disease emergency? And what programs did they advocate to improve national preparedness? The story is a complex one, involving the migration of techniques initially developed in the military and civil defense to other areas of governmental intervention.

The analysis in this chapter focuses not on widespread public discussion of disease threats but rather on particular sites of expertise where a novel way of understanding and intervening in potential future events was developed and deployed. In particular it focuses on the role of scenario-based exercises in constituting infectious disease as a problem of preparedness. This technique served two important functions: first, to provoke an affect of urgency among health and security officials in the absence of the event itself; and second, to generate knowledge about vulnerabilities in the government's response capacity that could then guide anticipatory intervention.

NATIONAL SECURITY AND PUBLIC HEALTH

In his spring 2006 congressional testimony on avian flu preparedness, former White House Homeland Security Advisor Richard Falkenrath declared: "When viewed in comparison to all other conceivable threats to U.S. national security, the catastrophic disease threat is and for the foreseeable future will remain the greatest danger we face."[9] Given Falkenrath's background as an expert in nuclear proliferation and counter-terrorism, this was a striking statement, a clear affirmation that national security strategists must now turn their attention to a subject that had, until recently, remained mainly under the purview of public health.

This claim was by no means the first time that national security had been linked to public health.[10] Early Cold War concerns about the threat of biological warfare led to the establishment of the Epidemic Intelligence Service in the U.S. Communicable Disease Center (the forerunner to the Centers for Disease Control and Prevention [CDC]).[11] And infectious disease specialists have regularly been involved in the U.S. military's foreign interventions, from the Spanish American war to the Vietnam War. To understand the significance of Falkenrath's statement—and its difference from prior such conjunctures—it will be useful to develop a schematic distinction among forms of collective security.

The first two forms are familiar: national security refers to practices oriented to the defense of state sovereignty against foreign and domestic enemies using military or diplomatic means. Population security involves measures to protect the national population against regularly occurring internal threats, such as illness, industrial accidents, or infirmity. Into the late twentieth century, these two formations—warfare and welfare— were the predominant governmental means of addressing collective security problems in the United States. However, a number of current security-related initiatives, such as pandemic preparedness or critical infrastructure protection, do not fit neatly into either of these familiar security frameworks. In recent years, a third form, which we can term "vital systems security," has become increasingly central to the government of security threats (see Table 2.1).

Vital systems security targets a distinctive type of threat: the event whose probability cannot be calculated but whose consequences are potentially catastrophic. Its object of protection is not the sovereignty of the nation-state or the health of the national population but rather the critical systems that underpin social and economic life. Vital systems security measures do not seek information about a foreign enemy or about regularly occurring events but, rather, use techniques of imaginative enactment to generate knowledge about internal system vulnerabilities. The interventions of this form of security do not focus on defending against foreign enemies or modulating the living conditions of the population; instead, they seek to ensure the continuous functioning of critical systems in the event of disaster.

Vital systems security did not appear whole cloth but emerged out of one arena of national security—civilian and defense mobilization for

Table 2.1. Forms of Collective Security

	Sovereign State Security	Population Security	Vital Systems Security
Moment of articulation	Seventeenth-century territorial monarchies	Nineteenth-century urban hygiene	Mid-twentieth-century civil defense
Normative rationality	Interdiction	Risk assessment	Preparedness
Types of threat	Adversaries	Regularly occurring hazards	Unpredictable, potentially catastrophic events
Exemplary form of knowledge	Strategy	Statistics	Imaginative enactment
Operation	Deter or defend against enemy	Distribute risk	Mitigate vulnerabilities

war—beginning in the mid-twentieth century. Many of its techniques were initially developed to manage the threat of nuclear attack during the Cold War but were gradually extended to approach other potential catastrophes, ranging from natural disasters to terrorism to epidemics. These different forms of collective security imply different ways of reasoning about disease. As we will see, when infectious disease is approached as a problem of population security, interventions are structured by a logic of prevention, whereas when it is taken up from the perspective of vital systems security, the guiding logic is one of preparedness.[12]

Swine Flu and the Limits of Population Security

The object of knowledge and intervention for classical public health is the population, understood as a "global mass" affected by processes characteristic of life, such as birth, sickness, and death.[13] Expert knowledge about the well-being of the population, as generated in fields like demography, epidemiology, and economics, tracks regularities in the occurrence of these events. Experiences such as the onset of disease "are aleatory and unpredictable when taken in themselves or individually," as Michel Foucault put it in his lectures on biopolitics, but "at the collective level, display constants that are easy, or at least possible, to establish."[14] Gathering statistical knowledge of the rate of occurrence of disease or death within a population makes such collective regularities visible. In turn, public health interventions seek to know and manage these regularities, to decrease mortality and increase longevity, to "optimize a state of life."

Modern public health measures have historically been justified based on the statistical analysis of patterns of disease incidence in a population. The case of nineteenth-century Britain is instructive. Beginning in the middle decades of the century, British public health reformers carefully tracked the collective incidence of disease to make the argument that, as historian George Rosen writes, "health was affected for better or worse by the state of the physical or social environment."[15] Such knowledge of disease incidence was cumulative and calculative. Advocates for health reform gathered and analyzed vital statistics—rates of birth, death, and disease as they varied among social classes—to demonstrate the economic rationality of hygienic measures such as the provision of clean water to urban slums or the removal of waste from streets. The argument was that the benefits of measures to increase the living standards of the poor would outweigh their cost. As social reformer Edwin Chadwick put it in his famous 1842 report, *An Inquiry into the Sanitary Conditions of the Labouring Population of Great Britain*, "The expenditures necessary to the adoption and maintenance of measures of prevention would ultimately amount to less than the cost of disease now constantly expanded."[16]

If this initial mode of population security emphasized improvements in living conditions such as sanitation infrastructure and urban housing, a next iteration intervened more directly in human biological life. The rise of bacteriology in the late nineteenth century helped lead to the systematic practice of immunization against a growing number of infectious diseases. Until the early twentieth century, smallpox was the only disease for which immunization was widely practiced. Beginning in the 1920s, it became possible to immunize populations against an increasing number of scourges, including diphtheria, tetanus, and whooping cough. But again, health policy decisions were in principle based on knowledge of the historical incidence of disease in a given population. For instance, as Rosen explains, in

designing New York City's childhood vaccination campaign against diphtheria in the 1920s, it was "necessary to know the natural history of diphtheria within the community: How many children of different ages had already
acquired immunity, how many were well carriers, and what children were
highly susceptible?"[17] Such knowledge about comparative rates of incidence
among specific subpopulations would, it was hoped, make it possible to efficiently target interventions at the most at-risk children.

   Given public health authorities' reliance on statistical knowledge of risk to
design and justify measures to prevent infectious disease, they tend to have
difficulty approaching events whose likelihood is difficult or impossible to
calculate. How, then, do health officials take responsible action when faced
with the prospect of a rare or unprecedented disease outbreak—one for
which the probable course is not yet known but which could have catastrophic consequences? Let us return to the situation with which the chapter
began: the apparent outbreak of swine flu in 1976. As we will see, the guiding
logic of classical public health structured the way that the threat was taken
up by government officials—and helped lead to an eventual "fiasco."

   In January 1976, federal health officials learned that a soldier at Fort
Dix had died of an unfamiliar strain of swine flu, a type of influenza virus
that typically infects pigs but that can cross the species barrier to cause
disease in humans. Moreover, the Army reported several other cases of the
same type of flu at Fort Dix, and so the virus appeared to be both virulent
and capable of human-to-human transmission. But there was no way of
knowing, at this early stage, whether the cases were a sign of an impend-
ing pandemic. Some influenza virologists hypothesized that molecular
transformations in the influenza virus leading to human pandemics happened approximately once per decade. The previous one had occurred in
1968. In the worst case, these experts believed, the damage wrought by the
new subtype could be comparable to that of the 1918 influenza pandemic,
which had killed an estimated fifty million people around the world.

   There were no government plans in place for response to a potential flu
pandemic. For this reason, it was not immediately clear what options were
available to health authorities. A catastrophe on the scale of the 1918 pandemic was by no means predictable, but it was possible. Edwin Kilbourne,
a leading influenza virologist, warned public health officials to plan
without delay for an imminent disaster. Given the nature of the threat and

the response measures available, there seemed to be only one possible course of action: an urgent program to immunize the entire U.S. population in advance of the next flu season. Such an option was both expensive and practically daunting. It would require producing and distributing enough vaccine to immunize more than two hundred million people within a matter of months. This was a new technical possibility: only recently could enough vaccine be rapidly produced to envision mass immunization. But given the time constraints, to successfully implement the program a decision would have to be made immediately.

Government health officials were thus faced, for the first time, with the opportunity to intervene in advance of a possible influenza pandemic. This situation presented a conceptual and practical challenge for public health expertise. As noted earlier, modern public health institutions were set up to monitor and respond to actual, rather than potential, disease incidence. Health authorities rely on epidemiological data about the timing, location and severity of outbreaks to design effective interventions and justify the allocation of resources. For this reason, in the wake of the initial swine flu reports, authorities had difficulty in approaching a foreseeable, but not statistically calculable, event. A later report described the situation in which they found themselves: "With a pandemic possible and time to do something about it, and lacking the time to disprove it, then *something* would have to be done."[18]

On March 10, CDC officials met in Atlanta with members of the Advisory Committee on Immunization Practices (ACIP). Each year, ACIP uses updated virological and epidemiological data to generate recommendations for the CDC on which strains of influenza to vaccinate against and which at-risk subpopulations to target in vaccination campaigns. In the case of swine flu, ACIP found that because the general population did not have any immunity to this subtype, a vaccination program could not be limited to high-risk groups. One of the committee members summed up the situation: first, there was evidence of a new strain of flu that could be transmitted among humans; second, all previous new strains had been followed by pandemics; and third, for the first time ever, there was both the knowledge and the time to provide for mass immunization.

One question was raised during the meeting, but not pursued further: epidemiologist Russell Alexander asked whether it might make sense to mass produce the vaccine and then stockpile it rather than moving directly to vaccination of the entire population. CDC director David Sencer argued that the virus would spread too quickly and that distribution logistics were too complex to consider waiting for convincing evidence of an emerging pandemic before beginning vaccination. CDC staff members were also concerned about future blame: if the Committee chose not to recommend vaccination and then a deadly pandemic followed, they would face biting criticism, argued one. It would be said that "they had the opportunity to save life," but "they did nothing."[19]

Following the ACIP meeting, Sencer composed a strongly worded memorandum to his superiors at the Department of Health, summarizing the advisory committee's recommendations. Given what he called a "strong possibility" of widespread swine influenza that could be highly virulent, the committee recommended a plan to immunize 213 million people in three months, at a cost of $134 million. The tone of Sencer's memo was urgent: "The situation is one of 'go or no go' . . . there is barely enough time. . . . A decision must be made now."[20] In turn, the Secretary of Health wrote a note to President Gerald Ford, shifting Sencer's conditional into the future tense, from possibility into apparent certainty: "There is evidence there will be a major epidemic this coming fall." The secretary's note alluded in particular to the return of the virus responsible for the 1918 pandemic: "The indication is that we will see a return of 1918 flu virus that is the most virulent form of flu." In such a case, the forecast was dire: "In 1918 a half a million people died" in the United States. "The projections are that this virus will kill one million Americans in 1976."[21]

With these grim numbers in hand, President Ford consulted with a number of leading authorities in virology and public health, including polio vaccine pioneers Jonas Salk and Alfred Sabin. The experts urged him to follow the CDC recommendation for a mass vaccination campaign. The president publicly announced the adoption of the National Influenza Immunization Program on March 24, using precautionary terms: "No one knows exactly how serious this threat could be. Nevertheless we cannot afford to take a chance with the health of the nation."[22] The projections of a potentially catastrophic event, based on the uncertain analogy to the 1918 pandemic, had placed responsibility for implementing prevention measures squarely on the president's shoulders.

Outside of the administration and its circle of public health advisors, there was sharp criticism of the immunization program. The New Jersey state epidemiologist warned of the possibility of dangerous side effects from the vaccine. Editorials from the *New York Times* were repeatedly skeptical of the program and accused the administration of engaging in politics at the expense of science. In advance of a major meeting of program participants in Atlanta, Alexander wrote to Sencer to again recommend the alternative of stockpiling vaccines "along the lines of military defense," and at the same time developing "well worked-out contingency plans" so that immunization could be rapidly carried out if the pandemic struck.[23] His suggestion, in other words, was to use military logistics methods to carve out an intermediary period of potential intervention in anticipation of the onset of the actual event. CDC officials did not consider the proposal seriously—such preparedness measures were not yet part of the shared toolkit of public health.

The goal of the immunization program was to begin vaccinations in August and finish before the end of winter. Field trials of the vaccine launched in April. By June, the epidemic had not yet appeared. At an ACIP meeting in Bethesda that month, virologist Alfred Sabin seconded Alexander's suggestion to stockpile supplies of vaccine rather than going forward with mass vaccination. Sencer countered that there was "no rational basis for a general 'stockpiling' concept." Because of "jet spread," he argued, the flu would move too fast. An unexpected blow to the program came in the summer: vaccine manufacturers announced that they would not bottle the vaccine without liability insurance. Insurers, in turn, were unwilling to offer such coverage given uncertainties about the health risks of the vaccine itself. "These questions defied actuaries," as the later report on the program put it. "There was no experience" on which to base a policy. "They were in the business to spread risk, not take it."[24] Once the issue of liability was addressed through Congressional passage of legislation to indemnify vaccine manufacturers and the immunization program began, further problems arose. The federal government had difficulty with the logistics of vaccine distribution, and there was also wide variation in state governments' capacity to implement the program.

It then became clear that CDC had not seriously considered how to manage the risk of severe side effects from the vaccine. When several elderly vaccine recipients died shortly after receiving their shot, the agency announced that a certain number of such deaths were to be "expected."[25] Despite these various setbacks, by December 1976, forty million people had been immunized, although these vaccinations were oddly distributed given the variation in individual states' execution of the plan. Then, in the middle of the month, Minnesota health officials reported multiple cases of Guillain-Barré syndrome, a severe neurological condition, among vaccine recipients. Although there was no definitive link between the vaccine and the syndrome, by this point it was clear that the anticipated epidemic was not coming, and the program was suspended.[26] The *New York Times* editorialized: "Swine Flu Fiasco."

A later report commissioned by the National Research Council did not fault the administration's decision to go ahead with the program: after all, public health experts had been nearly unanimous in their recommendations. But the report did suggest that one source of the program's failure was its administrators' lack of foresight. Federal health officials did not have contingency plans in place and so reacted in an ad hoc manner as unexpected events occurred. Moreover, officials had not envisioned and planned for potential problems such as manufacturers' liability protection, variations in state distribution capacities, and side effects of the vaccine. Given the public health rationality of prevention and the classical tools of population security, there had been "no choice" but to go forward with mass vaccination. Health officials did not have a mechanism with which to engage in responsible, but provisional, action under conditions of urgency and uncertainty.

EMERGENCY PREPAREDNESS AND
THE VULNERABLE SYSTEM

During this period, but still outside of the world of public health, a method was being developed for dealing flexibly with potential crisis situations. Over the prior two decades, the field of civil defense and defense mobilization had expanded its purview from an initial focus on planning for nuclear war to a more general form of emergency preparedness. Although in its inception, emergency preparedness was not institutionally linked to public health, the field would eventually add to its portfolio the threat of catastrophic disease.

Much of this process initially took place in government agencies devoted to preparing for an enemy nuclear attack. Beginning in the 1950s, civil defense and mobilization planners developed techniques of nuclear preparedness such as computer-based simulations of attack patterns, urban vulnerability mapping, and the administrative coordination of emergency response across multiple jurisdictions.[27] Over the course of the 1960s and early 1970s, such techniques were applied to a range of other potential emergencies, including natural disasters, economic crises, and terrorist attacks.

One of the defense mobilization specialists who followed this trajectory was the applied mathematician Robert H. Kupperman. Kupperman served as Assistant Director of the Office of Emergency Preparedness (OEP), a successor agency to the Office of Defense Mobilization, in the late 1960s and early 1970s. Mobilization planners had long been concerned with the vulnerability of vital industrial production systems to enemy attack.[28] At OEP, Kupperman's task was to bring sophisticated modeling techniques to bear on problems of emergency planning and system vulnerability. For example, he developed network vulnerability models to improve the postattack survivability of critical systems such as oil pipelines, railways, and telecommunications networks.

Kupperman's intellectual background was in operations research, a technical field dating from World War II efforts to introduce quantitative analysis to military practice. Operations research developed mathematical tools for analyzing and optimizing complex systems. This meant seeing multiple, heterogeneous elements as part of a coherent system whose behavior was, as one of the field's pioneers, Jay Forrester, put it, "a consequence of the interaction of its parts."[29] For instance, in studying the efficiency of allied bombing campaigns during World War II, operations researchers assembled data on specific bombing runs, looking at the interaction of multiple variables such as altitude, speed, number and formation of bombings, weather, and light. "In general," as historian Thomas Hughes observes, "advocates of the systems approach perceived, conceived of, or created a world made up of systems." The systems view gained prominence in the 1950s in settings including the RAND Corporation and the Defense Department under Robert McNamara. Less visibly, systems thinking shaped the reflections of postwar mobilization planners on how to ramp up industrial production in the lead up to a future total war. Beginning with the economic analysis of enemy industrial production systems during World War II as part of air targeting efforts, one branch of systems thinking focused on the vulnerability of vital systems to catastrophic interruption. Similarly, Kupperman's experiences in the Office of Emergency Preparedness directed his attention to the vulnerability of critical systems to sudden and unexpected events.

Based in the Systems Evaluation Division of OEP, Kupperman participated in governmental response to a number of domestic emergencies in the early 1970s, including the wage-price freeze of 1970, the devastation caused by Hurricane Agnes in 1972, a rash of domestic and international terrorist incidents, and the 1973 energy crisis. In this context, he developed an interest in the common structure of crisis situations and in the introduction of tools that could be used to prepare for them in advance. Kupperman argued that the numerous crises faced by government officials, however diverse, shared a number of common traits: a paucity of accurate information as the crisis unfolded, the difficulty of communication among decision-makers, and a confusing array of authorities seeking to take charge. Such situations involved uncertainty about what was unfolding coupled with an urgent demand for immediate intervention to alleviate the crisis. Flexibility for government decision-makers depended on the extent to which the emergency manager had envisioned the crisis situation in advance and had invested in preparation for it. The apparent recent upsurge in emergencies demonstrated the contemporary importance of such foresight. "As we begin to recognize the complex problems that threaten every nation with disaster," he and two of his OEP colleagues asked in a 1975 article in the journal *Science*, "can we continue to trust the ad hoc processes of instant reaction to muddle through?"[30]

After leaving OEP, Kupperman continued to reflect on how to improve governmental readiness for future crises, especially through his work at a Washington, D.C., think tank, the Center for Strategic and International Studies (CSIS), beginning in the late 1970s. There he was the coauthor, with national security expert James Woolsey, of a 1984 CSIS report on "crisis management in a society of networks," entitled *America's Hidden Vulnerabilities*. The report pointed to the nation's dependence on a sophisticated and intricate set of systems, or networks, for energy distribution, communication, and transportation. It noted recent disruptions of these systems, and warned: "A serious potential exists . . . for much more serious disabling of networks crucial to life support, economic stability, and national defense."[31] Kupperman and Woolsey recommended a number of measures that could help ensure the continued functioning of vital systems in the event of emergency, including improving system resilience, building in redundancy, stockpiling spare parts, performing risk analysis as a means of prioritizing resource allocation, and running scenario-based exercises to test the system. A final key element of crisis management, according to the report, was the specification in advance of the distribution of management responsibilities during the crisis situation itself.[32]

At CSIS, Kupperman and his colleagues sought to persuade national security officials of the problem of system vulnerability and of the urgent need to have in place a portfolio of techniques for managing potential future crises. One of their approaches was to invite government officials to participate in training simulations. As Woolsey and Kupperman wrote, crisis planning should involve the operating teams and managers so that "these critical personnel gain an increased understanding of how the system works, and, particularly valuable, how it is likely to behave under abnormal conditions." Simulations were a useful technique for transmitting such an understanding: "Training with crisis games and emergency exercises will augment this benefit significantly."[33]

Writing in the early 1980s about the vulnerability of collective life to catastrophic disruption, Kupperman again emphasized the role of simulation exercises in training for crisis management: "Ideally, when a real crisis hits, no difference should exist, either operationally or emotionally, between the current reality and the previous training simulations."[34] To design an effective training exercise required detailed information about the imagined future situation to be planned for: the speed of a toxic cloud under given weather conditions, the pattern of outbreak of an epidemic, the scale of impact of a large earthquake in a specific urban setting. Successful simulations not only exercised the system of emergency response and produced knowledge about needed capabilities but also generated a sense of urgency among participants.

At CSIS, Kupperman and a group of colleagues promoted the use of a specific technique they called the "crisis simulation," which was based on the RAND political exercises of the 1960s described in Chapter 1. The CSIS group's objective in developing these simulations was not to prevent future crises but rather to improve leaders' decision-making processes once such an event was under way. Simulations achieved this by exposing current gaps in readiness—thus generating awareness of what had to be considered before a crisis unfolded for future response to its occurrence to be adequate. In a 1987 interview, Kupperman explained that a well-designed crisis simulation had four key elements: first, a plausible scenario; second, a rapid sequence of events, leading to a feeling of intense pressure; third, experienced participants; and fourth, a "control staff" whose task was to simulate the real world.[35]

Like his predecessors at RAND, Kupperman noted that participants' absorption in the exercise, and therefore the capacity of the exercise to generate useful insights, depended upon its realism: "We try to make the players feel personally responsible," he said. "We create a twilight zone, they know it's not real, but they're not quite sure." The CSIS exercise designers emphasized the central role of the "control strategy" in creating a realistic feeling of crisis in which unpredictable events unfolded in real time and required immediate response. The reality effect of the exercise depended on the interventions, during the event, of the control group—the behind-the-scenes figures who supplied the real-world results of the participants' interventions. It was the control group that decided how the external world would respond, and so structured the experience of contingency that fostered participants' felt sense of reality. Such outside forces demonstrated to players their inability to fully control the outcome of the crisis situation, generating the anxiety and sense of responsibility crucial to an effective exercise.

There is a long history of reflection on how to govern certain kinds of crisis situations, extending from early modern quarantine plans to Cold War civil defense exercises. What was perhaps distinctive to the CSIS simulation was the application of the method of imaginative enactment to the generic crisis situation in order to generate knowledge about internal system-vulnerabilities. As we will see, this technique would eventually help convince national security officials to think seriously about biological threats. It would also help to make visible the elements of a new object of knowledge and intervention: the public health infrastructure.

DISEASE AS A NATIONAL SECURITY THREAT

In the mid-1990s, a group of advocates for renewed biodefense measures began to argue that the United States was dangerously vulnerable to a biological attack. They hypothesized an association among rogue states, terrorist organizations, and the global proliferation of biological weapons. Reports during the 1990s about secret Soviet and Iraqi bioweapons programs, along with the Aum Shinrikyo subway attack in 1995, lent credibility to calls for new biodefense measures focused on the threat of bioterrorism. On the one hand, according to biodefense advocates, the increasing accessibility of biological knowledge and the proliferation of biological weapons made an attack highly plausible. On the other hand, a lack of investment in biodefense measures and the disrepair of the nation's public health system meant that the United States was woefully unprepared for such an attack.

Prominent among the early biodefense advocates were scientists such as the epidemiologist Donald A. Henderson, who had directed the World Health Organization's successful smallpox eradication program, as well as national security specialists such as Richard A. Clarke, counter-terrorism adviser under Presidents George H.W. Bush and Bill Clinton. These experts argued that adequate preparation for a biological attack would require a massive infusion of resources into both biomedical research and public health response capacity.[36] More broadly, they maintained, it would be necessary to incorporate the agencies and institutions of the life sciences and public health into the national security establishment. In 1998, Henderson founded the Johns Hopkins Center for Civilian Biodefense Studies, which became a leading center of knowledge production around the new biological threat.

The chief concern among biodefense experts at this point was the possibility of a bioterrorist attack using smallpox virus. On the one hand, recent revelations from Soviet defector Ken Alibek about a vast Soviet bioweapons program raised the question of whether rogue states or terrorist groups might have smallpox stocks in hand. On the other hand, the U.S.

population was highly susceptible to a smallpox attack because routine vaccination had ended in 1972 and existing vaccine supplies were limited. Nobel prize–winning biologist Joshua Lederberg, a prominent advocate for greater attention to biodefense, argued that "the most likely source of supply for possible bioterrorists" came from the "laboratories of a hundred countries from the time that smallpox was a common disease."[37] At a 1999 meeting of government biodefense experts, participants were unanimous that smallpox was the primary biological threat to address—not because of the probability of an attack but because of the virulence and transmissibility of the virus alongside the vulnerability of the population. "The likelihood of an attack is small," commented Henderson, "but were it to occur it would be a real catastrophe."[38]

The CDC initiated several programs in response to the perceived threat of a biological attack. Among these was the establishment of the Office of Bioterrorism Preparedness and Response, which provided $40 million per year in bioterrorism preparedness grants to local public health departments. However, critics argued that these measures were not nearly enough. For instance, Tara O'Toole of the Hopkins Biodefense Center pointed to numerous vulnerabilities within the public health and medical response systems, to the absence of essential medical counter-measures to treat select pathogens, and to political decision-makers' unfamiliarity with infectious disease control and public health practices.[39]

Because they were describing an unprecedented event, biodefense advocates' claims about the characteristics of the biological threat typically took the form of the conditional—of what *would* happen in the event of an attack.[40] Henderson described the scenario of an aerosol release of a biological agent such as anthrax as follows: "No one would know until days or weeks later that anyone had been infected (depending on the microbe). Then patients would begin appearing in emergency rooms and physicians' offices with symptoms of a strange disease that few physicians had ever seen."[41] But such imaginative projections did not by themselves transmit to government officials the sense of urgency felt by figures such as Henderson and O'Toole to actually implement policies to mitigate what they saw as the nation's vulnerability to a biological attack.

The threat of bioterrorism had to compete in a crowded terrain of emerging security concerns, each vying to fill in what Senator Sam Nunn called the "threat blank" left by the end of the Cold War. Prospective national security threats in the late 1990s included nuclear proliferation, asymmetric warfare, "netwar," the Y2K bug, and rising economic powers such as China. There were at least two impediments to convincing policy-makers of the urgency and severity of the biological threat. First, defense strategists were not accustomed to thinking about disease in terms of national security. "We are used to thinking about health problems as naturally occurring problems outside the framework of a malicious actor," as James Woolsey put it. With disease as a tool of attack, "we are in a world we haven't ever really been in before."[42] And second, many security officials were not yet convinced that the threat was credible: a mass biological attack was an event that had never occurred, and its future likelihood was difficult if not impossible to assess.

A major task for biodefense advocates in this period was, then, to convince government officials of the seriousness of the security threat posed by a bioweapons attack. As part of this effort, advocates developed a scenario-based exercise that could serve as a pedagogical tool for public officials charged with thinking about and anticipating security threats. On June 22–23, 2001, the Hopkins Center for Biodefense, in collaboration with Kupperman's former think tank, the Center for Strategic and International Studies (CSIS), and the ANSER Institute for Homeland Security, held an exercise called "Dark Winter," which simulated a large-scale smallpox attack on the United States. According to its designers, the aim of the exercise was "to increase awareness of the scope and character of the threat posed by biological weapons among senior national security experts and to catalyze actions that would improve prevention and response strategies."[43] In other words, the exercise sought to constitute the possibility of a biological attack as a significant national security threat.

Although the Dark Winter exercise inherited much of its structure from its Cold War era precursors, there was at least one significant difference. As opposed to the RAND political exercises of the 1960s, in Dark Winter there was no red team against which the U.S. leaders played: in the case of a bioterrorist attack, there was no rational adversary whose actions would have to be understood and managed in a crisis situation. Whereas the strategizing enemy had been a central actor in the RAND exercises as well as the CSIS crisis simulations of the 1980s, "Nature" was now the only opponent. The central problem for exercise participants had shifted: from anticipating and managing enemy motivations and intentions in a diplomatic crisis to understanding the nation's internal vulnerabilities to an undeterrable external threat.

The organizers recruited twelve prominent public figures to serve as role players. These were all "accomplished individual(s) who serve or have served in high level government or military positions," and included eminent national security authority Sam Nunn, former chairman of the Senate Committee on Armed Services and chairman of the Board of Trustees of CSIS, as the president; former presidential adviser David Gergen as national security adviser; and CSIS veteran James Woolsey as director of the CIA. These individuals were chosen both because of their firsthand knowledge of how officials would likely react to the events in question and because their analyses of the lessons of the experience would likely be credible to a wide range of current officials.

The exercise took place in three segments over two days, depicting a time span of two weeks after the initial biological attack. It was held before an audience of more than a hundred observers, including national security analysts and members of the press. Although the scenario's designers used historical data on the transmission patterns of actual past smallpox outbreaks to structure the exercise, the point of using such data was not so much to accurately model how such an event would unfold as to create a plausible scenario—and specifically, one that had a poor outcome. A critical question in designing the exercise, for example, was the rate of disease transmission assumed. Historically, the rate of smallpox transmission fluctuates widely in relation to multiple contextual factors. To determine the rate to be assumed in the scenario, the exercise designers analyzed thirty-four European outbreaks of smallpox between 1958 and 1973, choosing the case of a 1972 outbreak in Yugoslavia as their model not because its transmission rate was the most likely but because this rate would yield a cascading crisis.[44]

The designers structured the exercise to direct participants' attention to certain key issues that had been identified by biodefense specialists in advance: the limited number of vaccine doses that would be available in the wake an attack, the need for information systems to track the spread of the disease, and the lack of existing plans for coordinating emergency response among federal and state officials. To shape how events unfolded over the course of the simulation, as in the RAND political exercises, "controllers played the roles of deputies or special assistants, providing briefings of facts and policy options to participants throughout the meeting as needed."[45]

The first meeting of the National Security Council laid out the situation for participants. There were reports of an outbreak of smallpox in Oklahoma City, assumed to be the result of a terrorist attack. Initial questions for the council were technical: "With only twelve million doses of vaccine available, what is the best strategy to contain the outbreak? Should there be a national or a state vaccination policy? Is ring vaccination or mass immunization the best policy?" The participants found that they did not have enough information about the scale of the attack to come up with a solution, especially given limited vaccine stocks. This sense of uncertainty about appropriate action had been built into the assumptions of the exercise: there was in fact no possible decision that could avert disaster.

By the second meeting of the National Security Council, the situation looked increasingly grim. "Only 1.25 million doses of vaccine remain, and public unrest grows as the vaccine supply dwindles," participants were informed. "Vaccine distribution efforts vary from state to state, are often chaotic, and lead to violence in some areas" read the transcript. International borders were closed, leading to trade disruption and food shortages. Simulated twenty-four-hour news coverage, periodically shown as video clips to participants, sharply criticized the government's response to the outbreak. The news clips included graphic images of dying American smallpox victims.

As vaccine stocks were depleted and crowds fought over remaining doses, advisers broached the prospect of using the National Guard to enforce quarantine. But who had the authority to make such a decision? In one exchange among participants, a National Security Council member argued that the president should federalize the National Guard, as states had begun to seal their borders. "That's not your function," objected a governor, defending states' rights. The attorney general responded, "Mr. President, this question got settled at Appomattox. You need to federalize the National Guard." The president then interjected: "We're going to have absolute chaos if we start having war between the federal government and the state government." Thus, the structured improvisation built into the exercise guided participants to formulate the vulnerabilities presented by the threat of a biological attack.

Meanwhile, civil unrest intensified. "With vaccine in short supply, increasingly anxious crowds mob vaccination clinics," reported the simulated news program. "Riots around a vaccination site in Philadelphia left two dead. At another vaccination site, angry citizens overwhelmed vaccinators."[46] By the third meeting, there had been hundreds of smallpox deaths, and the situation was growing still worse as the disease continued to spread. The exercise ended as the disaster escalated: there were no doses of smallpox vaccine remaining, and none were expected for at least four weeks. The Director of CSIS, John Hamre, later narrated the final stage of the exercise: "In the last 48 hours there were 14,000 cases. We now have over 1,000 dead, another 5,000 that we expect to be dead within weeks. There are 200 people who died from the vaccination, because there is a small percentage [of risk], and we have administered 12 million doses. . . . At this stage the medical system is overwhelmed completely."[47]

REALISM AND AFFECT

One of the objectives of the exercise was to give political leaders a *feeling* of how a biological attack would likely play out and how little prepared they were for such an event. Its circle of influence extended outward through a series of briefings that included a "documentary" video portraying the simulated outbreak as it unfolded. Vice President Dick Cheney, Homeland Security Secretary Tom Ridge, and key congressional leaders were among those briefed. At a congressional hearing where the video was to be shown, Hamre warned the committee chairman: "It is not pleasant. Let me also emphasize, sir, this is a simulation. This had frightening qualities of being real, as a matter of fact too real."[48] After watching the video, the chairman described his reaction: "I felt like I've been in the middle of a movie, and maybe that's why I was anxious. I wanted to know how it turned out. And so I asked my staff how did we finally get a handle on it, you know, 12 million vaccines out, the disease spreading? And the response was we did not get a handle on it."[49] Again, the dire outcome was built into the exercise design, given the designers' assumptions about the scale of the attack, the disease transmission rate, and the lack of available vaccine stocks.

In their congressional testimony on the need for improved bioterrorism preparedness, Dark Winter participants reported on their own experience of the exercise. Sam Nunn reflected on the problem of how to enforce quarantine given the absence of effective treatments: "It is a terrible dilemma. Because you know that your vaccine is going to give out, and you know the only other strategy is isolation, but you don't know who to isolate. That is the horror of this situation."[50] The event also revealed critical political vulnerabilities. As Hamre testified, "We thought that we were going to be spending our time with the mechanisms of government. We ended up spending our time saying, how do we save democracy in America? Because it is that serious, and it is that big."[51] Governor Frank Keating of Oklahoma was stunned at the lack of preparedness demonstrated by the exercise: "We think an enemy of the United States could attack us with smallpox or with anthrax . . . and we really don't prepare for it, we have no vaccines for it— that's astonishing."[52] Dark Winter was successful in that it convinced participants and later briefing audiences of the urgent need for advanced planning to be able to effectively govern in the event of a biological emergency.

The exercise imparted detailed knowledge about existing vulnerabilities in response capacity. First, officials did not have real-time "situational awareness" of the various aspects of the crisis while it unfolded: as the exercise designers wrote, "few systems exist that can provide a rapid flow of the medical and public health information needed in a public health emergency."[53] Second, without available stockpiles of medical countermeasures, emergency responders could not properly manage the crisis. And third, the exercise demonstrated the wide gulf between public health and national security expertise: "It isn't just [a matter of] buying more vaccine," said Woolsey. "It's a question of how we integrate these public health and national security communities in ways that allow us to deal with various facets of the problem."[54]

In their testimony, participants pointed toward policy measures that would address these lacunae. Nunn argued that first responders must be vaccinated against smallpox well in advance of an attack: "Every one of those people you are trying to mobilize is going to have to be vaccinated.

You can't expect them to go in there and expose themselves and their family to smallpox or any other deadly disease without vaccinations."[55] Hauer, a former New York City emergency manager, spoke of the need to address the problem of rapid vaccine distribution in an urban context: "The logistical infrastructure necessary to vaccinate the people of New York City, Los Angeles, Chicago is just—would be mind-boggling."[56]

But the broader lesson of Dark Winter was the need to imaginatively enact a future biological attack to be able to adequately plan for it in the present. As Hamre said, "We didn't have the strategy at the table on how to deal with this, because we have never thought our way through it before, and systematically thinking our way through this kind of a crisis is now going to become a key imperative. It clearly is going to require many more exercises."[57] And indeed, among the initiatives funded during the rapid increase in federal support for civilian biodefense of the early 2000s was a nationwide program of public health preparedness exercises, designed and run by the RAND Corporation under contract from the CDC.[58]

TOWARD PUBLIC HEALTH PREPAREDNESS

Just before the Dark Winter exercise, in June 2001, the CDC's ACIP had addressed the question of whether to implement a "pre-event vaccination" program for first responders in preparation for a potential smallpox attack. As background to its consideration, the committee cited heightened growing international concern "regarding the potential use of smallpox (variola) virus as a bioterrorism agent." However, the question of whether to recommend pre-event vaccination did not easily lend itself to resolution through the committee's standard method of evaluation, risk-benefit analysis. On the one hand, it was known that receiving the vaccine carried a risk of serious, even life-threatening, adverse effects. But it was not possible to quantitatively weigh that risk against the possible benefits of vaccination. There was no data available on which to make a calculation of the benefits of such a program in the absence of any actual incidence of the disease. As the committee reported, "The risk of smallpox occurring as a result of a deliberate release by terrorists is considered low, and the population at risk for such an exposure cannot be determined."[59] Given the difficulty of making a credible risk assessment, the committee declined to recommend a pre-event vaccination program.

Less than a year later, this issue returned to the committee. After the events of fall 2001—the attacks of September 11, followed by a series of anthrax attacks delivered through the mail—the Bush administration became urgently focused on bioterrorism preparedness. The lessons learned from the Dark Winter exercise helped direct this sense of urgency. Recall the argument by former senator Sam Nunn that first responders must be vaccinated against smallpox in advance of a potential attack. In early 2002, the White House asked CDC to develop such a plan for small-pox vaccination. In turn, CDC requested that its expert committee once again take up the question of pre-event vaccination. The committee's delib-erations show how the newly articulated demand for bioterrorism prepar-edness came into tension with the traditional rationality of public health. The transcript of the June 2002 ACIP meeting indicates that the commit-tee's infectious disease specialists were not accustomed to thinking in terms of worst-case scenarios; rather, they wanted statistical data that could be taken up as part of a technical risk assessment. "To make . . . deci-sions, the ACIP needs data," read the meeting's minutes. "Those on vaccine efficacy and safety are in hand, but not for the risk of disease. Does anyone have more information on this that they can share? Without it, should the ACIP even make this decision?"[60]

The committee was faced with the prospect of a future event that was conceivable but that had never occurred. Without data on its probability, its members again complained that they did not have the means to make a risk assessment. Nonetheless, given pressures from the Bush adminis-tration in the context of the lead-up to the Iraq War, the CDC emerged with a plan for the voluntary immunization of an estimated one million emergency responders and health care workers, known as the Smallpox Vaccination Program. However, the program lacked credibility for the tar-geted population, the vast majority of whom failed to volunteer for vacci-nation once the program began. For emergency responders and health care workers, the threat of a smallpox attack was not credible enough to make it worthwhile to take the risk of receiving the vaccine, given its known side effects. The program was suspended in 2003 after having immunized just thirty thousand health and emergency workers—roughly 3 percent of its initial target.[61]

More generally, in the period after the September 11 attacks and the anthrax letters, government support for bioterrorism preparedness increased markedly.[62] Hundreds of millions of federal dollars were sent to states to build local public health infrastructure, and the National Institutes of Health received substantial funds for basic research on select pathogens. In late 2001, Donald A. Henderson of the Hopkins Center for Biodefense was appointed to direct the newly established Office of Public Health Preparedness within the U.S. Department of Health and Human Services (HHS). In the following years, as HHS official Stewart Simonson later recalled, Henderson "became the architect of the post-9/11 HHS public health preparedness program," which sought to address both the threat of a biological attack and the threat of an emerging disease pandemic.[63]

Although federal public health preparedness efforts initially focused primarily on bioterrorist threats such as smallpox and anthrax, their emphasis gradually shifted to include dangers posed by "nature" as well—in particular, the threat of pandemic influenza. HHS had begun to develop pandemic preparedness plans in 1999, soon after the initial appearance of H5N1 avian influenza in Hong Kong in 1997. In the early 2000s, Simonson took an active interest in drawing the attention of government officials to the pandemic threat. In 2002, he invited the historian Alfred Crosby, author of *America's Forgotten Pandemic: The Influenza of 1918*, to brief HHS staff on the potential impact of a future pandemic. "What became clear to everyone present," Simonson later recalled, "was that we were not ready for a 1918-like event, not even close."[64] The 1918 influenza pandemic became a template for the scenario of a future influenza pandemic. To plan for the possibility of such an event, HHS decided to focus on two dimensions of public health preparedness: first, early warning—specifically, closing gaps in global influenza surveillance by forging partnerships with transnational institutions such as the Pasteur Institute; second, medical countermeasures—improving influenza vaccine production capacity and adding millions of doses of antiviral drugs to the Strategic National Stockpile, which had been established in 1999 to store drugs and vaccines for select bioweapons agents such as anthrax and smallpox. The National Institutes of Health also added funding for basic virology research on influenza transmission and virulence to the agency's biodefense research portfolio—a program whose significance we turn to in Chapter 5.

With an eye toward the transnational dimension of the problem of early warning, in late 2001, HHS Secretary Tommy Thompson established a group for the international coordination of public health preparedness. Under the rubric of the "Global Health Security Initiative" (GHSI), the group brought together health ministers from advanced industrial countries in Europe, North America, and Asia who initially pledged to strengthen preparedness and response policies for chemical, biological, and nuclear emergencies.[65] Late in 2002, at the time of Simonson's efforts to galvanize attention to the pandemic threat, the GHSI mandate was broadened to include pandemic influenza preparedness as well. Also around this time, HHS representatives began to regularly participate in World Health Organization meetings on influenza surveillance and preparedness. In May 2005, a staff member from the HHS Office of Public Health Preparedness led an effort to gain adoption of a resolution at the World Health Assembly supporting expedited pandemic influenza planning.[66] We return to the story of the global extension of pandemic preparedness efforts in Chapter 3.

In the U.S. political context, pandemic preparedness gained initial momentum as a priority for legislative support in 2004, due to two events: first, the reemergence and spread of highly pathogenic avian influenza (H5N1) over the prior year in East Asia; second, a highly publicized failure in the production of seasonal flu vaccine in the United States. At this point, Simonson later recalled, "it became a political liability to ignore influenza preparedness." As a result, Congress agreed to the HHS budget request for $100 million in 2005 to support development of a cell culture technique to enhance the efficiency of vaccine production and to purchase stocks of the antiviral drug Tamiflu as part of the Strategic National Stockpile (SNS).

Meanwhile, the Public Health Preparedness office continued its effort to spark concern about the issue among key congressional leaders. Soon after its release in 2005, HHS staff distributed highlighted copies of journalist John Barry's book on the 1918 pandemic, *The Great Influenza*, to members of major congressional committees and held a series of briefings on the pandemic threat. In June 2005, two members of the Senate Foreign Relations Committee, Barack Obama and Richard Lugar, coauthored an opinion piece in the *New York Times* advocating for attention to the specter of avian influenza. In addition to major national security threats such as "nuclear proliferation, rogue states and global terrorism," they wrote, "another kind of threat lurks beyond our shores, one from nature, not humans—an avian flu pandemic."

Senators Obama and Lugar argued that to adequately address the pandemic threat it was necessary to develop a "permanent framework for curtailing the spread of future infectious diseases." They laid out the elements of a public health preparedness system: it would require coordination among multiple actors including public health officials, the pharmaceutical industry, foreign governments, and international organizations. Its features would include increased disease surveillance and response capacity around the world, stockpiling of antiviral drug doses, domestic emergency planning to protect the population as well as "core public functions" in the case of a pandemic, investments in influenza vaccine and antiviral drug research, and incentives for nations to report outbreaks quickly.

Meanwhile, Simonson later recalled, the Bush administration was "focused like a laser on pandemic preparedness" due to the strong advocacy of HHS officials. In 2005, the White House Homeland Security Council led an interagency effort to develop a national pandemic plan, "which covered all departments and sections of critical infrastructure."[67] In a closed-door briefing for members of Congress in September, Secretary of Health Mike Leavitt warned that an influenza pandemic could cause up to two million deaths and ten million hospitalizations in the United States. Senate Minority Leader Harry Reid reported that Levitt's scenario had "scared the hell out of me."[68] The following day, the Senate voted to provide a $3.9 billion appropriation for federal influenza preparedness planning.

Such congressional attention to preparedness was further galvanized by the failed governmental response to Hurricane Katrina in August. As health preparedness expert Irwin Redlener explained in the aftermath of the hurricane, the government could not "tolerate another tragically inadequate response to a major disaster." An influenza pandemic, he continued, was the "next big catastrophe that we can reasonably expect, and the country is phenomenally not prepared for this."[69] For critics of the administration's emergency response, Hurricane Katrina served as a real-life exercise demonstrating gaps in the system of national preparedness. The failed response to the hurricane also indicated that while security planners had been focused on the threat of terrorism, the problem of how to govern emergencies was much broader: the rubric of "all-hazards" planning that had initially structured federal emergency management returned to the fore.

In congressional hearings over the following months, the problem of avian influenza was cast in terms of the vulnerability of the nation's public health infrastructure. According to Sen. Richard Burr, Chairman of the Subcommittee on Public Health Preparedness, Katrina "exposed an unstable public health infrastructure at all levels of government during an emergency event."[70] The challenge at hand, argued Burr, was akin to the project of constructing the national highway infrastructure in the 1950s. "For the purpose of a national public health and defense we need a national standardized public health system," he said. Such a system would have to do more than prepare for known threats: "The question is, are we smart enough to design a template that enables us to address the threats that we don't know about for tomorrow?"

What were the necessary elements of such a system for anticipating the unexpected? These elements could be made visible through an analysis of current gaps in response capability. "There are multiple holes in our capacity to respond," said Rep. Henry Waxman. "We need to increase our vaccine production capacity, strengthen our public health infrastructure, create adequate hospital surge capacity and draft contingency plans that will ensure the continued operation of important government functions."[71] The task was to constitute an effective public health preparedness system, based on knowledge of current vulnerabilities.

According to many officials, the most serious vulnerability Hurricane Katrina had exposed was that of the locus of government authority in an emergency situation. For some, the main problem was the incompetence of federal leadership, as exemplified by the infamous director of the Federal Emergency Management Agency, Mike Brown. For others, the problem was that local authorities were not up to the task of coordinating government response. Former Homeland Security Advisor Richard Falkenrath argued that government health authorities would be incapable of adequately responding to a catastrophic disease event. The U.S. Health Department, he said, "is simply not going to be able to meet the American people's expectation of the federal government in a truly catastrophic disease contingency such as a high lethal pandemic or major bioterrorist attack."[72] Falkenrath was especially concerned about the scenario of civil unrest resulting from "shortages in vital, life-saving counter-measures to the disease in question"—precisely the premise of Dark Winter. He focused on the logistics of medication distribution from existing stocks as the critical challenge: "I mean something very, very specific, which is to prepare to distribute life-saving medications to extremely large populations, very, very quickly, when they are afraid, because there is a communicable disease out there that they do not know how to deal with."

Falkenrath cited evidence from scenario-based exercises to validate his claim that government health agencies did not have the operational capabilities to distribute essential medical supplies in a crisis situation: "This extraordinary national deficiency was first revealed during the first TOPOFF exercise in May 2000 at which I was an observer," and "in a wide variety of smaller scale table top exercises and simulations." He continued: "The implication is inescapable: the plans, if put to the severe test of a catastrophic disease scenario in the near future, will fail." There was a clear policy implication, according to Falkenrath: the National Response Plan should be amended to assign Emergency Support Function #8, the mechanism for coordinating government response to a public health emergency, to the military in a catastrophic disease incident, at the order of the president: "Only the Department of Defense has the planning, logistics, and personnel resources needed to conduct nationwide medical relief operations in a full-scale catastrophic disease scenario." In the absence of an actual health emergency, the results of scenario-based exercises were used to authorize claims about what was likely to happen if the anticipated event did occur, and what policy changes were therefore needed in advance.

But such claims did not go uncontested. Tara O'Toole of the Center for Biosecurity drew a very different lesson from Hurricane Katrina: "What we have to do, and what the main point of planning is, as we have learned in all of the emergency preparedness done so far, is that we have to start talking with each other."[73] She disagreed with Falkenrath about the role of the military in a health emergency: "I think it would be a big mistake to . . . plan to put DOD in charge whenever we have a big bad thing happening." While acknowledging the need to "rethink federalism," O'Toole argued that the federal role should be one of creating infrastructure to enable local response: "What the feds have to do is create the capacity to plug in and that's where they ought to be focusing on. But I don't think we want the DOD to suddenly become everybody's responder in cases of dire need."[74] The debate recapitulated long-standing discussions of the appropriate organization for emergency management—centralized versus distributed, military versus civilian—going back to the Cold War civil defense era.[75] In the end, the HHS emerged victorious in the struggle, as it was officially assigned Emergency Support Function #8 in the summer of 2007.[76]

One thing that all parties could agree on was that public health and emergency management agencies must engage in more training exercises. In a congressional hearing on pandemic preparedness, a representative of the American College of Emergency Physicians testified: "We need to train the hospital and health care workers to more long-term pandemic scenarios. And then we need to take these lessons learned, the best practices and lessons learned, and disseminate."[77] The Health Commissioner of Duchess County New York concurred: "I think over the last five years we've built the framework of a system that we can carry forward . . . but we need to strengthen that and continue to have strategic exercises community wide, not just public health departments, but every single community drill to include as many partners as possible so that we can learn from each other."[78] And an emergency health official from Virginia explained, "We have been working very closely with DHS in terms of developing metrics as well as with the CDC and DHHS, but we need to assure that we have the exercises and events to test our plans and that's really the test of preparedness."[79]

By the end of 2006, Congress had moved to address the problem of public health preparedness in a more sustained and comprehensive way, with the passage of the Pandemic and All-Hazards Preparedness Act. Health security experts hailed the bill's passage as a "milestone" piece of public health legislation.[80] The bill included a range of measures, from the reorganization of federal health administration, to funding for local and state health agencies, the training of epidemiological investigators, and a novel biomedical research initiative. A key issue the bill sought to address was how to create an integrated system of public health preparedness, one that extended from disease detection to vaccine production to the relations among the various government agencies that would be charged with response. This system was focused not specifically on pandemic flu but on a generic form of biological threat: the unpredictable, but potentially catastrophic, disease event.

There was general agreement among preparedness advocates that addressing this threat was not simply a matter of public health but also one of national security. Although the link between national security and public health was not in itself new, what was distinctive about these measures was the attempt to integrate the institutions, forms of knowledge, and techniques of intervention developed in the period of modern public health into a system of national preparedness.

In closing, let us return briefly to the 1976 swine flu vaccination campaign described at the outset of the chapter, comparing it to the pandemic preparedness measures enacted three decades later. Along with the contrast in their scale, the two technical and political responses differed in their approach to disease threat. First, in the way of conceptualizing the threat to be managed: the 2005–2006 measures targeted not only the specific threat of a new and virulent strain of influenza but also the generic "catastrophic disease threat." Second, the site of intervention was distinct: whereas the 1976 campaign was aimed at the national population using classical methods of public health, the later plans targeted multiple elements of the "public health infrastructure," both within the United States and globally, including disease surveillance capacity, the ability to produce and distribute medical countermeasures, and the administrative organization of emergency response. And third, the prominent form of knowledge used to authorize expert claims about needed interventions had changed: rather than the statistical calculation of risk based on historical patterns of disease incidence, the emphasis of experts was on knowledge of system-vulnerabilities gathered through the imaginative enactment of singular events.

The first two chapters of this book have focused on developments in the United States: the extension of a style of reasoning and set of techniques from nuclear preparedness to a broad range potential threats ranging from natural disasters, to terrorism, to pandemics. But the specter of emerging disease, initially articulated in the late 1980s and then becoming highly visible by the early 2000s, pointed to the need for a different scale of preparedness efforts. Emerging disease specialists warned that mitigating vulnerabilities in the United States was not only a matter of investing in national pandemic preparedness measures such as maintaining antiviral stockpiles, managing hospital surge capacity, and training health officials in risk communication. In addition, given the potential for the rapid spread of a new disease across national borders, the detection and containment of a future outbreak at its site of emergence might prove crucial to averting a catastrophe in the United States. This was the background to the U.S. Department of Health and Human Services' investment in the Global Health Security Initiative in the early 2000s. Such efforts bore fruit at the international level with the official adoption of the strategy of "global public health security" by WHO member nations in 2007. In the next chapter, we turn to some of the tensions that soon arose around this new conceptualization of the problem of global health.

3 Two Regimes of Global Health

In an opinion piece published in the *Washington Post* in August 2008, diplomat Richard Holbrooke and journalist Laurie Garrett mounted a sharp attack on what they called "viral sovereignty."[1] With this term, the authors referred to the "extremely dangerous" idea that sovereign states could exercise ownership rights over samples of viruses found in their territory. Specifically, Holbrooke and Garrett were incensed by the Indonesian government's refusal to share isolates of the H5N1 avian influenza virus with the World Health Organization's (WHO) Global Influenza Surveillance Network (GISN). For more than fifty years, this network had collected samples of flu viruses from national laboratories and used these samples to determine the composition of yearly flu vaccines. More recently, the network had tracked the molecular transformations of the H5N1 virus over time and space as a means of assessing the risk of a deadly global pandemic.[2] International health experts feared that this strain of avian influenza, which had already proven highly virulent, would mutate to become easily transmissible among humans, in which case a worldwide calamity could be at hand. GISN thus served as a mechanism of global alert enabling influenza specialists to track genetic changes in the virus that could lead to a catastrophic disease event. Meanwhile, there was also an unofficial use of the viral samples gathered through the network: as the basis for H5N1 vaccine candidates developed by pharmaceutical companies.

As the country where the most human cases of avian influenza had been reported, Indonesia was a potential epicenter of such an outbreak. For this reason, the country's decision to withhold samples of the virus from WHO threatened to undermine GISN's function as a pandemic early warning system and as a source of viral isolates for use in vaccine development. From Holbrooke and Garrett's perspective, the Indonesian state's claim to sovereignty over the virus posed a significant threat to global health. They drew on the language of the free software movement to make a case against the Indonesian position. "In this age of globalization," they wrote, "failure to make viral samples open-source risks allowing the emergence of a new strain of influenza that could go unnoticed until it is capable of exacting the sort of toll taken by the pandemic that killed tens of millions in 1918." According to Garrett and Holbrooke, Indonesia had not only a moral but also a legal obligation to share its viruses with WHO. They argued that the country's action was a violation of the newly revised International Health Regulations (IHR), which held the status of an international treaty for WHO member states and underpinned the WHO strategy for achieving "global public health security."

The opinion piece suggested that the rational and beneficent technocracy of the WHO was faced with antiscientific demagoguery that threatened the world's health. Holbrooke and Garrett painted a picture of Indonesian Health Minister Siti Fadilah Supari as an irrational populist who sought to make domestic political gains through unfounded attacks on the United States and the international health community. Indonesia, they wrote, was withholding the virus samples based on the "dangerous folly" that these materials should be protected through the same legal mechanism that the United Nations Food and Agriculture Organization used to guarantee poor countries' rights of ownership to indigenous agricultural resources, the Convention on Biological Diversity. Further, Holbrooke and Garrett rebuked Supari's "outlandish claims" that the U.S. government was planning to use Indonesia's H5N1 samples to design biological warfare agents.[3]

The controversy over influenza virus sharing was, it turned out, somewhat more complicated than Holbrooke and Garrett allowed. Beginning in early 2007, at Supari's behest, the Indonesian Health Ministry had stopped sharing isolates of H5N1 found in human victims of the virus with the influenza surveillance network. The source of Supari's ire was the discovery that an Australian pharmaceutical company planned to develop and patent a vaccine against avian influenza using an Indonesian strain of the virus that had been acquired via the WHO sharing network. Such a vaccine, Supari and others noted, would not be affordable for most Indonesians in the event of a deadly pandemic. More generally, given the limited amount of vaccine that could be produced in time to manage such a pandemic—estimates were in the range of five hundred million doses— experts acknowledged that developing countries would have little access to such a vaccine. Through advance purchase agreements with vaccine manufacturers, government health agencies in North America and Europe had guaranteed that their citizens would have priority in the global distribution of a pandemic vaccine. In other words, while Indonesia had been delivering virus samples to WHO as part of a collective early warning mechanism (i.e., GISN), they would not be beneficiaries of the biomedical response apparatus that had been constructed to prepare for a deadly global outbreak. For the Indonesian health minister, this situation indicated a dark "conspiracy between superpower nations and global organizations" such as WHO.[4]

Although less suspicious of U.S. and WHO intentions than Supari, a number of Western journalists and scientists were sympathetic to the Indonesian position, on the grounds of equity in the global distribution of essential medicines. A *Time* magazine article noted that "they had a point; poor developing nations are often priced out of needed medicines, and they're likely to be last in line for vaccine during a pandemic."[5] An editorial in the *Lancet* argued, "To ensure global health security, countries have to protect the wellbeing not only of their own patients but also those of fellow nations."[6] Anxious to ensure the functioning of its influenza surveillance apparatus, WHO was willing to strike a bargain: at a World Health Assembly meeting in February 2007, members agreed to explore ways of helping poorer countries to build vaccine production capacity. "We have been in discussions with the Ministry of Health since November of last year," said David Heymann, head of the WHO communicable diseases branch, describing the agency's interactions with Indonesian health officials. "We will continue to work with them and with all countries to ensure this virus will remain somehow a public good."[7] But the financial and technical details of how a system for ensuring equitable vaccine access would function were opaque, and the issue remained unresolved. In October 2008, as Indonesia continued to withhold the vast majority of its virus samples from GISN, *Agence France-Presse* reported that "Supari does appear to be vindicated by a flood of patents being lodged on the samples of H5N1 that have made it out of Indonesia, with companies in developed countries claiming ownership over viral DNA taken from sick Indonesians."[8] The Australian drug company CSL acknowledged that it had used Indonesian bird flu strains to develop a trial vaccine for H5N1 but insisted that it had no obligation to compensate Indonesia or guarantee its citizens access to the vaccine in the event of a pandemic.

International law experts saw the virus-sharing controversy as an early test of how well the revised IHR would function in regulating national health agencies. According to the new regulations, all signatories were required to provide WHO with "public health information" about events that might constitute a public health emergency of international concern.[9] In the case of the virus-sharing controversy, the central legal question was whether biological materials such as H5N1 isolates constituted such "public health information." Plausible arguments could be made on both sides. At the May 2007 meeting of the World Health Assembly, Director-General Chan stated, "Countries that did not share avian influenza virus would fail the IHR."[10] The U.S. delegation agreed: "All nations have a responsibility under the revised IHRs to share data and virus samples on a timely basis and without preconditions."[11] Thus, the United States continued, "our view is that withholding influenza viruses from GISN greatly threatens global public health and will violate the legal obligations we have all agreed to undertake through our adherence to IHRs." However, the relevance of the revised IHR to the specific issue of virus sharing was ambiguous: the new regulations explicitly referred only to a requirement to share public health *information*, such as case reports and fatality rates, and an argument could be made that biological materials such as virus samples were distinct from such information.[12]

In any case, the Indonesian Health Minister's response came from outside the legal framework of IHR. Rather, Supari argued that the virus sharing system was ethically compromised and in need of reform. "We want to change the global virus sharing mechanism to be fair, transparent and equitable," she said in an interview defending the Indonesian government's decision to withhold the virus.[13] "What we mean by fair is that any virus sharing should be accompanied by benefits derived from the shared virus, and these benefits should be coming from the vaccine producing countries." Supari was speaking from within a different technical and political framework than that of the International Health Regulations. In speaking of benefits-sharing, Supari was invoking a mechanism intended to encourage economic development and natural resource preservation—the Convention on Biological Diversity—to ground a rhetoric of national sovereignty that ran counter to the transnational authority of WHO.[14] But as we will see, her attack on the high price of patented vaccines also resonated with demands for equal access to life-saving medicines coming out of the humanitarian global health movement.

A system of alert and response designed to prepare for catastrophic disease outbreaks at a global scale was facing a very different demand: a call for access to essential medicines based on a vision of global equity. The potential for a deadly outbreak of avian influenza had led to an encounter between two ways of conceptualizing the problem of global health—an encounter that was taking place in the absence of an actual pandemic emergency. At stake was not only the issue of how best to respond to a global outbreak of H5N1 but, more broadly, how to define the political obligation to care for the population's health in an interconnected world in which the capability of national public health authorities to protect their citizens' well-being was increasingly in question.

Global health security focuses on "emerging infectious diseases," whether naturally occurring or manmade, which are seen to threaten wealthy countries and which typically (although not always) emanate from Asia, sub-Saharan Africa, or Latin America. Examples of emerging diseases include severe acute respiratory syndrome (SARS), Ebola, and highly pathogenic avian influenza; but what is crucial is that this regime is oriented toward outbreak events that *have not yet occurred*—and may never occur. For this reason, global health security develops techniques of preparedness for potential events whose likelihood is incalculable but that threaten catastrophic political, economic, and health consequences. Its advocates seek to create a real-time, global disease surveillance system that can provide early warning of potential outbreaks, and to link such early warning to systems of rapid response designed to protect against their spread to the rest of the world. To create such an apparatus, global health security initiatives draw together various organizations including multilateral health agencies, national disease control institutes, and collaborative reference laboratories, and they assemble diverse technical elements such as disease surveillance methods, emergency operations centers, and vaccine distribution systems.

Humanitarian biomedicine, in contrast, targets diseases such as malaria and tuberculosis (TB) that currently afflict large numbers of people in places where treatment is difficult or impossible to access. The objective of humanitarian biomedicine is to alleviate the suffering of individuals, independent of national and social identity. Such intervention is seen as necessary in settings where public health infrastructure has broken down or is nonexistent. Advocates for humanitarian biomedicine seek to develop linkages outside of the state—among nongovernmental organizations (NGOs), activists, scientific researchers, and local health workers. Their object of intervention is not the national population of classical public health but rather individual human lives regardless of territorial borders. As a social and technical project, this regime of global health seeks to bring advanced diagnostic and pharmaceutical interventions to those in need. Such a project involves both enabling access to existing medical technologies and encouraging the development of new treatments addressed to neglected diseases—that is, to conditions that are not targeted by the pharmaceutical industry due to a lack of effective demand. Whereas global health security develops prophylaxis against potential threats to the populations of wealthy countries, humanitarian biomedicine invests resources to mitigate present suffering in other parts of the world.

Each of these two regimes is global in the sense that it strives to transcend certain limitations posed by the national governance of public health. Within each regime, actors work to craft a space of the global that can be a site of knowledge and intervention.[15] However, the type of ethical relationship implied by a project of global health depends on the regime in which the question is posed: the connection between health advocates and the afflicted (or potentially afflicted) can be one of either moral obli-

Table 3.1. Regimes of Global Health

	Global Health Security	Humanitarian Biomedicine
Type of threat	Emerging infectious diseases that threaten global circulation	Neglected diseases that afflict poor countries
Source of pathogenicity	Social and ecological transformations linked to globalization processes	Failure of development; lack of access to health care
Organizations and actors	National and international health agencies; technocrats	Nongovernmental organizations, philanthropies, activists
Technopolitical interventions	Global disease surveillance; building response capacity; biomedical countermeasures	Provide access to essential medicines; vaccine and drug research on neglected diseases
Target of intervention	National public health infrastructures	Suffering individuals
Ethical stance	Self-protection	Common humanity

gation to the other or protection against risk to the self. Global health is, in this sense, a contested ethical, political and technical zone whose contours are still under construction (see Table 3.1).

REGIMES OF GLOBAL HEALTH

These regimes have each emerged in response to a crisis of existing, nation-state–based systems of public health. For global health security, this crisis comes from the recognition that existing national public health systems are inadequate to prepare for the catastrophic threat of emerging infectious diseases. Such diseases outstrip the capabilities of modern public health systems, which were designed to manage known diseases that occur with a certain regularity in a national population. For humanitarian biomedicine, in contrast, the crisis comes from the failure of international development efforts to provide adequate health infrastructure to lessen the burden of treatable, but still deadly maladies in poor countries. From this perspective, suffering is the result of political and technical failure rather than disease emergence per se. For humanitarian biomedicine, especially in the context of poor countries lacking basic public health infrastructure, human suffering demands urgent and immediate response outside of the framework of state sovereignty.

Despite their differences, each of these regimes of global health has borrowed certain aspects of earlier public health formations, adapting them for new uses in the post–Cold War era. Public health systems in Europe and North America were initially built in the mid-to-late nineteenth century in response to pathologies linked to industrialization and urban growth.[16] For these health systems, the object of knowledge and intervention was the population: its rates of death and disease, cycles of scarcity, and endemic levels of mortality. Public health advocates uncovered patterns of disease incidence linked to living conditions that could be reduced through technical interventions such as improved sanitation.[17] Statistical knowledge, generated in fields such as epidemiology and demography, made these collective regularities visible and justified policy interventions.

Cold War era international health efforts sought to forge collaborations among existing national health agencies.[18] International health in this period had two main currents: disease eradication and primary health care. The major international disease eradication efforts were the WHO-led malaria campaign beginning in 1955 (and abandoned by the early 1970s) and the more successful smallpox eradication campaign, also led by WHO, which was completed in 1977. Such initiatives can be termed "international" rather than "global" in that they required coordination between multilateral agencies and national health services. The other main current of Cold War era international health, primary health care, articulated health as a basic human right linked to social and economic development. Again, this vision was international rather than global: a functioning nation-state apparatus was seen as central to the delivery of basic primary care.

By the early 1990s, the primary health care model linked to the developmental state was in crisis. Funding dried out for primary health schemes in the context of the influence of World Bank–led reforms of national health systems. WHO shifted its energies toward vertically integrated public–private partnerships that focused on managing specific diseases, such as HIV/ AIDS, malaria, and tuberculosis, rather than on supporting the development of local public health infrastructures. The emphasis was on targeting the burden of a given disease. As a group of public health historians has suggested, competition between WHO and the World Bank over the field of primary care was one motivation for WHO's move toward such public–private global health initiatives.[19] The Gates Foundation also played a key early role in this shift, funding $1.7 billion worth of projects between 1998 and 2000. Gates was then joined in this type of disease-focused initiative by other philanthropic organizations, such as the Global Fund and the Clinton Global Initiative.

Contemporary regimes of global health take up aspects of earlier national and international public health programs but adapt them to a different set of circumstances. Global health security incorporates elements of existing national health systems and redirects them toward the goal of early detection and rapid containment of emerging infectious diseases. Given the focus of this regime on potential disease events whose likelihood cannot be calculated using statistical methods, it develops techniques of imaginative enactment that model the impact of a future outbreak. Global health security measures seek to ensure compliance from national governments in implementing measures to prepare for and respond to outbreaks that threaten global catastrophe. Like classical public health, humanitarian biomedicine is concerned with diseases that currently afflict populations, but it functions outside of a state apparatus; its object of concern is not the national collectivity but rather suffering individuals regardless of national borders. If a major political and ethical imperative motivating classical public health efforts was social solidarity, the central value driving humanitarian biomedicine is that of common humanity.

HUMANITARIAN BIOMEDICINE

The term "humanitarian biomedicine" refers not to a single, clearly articulated framework but rather to a congeries of actors and organizations with diverse histories, missions, and technical approaches.[20] They share what anthropologist Peter Redfield calls "a secular commitment to the value of human life," one that is practiced through medical intervention.[21] This ethical commitment underlies a sense of urgency to provide care to suffering victims of violence, disease, and political instability. The structure of intervention is one in which medical organizations and philanthropies from advanced industrial countries engage in focused projects of saving lives in the developing world—and these efforts explicitly seek to avoid political involvement.[22]

We can take as paradigmatic instances of humanitarian biomedicine two prominent though quite distinctive organizations: *Médecins sans Frontières* (MSF) and the Bill and Melinda Gates Foundation. In her analysis of MSF, sociologist Renée Fox has written that the organization's efforts are premised on the "conviction that the provision of medical care, service, and relief is a humane form of moral action," that medical practice has the capacity to heal the body politic as well as the human body.[23] MSF has an actively "global" sense of its mission, challenging the 'sacred principle' of the sovereignty of the state and claiming a new geopolitical order grounded in the Universal Declaration of Human Rights. In announcing an ambitious initiative to eradicate malaria, the Bill and Melinda Gates Foundation articulated a similar ethical stance, casting it in economic terms. As Melinda Gates put it, "The first reason to work to eradicate malaria is an ethical reason—the simple cost. Every life has equal worth. Sickness and death in Africa are just as awful as sickness and death in America."[24] This ethical rationale for malaria eradication—grounded in common humanity, outside of the politics of nation-states—can be contrasted with the developmentalist agenda at the heart of Cold War international health efforts, in which improving the health of a given population was inextricably tied to economic and political modernization within a nation-state framework.[25]

In a sense, the primary health movement's stance of a "right to health for all" was carried into humanitarian biomedicine. But for many of the philanthropic organizations at the heart of humanitarian biomedicine, this right could not be concretized by national governments, which were seen as beset with corruption and incapable of reliably enacting programs. Thus global health initiatives to combat specific diseases such as AIDS in the poor world often expressly detach aid from existing national health agencies, seeking to "govern through the non-governmental," as Manjari Mahajan puts it.[26] In turn, to govern global health from outside of the state, the knowledge practices that guide intervention, such as epidemiological modeling, must be transposable from local contexts—a characteristic that also structures the governance of global health security.

Given the desire to avoid political entanglement and to operate across multiple settings, humanitarian biomedicine tends to emphasize mobile and standardizable technical interventions such as drugs, vaccines, or bed nets. A prominent example is work by activist organizations as well as philanthropies and multilateral agencies to increase access to antiretroviral therapies,[27] as well as coordinated work to develop new treatments and protocols for treating neglected diseases in resource poor settings.[28] In some cases, humanitarian biomedicine has moved toward ambitious biotechnical projects, as in the Gates Foundation's funding of basic research in the genomics of drug resistant tuberculosis and malaria. Meanwhile, critics have argued that such an emphasis on technical approaches ignores the more fundamental sources of suffering in developing countries, the basic living conditions of the world's poor. As Anne-Emanuelle Birn writes, "In calling on the world's researchers to develop innovative solutions targeted to 'the most critical scientific challenges in global health,' the Gates Foundation has turned to a narrowly conceived understanding of health as a product of technical interventions divorced from economic, social, and political contexts."[29] In a similar vein, Redfield describes the limits of MSF's campaign to provide chronic care for AIDS patients in Uganda: "In identifying structural deficits in the global supply of pharmaceuticals, MSF has recognized poverty as a condition for which it offers no cure."[30]

GLOBAL HEALTH SECURITY

A 2007 report from WHO articulated the objects and aims of global health security.[31] The report, entitled *A Safer Future: Global Public Health Security in the 21st Century*, began by pointing to the success of traditional public health measures during the twentieth century in managing infectious diseases such as cholera and smallpox. But in recent decades, the report continued, there had been an alarming shift in the "delicate balance between humans and microbes."[32] A series of factors, including demographic changes, economic development, global travel and commerce, and conflict, had "heightened the risk of disease outbreaks" ranging from emerging and reemerging infectious diseases such as HIV/AIDS and drug-resistant tuberculosis to food-borne pathogens and bioterrorist attacks.[33]

The WHO report proposed a strategic framework for responding to this new landscape of threats, which it called "global public health security." The framework emphasized an arena of global health that was distinct from the predominantly national organization of traditional public health. "In the globalized world of the 21st century," the report began, simply stopping disease at national borders was not adequate. Nor was it sufficient to respond to diseases after they had become established in a population. Rather, it was necessary to prepare for unknown outbreaks in advance, something that could be achieved only "if there is immediate alert and response to disease outbreaks and other incidents that could spark epidemics or spread globally and if there are national systems in place for detection and response should such events occur across international borders."[34]

The articulation of the global health security framework was a culmination of two decades of increasing concern over the threat of emerging infectious disease. The problem of emerging infections was initially raised by a group of U.S.-based infectious disease specialists in the late 1980s and early 1990s.[35] In 1989, molecular biologist Joshua Lederberg and epidemiologist Stephen Morse organized a major conference at Rockefeller University on the topic, which led to a landmark edited volume, *Emerging Viruses*.[36] Lederberg and Morse shared an evolutionary understanding of disease emergence as the inevitable result of microbial adaptation in relation to global environmental transformations. According to this ecological vision, "Evolutionary processes operating on a global scale were responsible for the emergence of 'new' diseases," as historian Warwick Anderson has summarized. "As environments changed, as urbanization, deforestation, and human mobility increased, so, too, did disease patterns alter, with natural selection promoting the proliferation of microbes in new niches."[37]

Participants in the Rockefeller conference warned officials of a dangerous intersection. On one hand, novel pathogens were emerging, including viruses such as AIDS and Ebola and drug-resistant strains of familiar diseases such as tuberculosis and malaria. On the other hand, the scientists argued, public health systems worldwide had been allowed to decay with

the assumption that the problem of infectious disease had been con-
quered. Moreover, the emergence and spread of new infectious diseases
could be expected to continue, due to processes of global transformation,
including migration, urbanization, air travel, civil wars and refugee crises,
and environmental degradation. According to these experts, the AIDS crisis was a harbinger of a dangerous future in which deadly new diseases
were likely to appear with increasing frequency.

Over the ensuing years, warnings about the emerging disease threat
came from various quarters, including scientific reports by prominent
organizations such as the Institute of Medicine, the reporting of science
journalists such as Laurie Garrett, and the dire scenarios of writers such
as Richard Preston.[38] For a number of public health experts, the emerging
disease threat, particularly when combined with weakening national public health systems, marked a worrisome reversal in the history of public
health. At just the moment when it seemed that the threat posed by infectious disease had waned, and that the critical health problems of the
industrialized world now involved chronic disease, these experts warned,
we were witnessing a return of the microbe.

It is worth emphasizing the generative character of the category of
"emerging infectious disease" as it was articulated in this period. The category made it possible to bring the HIV/AIDS pandemic into relation with a
range of other microbial threats to health, such as Ebola, West Nile virus,
dengue, and drug-resistant strains of malaria and tuberculosis. It also
pointed toward the imperative to develop means of anticipatory response
that could manage a disparate set of disease threats. Initiatives that would
later come to be associated with global health security were first proposed
in response to this perceived need. In a 1990 essay, Stephen Morse called for
efforts to monitor and intervene in a world of threatening new microbes
spreading via networks of human and animal transit: "Knowledge of viral
traffic can help us identify where to look and what to look for, but only if
mechanisms are in place to deepen this knowledge and help put it into
action."[39]

In an initial stage of discussion, health authorities proposed to address
the threat of emerging disease by adapting tools of disease surveillance
that had been honed as part of Cold War era disease eradication efforts.
For instance, epidemiologist Donald A. Henderson had implemented

infectious disease surveillance techniques in the 1960s and 1970s as director of the WHO Smallpox Eradication Program. For Henderson, the appropriate strategy to address emerging diseases was not prevention, which was unfeasible, but rather vigilant monitoring and rapid containment. In his contribution to *Emerging Viruses*, he argued that pathogen emergence was inevitable and ongoing, that "mutation and change are facts of nature, that the world is increasingly interdependent, and that human health and survival will be challenged, ad infinitum, by new and mutant microbes, with unpredictable pathophysiological manifestations."[40] As a result, "we are uncertain as to what we should keep under surveillance, or even what we should look for." What we therefore need, he continued, is a system that can detect novelty: in the case of AIDS, such a detection system could have provided early warning of the new virus and made it possible to put in place measures to limit its spread. Henderson proposed the establishment of a network of global disease surveillance units to be run by the U.S. Centers for Disease Control and Prevention (CDC), which would be located in peri-urban areas in major cities in the tropics, where they could provide a "window on events in surrounding areas." This proposal, as we will see, was an early articulation of the disease surveillance system that would later be central to the WHO strategic framework of global public health security.

EPIDEMIC INTELLIGENCE

Henderson's model of real-time disease surveillance was a product of his background at the Epidemic Intelligence Service (EIS) based at the CDC.[41] The EIS approach, introduced in the 1950s by Henderson's mentor Alexander Langmuir, was one of hypervigilance, of "continued watchfulness over the distribution and trends of incidence through systematic consolidation and evaluation of morbidity and mortality data and other relevant data," as Langmuir put it.[42] Henderson had used this approach in tracking the worldwide incidence of smallpox as director of the WHO eradication program. His proposed global network of surveillance centers and reference laboratories sought to extend the approach to as-yet-unknown diseases, providing early warning for response to outbreaks of any kind—

whether natural or manmade. In the 1990s, Henderson and others connected the interest in emerging diseases among international health specialists with U.S. national security officials' concern about the threat of bioterrorism (see Chapter 2), suggesting that a global disease surveillance network could serve to address both problems. Thus, in a 1992 essay, epidemiologist Stephen Morse summarized the justification for "expanding permanent surveillance programs to detect outbreaks of disease" in terms of the shared needs of international health and national security: "A global capability for recognizing and responding to unexpected outbreaks of disease, by allowing the early identification and control of disease outbreaks, would simultaneously buttress defenses against both disease and CBTW [chemical, biological, and toxin warfare]."[43] The question remained, however, of how to create such a "global capability" given the national scale of most epidemiological reporting.

The approach articulated by Langmuir and Henderson of "continued watchfulness" for emerging infections was institutionalized at a global scale over the course of the 1990s as experts from the CDC brought the methods and assumptions of the Epidemic Intelligence Service into the World Health Organization. The career of epidemiologist David Heymann is instructive. Heymann began his professional service in EIS and in the 1970s worked with the CDC on disease outbreak containment in Africa and with WHO on the smallpox eradication program.[44] In the early years of the AIDS pandemic, he helped establish a WHO office to track the epidemiology of the disease in developing countries. He then returned to Africa in 1995 to lead the agency's response to a widely publicized Ebola outbreak in Congo. After this he was asked by the director of WHO to set up a program in emerging diseases. "At this time there was an imbalance in participation internationally in the control of emerging and re-emerging infectious diseases," he later recalled, "the burden was falling mainly on the USA."[45] Heymann worked to relieve this burden by adopting the CDC model of epidemic intelligence within a multilateral setting. At WHO, Heymann set up a global funding mechanism that broadened the agency's disease surveillance and response capacities following the CDC model. He and other WHO officials soon identified a specific problem to be addressed: how to ensure the compliance of national health agencies with the demands of global disease surveillance?

Recent experiences with outbreaks of "reemerging" diseases had focused international health authorities' attention on the problem of enforcing national compliance with international reporting requirements. In the wake of the 1995 Ebola outbreak, as well as catastrophic epidemics of cholera in Latin America and plague in India in the early 1990s, Heymann later recalled, a "need was identified" for stronger international coordination of surveillance and response.[46] A major problem for outbreak investigators was that national governments were often hesitant to report the occurrence of an infectious disease that could harm tourism and international trade. The case of a plague outbreak in Surat in 1994, in which Indian officials suppressed international reporting of the event, demonstrated the difficulty of getting countries to publicly acknowledge infectious disease emergencies.[47] Heymann described how WHO addressed this problem: "In our emerging diseases program our idea was to change the culture so that countries could see the advantage of reporting," but a practical means of encouraging such compliance was needed.

A potential tool for such enforcement soon arose from an unexpected source: the establishment, during the 1990s, of Internet-based reporting systems such as ProMED (Program for Monitoring Emerging Diseases) in the United States and GPHIN (Global Public Health Intelligence Network) in Canada that scoured international media for stories about possible outbreaks. The development of these digital information networks meant that global public health authorities did not have to rely exclusively on official, nation-state–based epidemiological reporting to learn about outbreak events.[48] In 2000, WHO established the Global Outbreak Alert and Response Network (GOARN), which linked together multiple existing surveillance and response systems and which eventually included 120 partners, including scientific institutions, laboratory networks, UN agencies, and NGOs. The resulting potential for the rapid circulation of information about infectious disease outbreaks across national borders undermined national governments' traditional monopoly on epidemiological knowledge, making possible a global form of disease surveillance.

The outbreak of SARS in 2002 in China provided Heymann and his colleagues in WHO's Communicable Disease branch with an opportunity to test the new disease reporting system. As a previously unknown, highly virulent infectious disease, SARS fit well into the category of emerging disease.[49] The Chinese government's initial reluctance to provide information on the outbreak to international health authorities led WHO to take advantage of its new capacity to analyze epidemiological data gathered from non-state sources: SARS was the first time the GOARN network identified and publicized a rapidly spreading epidemic. As opposed to recalcitrant national governments, Heymann later reflected, international scientists "are really willing to share information for the better public good."[50] GOARN made it possible to electronically link leading laboratory scientists, clinicians, and epidemiologists around the world in a "virtual network" that rapidly generated and circulated knowledge about SARS. WHO closely tracked the global spread of the virus and issued a series of recommendations concerning international travel restrictions. According to Heymann, who led the WHO response, this rapid reaction was critical to the containment of the epidemic by July 2003, although he also acknowledged the good fortune that SARS had turned out not to be as easily transmissible as initially feared.

The lesson Heymann drew from the experience of SARS echoed the earlier warnings of scientists such as Henderson and Lederberg: in a closely interconnected and interdependent world, "inadequate surveillance and response capacity in a single country can endanger the public health security of national populations and in the rest of the world."[51] Processes of social and environmental change, including transnational migration, ecological destruction, and increasing international travel, had generated novel biological, social, and political risks—risks that transcended national borders and therefore could not be ignored by wealthy countries. Only a global system of rapidly shared epidemiological information could provide adequate warning to mitigate such risks. National sovereignty must accede to the demands of global health security. As Holbrooke and Garrett would later argue, in calling for Indonesia to comply with WHO's influenza virus–sharing network, SARS had proven that "globally shared health risk demands absolute global transparency."

THE INTERNATIONAL HEALTH REGULATIONS

The space of emerging disease, initially carved out by AIDS and then expanded by SARS, was soon occupied by a new threat: the possibility that a highly pathogenic strain of H5N1 avian influenza would mutate or reassort to become easily transmissible among humans. The risk of such an event could not be calculated using statistical data on historical incidence (since it had never occurred), but its onset could, experts warned, be catastrophic. As of 2005, when global pandemic preparedness efforts intensified, an estimated 60 percent of those who had contracted H5N1 had died from the disease, and the virus was spreading globally among migratory waterfowl and domesticated poultry. Fortunately, the only way for humans to contract the disease seemed to be through close physical contact with infected birds. Given the rapid genetic evolution of influenza viruses, public health authorities were deeply alarmed by the prospect that a mutant strain of the virus could maintain this fatality ratio but gain the ability to spread easily among humans.

In an article entitled "The Next Pandemic?" journalist Laurie Garrett evoked both the dire scenario of an H5N1 pandemic and the uncertainty surrounding it: "In short, doom may loom. But note the 'may.' If the relentlessly evolving virus becomes capable of human-to-human transmission, develops a power of contagion typical of human influenzas, and maintains its extraordinary virulence, humanity could well face a pandemic unlike any ever witnessed. Or," she added, "nothing at all could happen."[52] Others were less circumspect in their warnings. "It is not a question of if, but when," declared infectious disease specialist Michael Osterholm.[53] "I believe an influenza pandemic will be like a 12 to 18 month global blizzard that will ultimately change the world as we know it today." The prospect of such global catastrophe lent urgency to the enactment of WHO's global public health security framework, including its adoption of major revisions to the venerable International Health Regulations (IHR).

According to legal scholar David Fidler, the 2005 IHR revision was "one of the most radical and far-reaching changes in international law on public health since the beginning of international health co-operation in the mid-nineteenth century."[54] For my purposes here, the revised regulations are best understood as a significant element in the emerging framework of global health security. The revised regulations instituted a new set of legal obligations for nation-states to accept global intervention in a world seen as under threat from ominous pathogens circulating ever more rapidly.

The IHR system, dating from the 1851 International Sanitary Law, defines states' mutual obligations in the event of an outbreak of a dangerous communicable disease. Historically, its function has been to guarantee the continued flow of international trade during epidemics, ensuring that individual countries not take overly restrictive measures in response to the threat of infection while also enabling intervention by international health authorities. In the context of increasing concern over emerging diseases in the 1990s and early 2000s, the existing IHR was seen as ineffectual for at least two reasons. For one, its list of reportable conditions was limited to the sources of the nineteenth-century epidemics that had initially led to the establishment of the regulations: cholera, plague, and yellow fever—a list that was of little relevance for the expansive category of emerging diseases. Second, the existing regulations did not have a legal mechanism to enforce national compliance with IHR reporting requirements.

The IHR revision process was initiated in 1995 in response to a perception among health authorities that WHO and its member states had neither the technical capacities nor adequate legal and administrative tools to deal with the threat posed by emerging infectious diseases. That year, the World Health Assembly adopted a resolution "requesting that the IHR be revised to take more effective account of the threat posed by the international spread of new and reemerging disease."[55] The revision of IHR became a vehicle for outbreak investigators from the world of epidemic intelligence to construct the global system of disease surveillance and response that Henderson and others had advocated. WHO authorities proposed three key innovations to IHR that would make it possible for the agency to manage a range of potential disease emergencies.

The first innovation responded to the problem of the narrow range of disease events covered by the existing IHR. Through the invention of the concept of the "Public Health Emergency of International Concern" (PHEIC), the revised regulations vastly expanded the kinds of events to which the regulations might apply. According to the "IHR Decision Instrument," naturally occurring infectious diseases such as pandemic influenza and Ebola, intentional releases of deadly pathogens such as smallpox, or environmental catastrophes such as those that occurred at Bhopal in 1984 and Chernobyl in 1986 could all provoke the official declaration of an international public health emergency. The IHR decision instrument was designed to guide states in determining what constituted a public health emergency that required the notification of WHO. However, as we will see, the pathway in the instrument defined as "any event of international public health concern" left considerable room for interpretation of the scope of the regulations.

The second major innovation in the revised IHR responded to the issue of national health agencies' monopoly on epidemiological data. The new regulations expanded the potential sources of authorized reports of outbreaks: whereas the prior IHR had restricted official disease reporting to national governments, the revised IHR authorized WHO to recognize reports from non-state sources such as digital and print media. In this way, state parties' unwillingness to report outbreaks would not necessarily impede the functioning of the system. The premise of this measure was that, with WHO's official recognition of nongovernmental monitors such as ProMED and GPHIN, reports of outbreaks could no longer be suppressed, and so it would be in the interest of national governments to allow international investigators into the country as soon as possible after an outbreak in order to undertake disease surveillance and response measures and to assure the public that responsible intervention was underway.

The third innovation of the revised IHR addressed the problem of poor countries' ability to monitor and respond to outbreaks. It required that all WHO member states build national capacity for infectious disease surveillance and response. The establishment of "national public health institutes" in each World Health Assembly member nation, on the model of the U.S. CDC, would make possible a distributed global network that relied on the functioning of nodes in each country. The task of these institutes was to "fulfill the public health functions necessary to meet the IHR core capacity requirements particularly in the area of surveillance standards, surveillance coordination, data analysis, data mapping, risk assessment, and reporting."[56] The impetus for creating such institutes as part of WHO's global health security framework should be distinguished from prior modernizing efforts to build public health systems in the developing world. The IHR requirement to establish national public health institutes did not necessarily imply strengthening basic infrastructure for managing existing health problems in the population; rather, it directed the development of outbreak detection and response systems according to the needs of global health security.[57] The revised IHR gave countries until 2016 to fulfill this obligation. However, it was unclear where the resources would come from to implement systems for detecting and containing outbreaks of emerging disease in poor countries that already had trouble managing the most common ones. As we will see in Chapter 6, this issue would come to the fore in the wake of the catastrophic Ebola epidemic of 2014 in West Africa.

MAKING THE PHEIC

The decision instrument used to recognize a "public health emergency of international concern" (PHEIC) is at the heart of the revised IHR's method for governing infectious disease outbreaks that threaten to spread across national borders. This technique of classification is a way of bringing a singular event—the outbreak—into a more general category, which in turn puts into motion a machinery of action steps that guide institutional actors and limit the scope of interpretation and debate. The classification process begins with the requirement that member states notify WHO of potential health emergencies. As noted earlier, the prior version of the International Health Regulations limited notification requirements to three specific diseases: cholera, plague, and yellow fever. Early in the revision process, the IHR project team pointed out that in the era of Ebola and HIV/AIDS, this narrow list of nineteenth-century scourges was outdated. Indeed, given the assumption that the emergence of novel pathogens was ongoing and inevitable, it was the wrong approach to begin with a list of known diseases: "In a world of emerging and re-emerging diseases, any disease list could become obsolete the day after it was printed."[58] As a 2002 progress report on the revision process put it: "The requirement to notify WHO must be broadened in scope."[59]

As an alternative to honing a finite list of diseases that would require notification, the IHR project team initially proposed the development of a "syndrome"-based notification requirement. The idea was that because previously unknown diseases could not be recognized by existing diagnostic systems, authorities should focus instead on the detection of anomalous syndromes. Under such a system, it would be possible to inform WHO of the need to monitor and respond to an outbreak even before a specific disease had been identified. Five potential syndromes were developed and field-tested in a 1999 pilot study. But WHO soon abandoned this approach: the IHR team concluded that syndromes could not substitute effectively for specific disease entities in a regulatory framework, first because it was difficult to report syndromes in the field, and second, because "syndromes could not be linked to preset rules" for control of the spread of an infectious disease.[60]

As an alternative, the IHR project team proposed an "even bolder" departure from the preexisting list: a decision tree or algorithm-based tool to guide heath authorities "in determining whether a public health risk is of urgent international importance."[61] In a 2002 progress report on the IHR revisions, WHO noted that "obtaining an agreement on such an algorithm will be one of the main tasks of the IHR project team." According to the report, WHO was working with the Swedish Institute of Infectious Diseases to define what type of "health-related events" would require national health authorities to notify WHO.[62] The Swedish Institute had been commissioned to consult with the IHR project team to "define what constitutes an urgent international public health event" and to "develop an operational framework" to be used within national health agencies to assess the international importance of a given event.[63] Coming out of this collaboration, an algorithm was developed and tested beginning in 2002 and, after some negotiation and amendment, was agreed to by a World Health Assembly Working Group, and adopted as Annex 2 of the revised IHR in 2005 (see Figure 3.1).

In the highly charged context of international outbreak detection and response, the purpose of the IHR decision instrument was to provide clearly defined rules for action.[64] Assuming the instrument operated properly, the decision as to whether a given health event should lead to notification of WHO would not be a matter of personal judgment or political debate but would happen automatically via adherence to the algorithm embedded in the decision tree. The finalized IHR decision instrument emphasized the possibility that an unknown pathogenic agent could lead to notification: it did not require that the event to be assessed "involve a particular disease or agent or even that the agent is known." Moreover, such an event could be "accidental, natural, or intentional." The instrument listed two basic categories of events that would automatically lead to

ANNEX 2
DECISION INSTRUMENT FOR THE ASSESSMENT AND NOTIFICATION OF EVENTS THAT MAY CONSTITUTE A PUBLIC HEALTH EMERGENCY OF INTERNATIONAL CONCERN

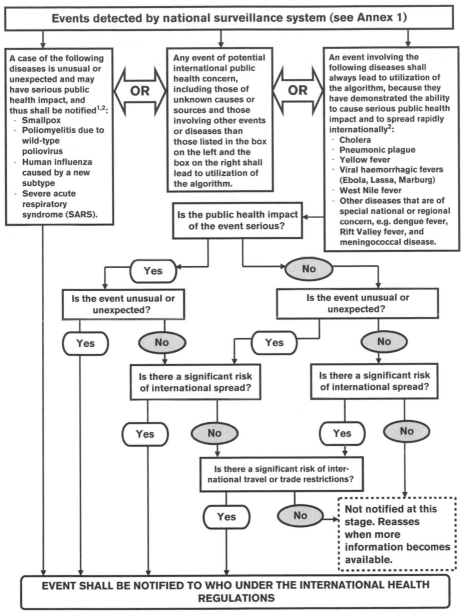

Figure 3.1. World Health Organization, International Health Regulations Decision Instrument.

notification: either (1) an event that fulfilled two of four public health criteria: seriousness, unusualness or unexpectedness, significant risk of international spread, or significant risk of travel or trade restrictions; or (2) an event involving one or more cases of four specific diseases to which WHO was especially attuned, given its eradication priorities and its attentiveness to dangerous emerging pathogens: smallpox, polio, SARS, or human influenza caused by a new subtype.

The 2005 WHO guidance for the use of the decision instrument defined a PHEIC as "an extraordinary event which is determined to constitute a public health risk to other states though the international spread of disease and to potentially require a coordinated international response."[65] The guidance emphasized that the notification by a national health agency to WHO of a *possible* PHEIC was not equivalent to the event's classification as an *actual* emergency. "It is important not to equate notification with the very rare situation of a PHEIC since the vast majority of events assessed as requiring notification to WHO will not ultimately be determined to be PHEICs." Rather, the notification requirement constituted a field of possible emergencies. The responsibility to determine whether a reported event should be officially declared a PHEIC lay with the director-general of WHO and required that an IHR Emergency Committee be convened. This committee would then advise WHO on recommended measures to be taken over the duration of the emergency.

THE THREAT OF INTERNATIONAL AIR TRAVEL

In their 2005 *New York Times* editorial on pandemic preparedness (see Chapter 2), Senators Barack Obama and Richard Lugar had, like others, emphasized a cosmopolitan condition of shared risk, in which international air travel brought Americans into a new kind of relation to other parts of the world: "In an age when you can board planes in Bangkok or Hong Kong and arrive in Chicago, Indianapolis or New York in hours, we must face the reality that these exotic killer diseases are not isolated health problems half a world away, but direct and immediate threats to security and prosperity here at home."[66] The system of international health regulations was historically designed to ensure the ongoing flow of international trade and tourism while at the same time alerting health officials to dangerous outbreaks that might cross borders. But it had been established in the very different context of nineteenth-century oceangoing travel. From the outset of reflection on the problem of emerging diseases in the late 1980s, the speed of international air travel was continually cited as a novel source of threat, requiring the development of new detection and response capabilities. One of the difficulties for WHO in revising the IHR lay in how to assure national governments that if they reported domestic outbreaks of dangerous infectious diseases and allowed international health specialists to monitor and contain them, their countries would not then face unreasonable restrictions on travel and trade.[67] Like the mid-nineteenth-century international sanitary conventions that it built on, the revised IHR was an attempt to balance liberalism and security in a globalizing world in which circulation was a source of both opportunity and danger.

Just before the official adoption of the revised IHR by WHO member states in 2007, the problem of how to regulate disease circulation in an age of mass international air travel appeared in an unexpected context: not the outbreak of a deadly new pathogen in a country of the Global South but rather the diagnosis of an American air traveler infected with an especially dangerous strain of drug-resistant tuberculosis.[68] In May, an Atlanta lawyer named Andrew Speaker was diagnosed with multidrug-resistant tuberculosis just before leaving on his honeymoon to Greece and Italy. According to CDC authorities, Speaker ignored the agency's recommendation against international travel and flew to Europe with his wife. The CDC then informed him by phone that a follow-up test had indicated a diagnosis of extensively drug-resistant tuberculosis (XDR-TB), a rare form of the disease that was classified by health officials as an "emerging pathogen." The CDC told Speaker that he would either have to remain in Europe for treatment, quarantined for an extended time in an Italian hospital or else pay his own way back to the United States on a private jet to avoid the risk of contagion—a prohibitively expensive alternative. Instead, without informing health officials, Speaker purchased a plane ticket to Montreal and was able to pass into through the Canadian border to the United States, even though he had been placed on a Department of Homeland Security watch list. The event briefly caused an international panic, as health officials worried that Speaker had exposed fellow passengers to the pathogen during the long trans-Atlantic flight, and it led to close scrutiny of U.S. border control measures.

From the perspective of the framework of global health security, the Speaker case was a test of the new public health preparedness system in the United States. As a *New York Times* reporter wrote, "The bizarre case calls into question preparations to deal with medical crises like influenza pandemics and even bioterror attacks."[69] Similarly, a *Los Angeles Times* editorial warned: "One day, a plane landing at LAX could carry a passenger infected with XXDR, a bioterror agent, Ebola or an emerging virus. Will we be ready?"[70] At congressional hearings on the incident in September 2007, critics of the CDC response described Speaker as a "walking biological weapon."[71] The chairman of the House Committee on Homeland Security pointed to a "breakdown at the intersection of homeland security and public health," and repeated the analogy between international travel by a passenger infected with drug-resistant TB and a biological attack: "This certainly raises questions about our homeland security if the government had this much trouble countering TB, let alone countering terrorism."[72]

The report by the House Committee on Homeland Security on the Speaker incident linked XDR-TB to the broad problem of emerging infectious disease, whose solution would require the integration of public health and national security: "The twin specters of diseases that are increasingly resistant or completely without current treatments and antimicrobials, and the ability of diseases to spread more quickly than ever before due to rapid transit and other enablers, place public health concerns squarely on the homeland, national, and transnational security agendas." The House report argued that the Speaker incident had exposed gaps in the U.S. public health preparedness system that needed to be urgently addressed: "How we address these gaps now will serve as a direct predictor of how well we will handle future events, especially those involving emerging, reemerging, and pandemic infectious disease."[73] The report honed in on WHO's revised International Health Regulations as a source of procedures that could have addressed a communication gap between U.S. and international health authorities. "Under the International Health Regulations, CDC should have informed the World Health Organization (WHO) that same day of this significant public health risk. Had the CDC informed the WHO earlier of the situation," the report speculated, "European authorities may well have been able to apprehend Mr. Speaker while he was still overseas."[74] Similarly, a leading tuberculosis specialist with WHO cited the IHR revision as a procedure that would have aided in managing the crisis: "If the International Health Regulations, 2006, had been in place," he suggested, "the relevant procedures outlined would have been followed correctly."[75]

However, the Speaker case was far from typical of the global problem posed by drug-resistant tuberculosis. In fact, drug-resistant TB was one of the central objects of attention for the regime of humanitarian biomedicine.[76] For advocates of humanitarian biomedicine, the incident was useful insofar as it drew attention to what they considered a scandalously under-reported issue: the increasing incidence of multidrug-resistant and XDR-TB in parts of the world with underfunded and deteriorating public health systems, such as South Africa and many of the countries of the former Soviet bloc. As one humanitarian activist urged, "We need to wake up and pay attention to what's happening with TB in other parts of the world. We need to start treating XDR-TB where it is, not just respond to one case of one American who will get the finest treatment."[77] For humanitarian biomedicine, the growing epidemic of drug-resistant TB in the Global South pointed to structural inequality and to the failures of public health systems to adequately manage a treatable, existing condition among the world's poor.[78]

Thus, if the specter of an airplane passenger with XDR-TB was understood as a practice run for a future bioterrorist attack, the conclusions to be drawn from the incident were quite different than if the passenger were seen as a sign of an existing health crisis, but one taking place outside of the public health and communication networks of wealthy nations. The same disease could look quite different, and provoke quite different responses, depending on whether it was taken up within the regime of global health security or that of humanitarian biomedicine.

CONCLUSION

The question of whether the revised IHR would live up to its billing as a radical transformation of international public heath to provide security against emerging pathogens depended at least in part on its capacity to force sovereign states to comply with the requirements of global disease surveillance. The issue of intellectual property rights in the case of Indonesian bird flu virus isolates indicated that an alternative regime of global health—one focused on the problem of access to essential medicines—could well complicate such efforts. Global health security did not address the major existing infectious disease problems of the developing world, which were linked to poverty and the lack of resources to devote to basic health infrastructure. Its focus on early detection and rapid containment of novel pathogens ignored the ongoing prevalence of treatable diseases in much of the world. As Fidler put it, "the strategy of global health security is essentially a defensive, reactive strategy," given its narrow emphasis on detection and response to outbreaks of emerging disease. "The new IHR are rules for global triage rather than global disease prevention."[79]

The program of global health security was inherently limited by its focus on prospective threats; it did not have any means to address, for example, the ongoing HIV/AIDS pandemic—and so it was suspect for advocates of humanitarian biomedicine, who were most concerned with existing health crises. It contained no provisions regarding medication access, prevention programs, or vaccine research and development for neglected diseases. As the physician and scientist Philippe Calain of Médecins sans Frontières wrote, describing the "epidemic intelligence" approach built into WHO-coordinated surveillance projects such as GOARN: "There is no escaping from the conclusion that the harvest of outbreak intelligence overseas is essentially geared to benefit wealthy nations."[80] Humanitarian biomedicine thus offered significant resources for a critique of what was missing from global health security. Nonetheless, each regime functioned relatively coherently on its own, leading to the question of whether, in fact, the two regimes might best be understood as complementary rather than inherently contradictory facets of contemporary global health governance. If so, humanitarian biomedicine could be seen as offering a philanthropic palliative to countries lacking public health infrastructure in exchange for the right of international health organizations to monitor their populations for outbreaks that threatened to spread rapidly along global circuits.

4 Real Time Biopolitics

When a new strain of influenza made its initial appearance in the spring of 2009, it seemed at first that it might be the outbreak that global health authorities had been anticipating. Early reports were that dozens had died from a mysterious respiratory ailment in Mexico, and hundreds more had been hospitalized. Young people were apparently especially susceptible to the virus, which was identified as influenza A/H1N1 (swine flu). The incidence of cases from around the United States suggested rapid transmission of the virus. It was possible that this was the beginning of a devastating global pandemic, but the key characteristics of the virus that would determine its trajectory—in particular, its case fatality ratio—were not yet known.

Within weeks, a global assemblage of public health actors, organizations, and technologies had taken hold of the virus, tracking its geographic extension through reference laboratories, mapping its genomic sequence, collating data on hospitalization and death rates, working to distribute antiviral medications and rapidly develop a vaccine, and, not least, communicating risk—and uncertainty—to the public.[1] Although some elements of this assemblage were decades old—for example, the Global Influenza Surveillance Network (GISN) and the egg-based technique of influenza vaccine production—others were fairly new, such as Internet-based reporting systems, molecular surveillance methods, and national pandemic preparedness plans. These various elements had been brought together through the World Health Organization's (WHO's) pandemic planning efforts, which began in the late 1990s but had intensified over the five years since the reemergence of H5N1 avian influenza in Asia.

In response to early epidemiological reports from Mexico, WHO Director-General Margaret Chan convened an Emergency Committee under the aegis of the International Health Regulations to advise her on how to manage the event. Based on the committee's recommendation, on April 25 Chan declared a Public Health Emergency of International Concern (PHEIC) and issued a Phase 3 alert according to the graduated alert system built into the WHO pandemic preparedness guidance.[2] The six-phase pandemic alert system was designed to guide national public health authorities in how to respond to each stage in the evolution of a potential influenza pandemic. For the time being, the Emergency Committee advised, since it was not possible to contain the rapidly spreading virus, national health authorities should focus on putting in place mitigation measures.

According to the preparedness guidance, the function of the pandemic alert system's phased approach was "to help countries and other stakeholders to anticipate when certain situations will require decisions and decide at which point main actions should be implemented."[3] The goal was to provide national health authorities with a range of options during the early and uncertain period of a possible pandemic. Recall the situation faced by Ford administration officials in 1976 after the appearance of swine flu, as they mulled whether to go forward with a mass immunization campaign (see Chapter 2). At that time, the director of the Centers for Disease Control (CDC) urged the administration to make an immediate and conclusive decision: "The situation is one of 'go or no go.'" In contrast, WHO's pandemic contingency plans sought to provide guideposts for flexible management of an unfolding situation. An early version of the pandemic preparedness guidance, released in 1999, described the twentieth-century history of pandemics and false alarms, including the 1976 swine flu episode, and concluded: "These different histories show the need for flexible contingency plans capable of responding efficiently to a pandemic threat."[4] One of the functions of the six-phase alert system, then, was to institute a capacity for adaptive response in relation to unfolding knowledge over the course of a pandemic. For this system to function, as we will see, it was crucial that authorities be able to assimilate new data about the event in near real time.

In late April, the WHO Emergency Committee raised the official pandemic alert level to Phase 5, indicating that national health agencies should shift from "preparedness" to "response" activities. Chan confidently announced that although the virus continued to spread rapidly, "the world is better prepared for an influenza pandemic that at any time in history" due to authorities' recent investment in preparedness measures.[5] She assured government officials and members of the public that her agency was tracking the virus at multiple registers: epidemiological, clinical, and virological. Finally, she advised national health ministries to activate their pandemic plans and to remain on high alert for outbreaks of influenza-like illness in the population.

In her statement declaring the change in alert level, Chan stated that "the biggest question, right now, is this: how severe will the pandemic be, especially now at the start?"[6] The question of how to assess severity in the early stages of a pandemic had been a topic of reflection for WHO planners as they revised their pandemic preparedness guidance in the years immediately before the H1N1 outbreak. The question of severity was critical because the degree of urgency of response at the outset of the pandemic hinged on knowledge of how deadly it was likely to be. The previous year, in 2008, the results of a WHO global consultation on pandemic control strategies had pointed to several challenges in assessing severity early in a pandemic, including national variations in public health infrastructure and the health status of populations, the "paucity of reliable and complete information" at the early stages of a pandemic, and the fact that the pathogenicity of the virus would likely change over time as the pandemic evolved. WHO pandemic planners decided that given the complexity of assessing severity across a variegated global health terrain, the alert system should no longer include the criterion of severity in its definition of a pandemic.[7] However, WHO would nonetheless try to make an early assessment by looking at a number of indicators of severity. Potential severity indicators included the case fatality rate, reports of unusually severe morbidity, unexpected mortality patterns, and unusual complications.

In the weeks immediately following the initial identification of H1N1, WHO experts sought to assess the severity of the virus based on epidemiological reports from countries where the disease was already prevalent. While the experience of the swine flu was reported to be highly severe in Mexico, information from the United States and Canada suggested a more moderate level of virulence. In teleconferences among international health officials, advisers cautioned that "it would take time for a fuller picture of the virus to emerge."[8] To fill in this picture, WHO sent data collection tables to national focal points—typically an official based in a government health ministry—to organize information on cases, seeking "consistent patterns of information about the characteristics of the pandemic virus." On May 29, 2009, just six weeks after the initial identification of the virus, WHO published a three-part framework for the global assessment of pandemic severity in order to harmonize results that were coming in from the diverse settings in which the pandemic was unfolding. The severity assessment framework included, first, virological characteristics, along with the epidemiological and clinical implications of these characteristics; second, the vulnerability of a given population, such as its preexisting levels of immunity and the prevalence of risk factors; and third, the institutional capacity for public health response in each country, including issues such as access to medical care.

In late May, the journal *Science* published an editorial on influenza specialists' response to the outbreak entitled "Epidemic Science in Real Time." One of its authors was Harvey Fineberg, who had also been a coauthor of the National Research Council's report on the 1976 swine flu affair (see Chapter 2) and was now president of the U.S. Institute of Medicine. The editorial described flu scientists' intensive work to track epidemiological patterns in the field and molecular sequences in the laboratory during the early course of the epidemic. According to the authors, novel technical capacities such as molecular surveillance were transforming the relation between epidemic science and health policy: "By conducting the right science and communicating expert judgment, scientists can enable policies to be adjusted appropriately as an epidemic scenario unfolds."[9] Similarly, Director-General Chan stated: "For the first time in history, we can track the evolution of a pandemic in real-time." The hope was that by combining epidemiological tools for monitoring the virus with administrative devices like the six-phase alert system, it would be possible for governments to adjust policies for managing the population's health in relation to unfolding events.

REAL TIME BIOPOLITICS

This description of the "real-time" interaction between epidemic science and government intervention during first weeks after the appearance H1N1 points to one of the innovations of public health preparedness: the invention of tools to monitor and respond to the onset of novel disease entities in the present. Such tools, oriented toward vigilant attention to biological transformation at the molecular level, involve a modulation in the political administration of collective life, what Michel Foucault called "biopolitics." In his writings and lectures from the late 1970s, Foucault developed the concept of biopolitics to describe governmental practices that gather systematic knowledge about humans as living beings, and that implement targeted interventions with the aim of increasing the well-being of populations. In a series of lectures on "Security, Territory, Population," he focused on the setting in which the problem of population initially appeared as a central object for governmental knowledge and intervention: late eighteenth and early nineteenth century Europe. The lectures characterize the operation of "security mechanisms," regulatory devices designed to manage threats to collective life.

The lectures demonstrate how security mechanisms work through a series of contrasts with "disciplinary mechanisms," which address threats by prohibiting them—by attempting to spatially block their encroachment. These schematic comparisons demonstrate how each of these mechanisms treats a given problem-space: the expanding early modern town, the threat of hunger in the countryside, and the scourge of infectious disease. The lectures suggest that security mechanisms arose at an historical moment in which disciplinary methods reached a limit of effectiveness: a technology of power that sought total control—discipline—proved incapable of dealing with a novel set of economic and social challenges linked to the integration of the town into existing structures of legitimate sovereignty. The invention of security mechanisms is thus related to the rise of liberal political rationality. In contrast to the restrictive and centralizing power of discipline, liberalism was articulated as an "art of government" that emphasized the free circulation of men and things and depended for its efficacy on mechanisms of security that could ensure the optimal regulation of such flows.

The distinction between disciplinary mechanisms and security mechanisms is well illustrated through a contrast between two approaches to the threat of epidemic disease. If disciplinary mechanisms such as quarantine seek to restrict the circulation of disease, isolating the sick from the healthy, security mechanisms allow disease to circulate but minimize its harm through regulatory interventions such as vaccination. Security mechanisms are, importantly, dependent on the accumulation of certain kinds of knowledge. Detailed information on historical patterns of disease incidence in a population is necessary to minimize the impact of epidemics. Thus, eighteenth-century advocates of smallpox inoculation conducted statistical analyses of mortality rates from the disease and of the efficacy of variolization in preventing death. Such analyses led to a transformation in the meaning of smallpox. First, the disease appeared no longer as an overall relation between a disease and a place but rather as "a distribution of cases in a population circumscribed in time or space."[10] Second, the analysis of the distribution of cases in a population made it possible to statistically calculate the probability, for an individual or for a specific group, of contracting the disease and dying from it: if one knew the age, town, or profession of a given person, one could determine the person's risk of morbidity and of mortality. Third, such calculation pointed to zones of particular danger: it was more dangerous to be under three years old than to be older; it was more dangerous to live in a town than in the countryside; and so on. Finally, through this lens of the statistical calculation of risk, the incidence of crisis—the sudden acceleration of disease incidence—became visible as a regularly occurring phenomenon.

This process of taking up the entire population in terms of its relative probability of mortality is characteristic of the operations of a security apparatus. Once sufficient knowledge has been gathered concerning differential rates of mortality, it then becomes possible to create targeted interventions that will reduce the incidence of disease to a more optimal level, even though the threat cannot be eliminated altogether. For instance, in the case of smallpox, one might seek to develop measures that can lower the heightened risk of childhood mortality to the level of the overall population.

The early history of public health involved the gradual adoption, within governmental practice, of this style of reasoning about infectious disease.

Beginning in the nineteenth century, European national governments began to publish vast amounts of statistical data on the vital characteristics of populations: their rates of marriage, birth, death, and disease.[11] The analysis of this data by statisticians revealed that although the future was contingent, there were nonetheless certain regularities according to which governments could rationally plan. This mode of calculation gradually became the standard for government policies addressing the management of collective risk, in arenas ranging from public health to industrial accidents. From within this form of rationality, the demonstration of risk calculation is necessary to render political decisions concerning future dangers legitimate, whether or not the potential hazard eventually appears.[12]

Such an approach to the assessment and management of disease risk can be termed "actuarial." Like insurance, it uses data on historical patterns of incidence to make calculations about future probabilities. However, it applies these methods with a different aim: to reveal the laws of human vitality, demonstrating that events that appear to be contingent at the individual level in fact correspond with regularities at the level of the collective.[13] Assembling such data, nineteenth-century European public health administrators designed actuarial devices to gauge the health of urban populations. For example, the "life table" or "biometer," invented in the 1840s by William Farr, head of the British General Register Office, made it possible to calculate the likelihood of mortality in any given year for each member of a particular age group.[14] Farr's biometer combined national census data with parish death registers, tracking a group of infants born at the same time over their life courses, and recording how many members of this group were still alive at periodic intervals until all of them had died. Such information could then be used to calculate the regularities of collective life, enabling government administrators to rationally plan for the future. Thus, using a biometer, one could determine the average life expectancy for all children born in 1841, no matter their individual circumstance and life trajectory. As Farr put it, "Although we know little the labours, the privations, the happiness or misery, the calm or tempests, which are prepared for the next generation of Europeans, we entertain little doubt that about 9000 of them will be found alive at the distant Census in 1921."[15] In the service of contributing to public health planning, actuarial devices like the biometer demonstrated the law-like regularities that underlay seemingly contingent vital phenomena such as birth, sickness and death.

Such devices could also reveal anomalies in rates of morbidity and mortality that pointed officials to potential targets of intervention, as in the calculation of smallpox risk according to age. In his research on the 1848 cholera outbreak in London, Farr analyzed the course of the epidemic numerically, building what he called a "sickness table" to determine the probability of recovery or death for each victim of the disease. As historian John Eyler describes the method, Farr did this "by extending the actuary's technique of discovering the law of mortality in a life table." One of Farr's sickness tables indicated that the risk of dying from cholera in the 1848 London epidemic was related to the elevation of one's residence; Farr hoped this would provide evidence to substantiate his miasmatic theory of disease causation. Even if his theory of disease transmission proved flawed, his actuarial method of determining relative risk would have a long career in public health.

The accumulation of vital statistics via actuarial devices made it possible for reformers to demonstrate the impact of social and environmental factors on life chances. For instance, French social reformer Louis-René Villermé combined tax data with death records to analyze the effects of housing conditions on comparative mortality rates during the 1832 cholera epidemic in Paris. His research demonstrated that "death is a social disease"—in other words, that social class corresponded in a regular fashion with susceptibility to the epidemic.[16] By the middle of the nineteenth century, then, the relation of social and environmental conditions to collective vitality had been made visible to political reflection through the accumulation and publication of statistical data on the health of populations.

SENTINEL DEVICES

The actuarial style of reasoning, oriented toward disease prevention through risk management, has remained predominant among experts in approaching public health problems into the present. However, in the last decades of the twentieth century, it began to coexist with a different approach to disease threats, one that emphasizes vigilant monitoring for the onset of an unpredictable but potentially catastrophic event. Sociologists Francis Chateauraynaud and Didier Torny have elaborated this distinction between two technocratic approaches to potential dangers, "risk management" and "vigilance." According to Chateauraynaud and Torny, risk management involves the creation of a common space of calculation through which planners can anticipate the likelihood of such dangers occurring. Vigilance, in contrast, assumes that the dangerous future cannot be known through calculation and that one must therefore be prepared for surprise. Rather than using the calculation of costs and benefits to guide or justify decisions concerning government intervention, vigilance enjoins one to intervene in a precautionary mode. For a decision-maker faced with the possibility of future catastrophe, having made a risk calculation may prove an insufficient shield from responsibility. As Chateauraynaud and Torny write, "It is no longer possible to say, without exposing oneself to criticism, that 'according to the calculations, the risk is negligible.'"[17] It is necessary to act now to interrupt the onset of a catastrophic event, or else one may be held accountable later for the results of present inaction.

Two types of security mechanism are at work here. If risk management leads to the invention of actuarial devices that assemble data on historical incidence in order to calculate the probable future, vigilance relies on sentinel devices that can provide early warning of an encroaching danger. An actuarial device is invented for a world in which the possible threats to collective life can be known through painstaking research in fields like epidemiology and demography; the task is one of accumulating enough statistical data to guide cost-effective intervention. A sentinel device, in contrast, is devised to stimulate and guide action when decision is imperative but knowledge is incomplete.

In a number of contemporary arenas in which potential future danger looms, one finds a proliferation of sentinel devices. These devices are especially useful for monitoring processes that are difficult to perceive directly but that may herald the onset of disaster. One can look, for example, at the use of techniques for tracking animal populations such as endangered fish species or threatened bee colonies, whose decline warns of ecological collapse,[18] or at the practice of collecting flu samples from migratory birds to detect mutations that could render the virus easily transmissible among humans.[19] In the field of global health security, sentinel devices are used to detect the appearance of unexpected or previously unknown pathogens. Examples here include efforts to test African bush meat for new zoonotic diseases based on the premise that such an effort could "stop the next pandemic before it starts," as well as syndromic surveillance systems, which look for signals of a disease outbreak even before doctors have made a diagnosis—for instance, by tracking anomalies in the number of emergency room visits or in the use of over-the-counter flu medicines in a given city, over a certain period of time.[20]

Such devices are designed to alert officials to a significant event as it unfolds in the present, but they typically provide little information about what is likely to happen next, and do not by themselves trigger an intervention. For this reason, they are often linked to already-formulated guidelines or protocols for taking authorized action in the face of uncertainty. In the case of influenza preparedness, preexisting pandemic plans, put into motion by the six phase alert system, enable officials to intervene rapidly in an urgent situation without engaging in complex and open-ended deliberation. Thus, sentinel devices do not usually operate in isolation but rather are integrated into a larger system of alert-and-response, one that can include preparedness plans that lay out a range of potential interventions as well as decision tools that guide action as the situation unfolds. In the case of the 2009 swine flu epidemic, as we will see, this system of vigilance came under sharp criticism from a group of actors who were invested in actuarial approaches to health threats.

ALERT AND RESPONSE

In the weeks after WHO raised the pandemic alert level to Phase 5, the H1N1 virus continued to spread globally. There was considerable uncertainty, however, about when officials should raise the level of alert to Phase 6, a "full global pandemic" and what exactly this shift would imply. A major issue, as noted earlier, was that the definition of the term "pandemic" in the WHO planning guidance referred only to the degree of global spread of the disease and did not include a threshold for the severity of the virus.[21] Even if the organization sought to account for severity in making a decision about whether to declare a Phase 6 pandemic, however, it was difficult to determine how virulent H5N1 was at this stage or how it might evolve before an anticipated wave of flu in the fall.

The question of how to define a pandemic had significant implications for public health policy. For a number of European and North American governments, the WHO declaration of a full pandemic would trigger advance-purchase agreements with pharmaceutical companies for millions of doses of a pandemic influenza vaccine. Government health agencies had entered into such agreements over the previous several years in order to secure supplies of vaccine in anticipation of a pandemic of the highly pathogenic avian influenza H5N1 virus. The assumption behind advance-purchase agreements was that in a future pandemic, it would take several months for vaccines to become available and that global supplies would be limited. In such a situation, national governments would be under intense pressure to ensure the availability of vaccine doses to their populations as soon as possible. The British government held a $236 million advance-purchase agreement with GlaxoSmithKline that guaranteed delivery of 132 million doses of vaccine to the United Kingdom in the event of a pandemic. And the United States had awarded Novartis a $486 million contract toward the construction of a vaccine factory that could produce 150 million doses for the U.S. population within six months of a pandemic declaration.[22] Worldwide capacity for production of a pandemic vaccine was estimated at somewhere between one and two billion doses, and the United States held preexisting contracts giving the federal government priority to purchase at least 600 million doses for American citizens (with the assumption that immunization would require two doses of vaccine).[23]

As the Indonesian health minister had argued in justifying her decision to withhold avian influenza virus samples from WHO's global surveillance system (see Chapter 3), wealthy countries held a near-monopoly on short-term vaccine supply in advance of the anticipated pandemic emergency, despite the premise that "global health security" sought to protect all populations. In May 2009, just a month after the initial detection of H1N1, WHO and the United Nations officials met to discuss how, under these circumstances, access to a pandemic vaccine might be provided to poor and middle-income countries. An official from the Pan American Health Organization commented on the likely shortage of vaccine in much of the world: "If you impose this kind of restriction to equitable access, then it's going to be a tremendous burden on how we control this outbreak."[24]

On June 11, Chan declared an alert level of Phase 6, or "full pandemic." At this point, the Emergency Committee described the severity of the pandemic as "moderate" but recommended that its level of severity continue to be closely monitored by looking at features such as the genetic makeup of the virus, the clinical course of illness, and its impact on health services. In her public statement, Chan emphasized WHO's ongoing vigilance as the event unfolded: "No previous pandemic has been detected so early or watched so closely, in real-time, right at the very beginning."[25] The capacity for such vigilance was, she said, the result of intensive work among national and international public health officials: "The world can now reap the benefits of investments, over the past five years, in pandemic preparedness." At the same time, the director-general warned about the inherent unpredictability of influenza: "The virus writes the rules and this one, like all influenza viruses, can change the rules, without rhyme or reason, at any time." Thus vigilant watchfulness for any changes in the virus' behavior would continue to be necessary.

Over the next several months, virologists and epidemiologists worked intensively to discover what the pandemic virus' "rules" were, in particular, its rules of transmissibility and virulence. Such knowledge was critical for evaluating the pandemic's potential severity and thus for making decisions about how urgently to implement containment and mitigation measures. A critical problem was the lack of quantitative data, at this early stage, concerning the overall incidence of H1N1 in the population—as distinct from the number of fatalities the virus had caused. This was the well-known "problem of the denominator." One could not calculate the all-important case-fatality ratio without knowing how many total cases of infection had resulted in a given number of deaths. In a commentary in the *New England Journal of Medicine* published in late May on "managing and reducing uncertainty" in the emerging pandemic, a team led by Harvard epidemiologist Marc Lipsitch made the case for immediate investment in serological surveys to track population-level exposure to the virus, which would make it possible to calculate the case-fatality ratio. "Without good incidence estimates," they wrote, "estimates of severity will continue to suffer from an uncertain denominator." This lack of knowledge about exposure also hindered the evaluation of treatment success: "[t]he effectiveness of control measures will be difficult to assess without accurate measures of local incidence."[26] Such molecular surveillance research was part of a broader effort, among experts and officials, to move from vigilance to risk management through the accumulation, sharing, and analysis of epidemiological data.

A Pandemic Evaluation Group within WHO reviewed new data as it came in from various regions, using indicators to try to assess the pandemic's severity: how many people were getting sick? Of these, how many were dying? What was the proportion of severe cases? How were national public health systems coping with outbreaks? However, as a later report noted, it remained the case that "severity was difficult to calculate in real time," for several reasons. First, there was not yet sufficient data available for some of these indicator variables. Second, baseline data for many of the variables were not known for many countries, which may have led to artifactual variability in reported severity throughout the pandemic. And third, "factors not related to the disease can affect the calculation of indicator variables"—for instance, national treatment protocols rather than disease severity per se structured rates of hospitalization; similarly, intensive care unit (ICU) admissions and ventilator use "were heavily influenced by ICU capacity and the availability of ventilators."[27]

As the pandemic unfolded in its early stages, policy decisions on issues such as school closure and vaccine composition—whether, for example, scarce vaccine supply should be expanded through the use of untested adjuvants—had to be made in the absence of fully elaborated data on risk. "In practice," as Lipsitch and his coauthors put it, "decisions have had to be made before definitive information was available on the severity, transmissibility, or natural history of the new H1N1 virus." Beginning in the late summer, the U.S. government spent $1.6 billion on 229 million doses of vaccine in what the *Washington Post* called "the most ambitious immunization campaign in U.S. history."[28] Health officials envisioned a possible shortage of vaccine given anticipated high public demand and long production time and so implemented a prioritization scheme that focused on maintaining essential services and on protecting vulnerable populations.[29] The vaccine prioritization scheme was part of the national preparedness plan that had been developed in 2005 in anticipation of a pandemic of H5N1 avian influenza (see Chapter 2).

When the U.S. vaccination program began in the fall, unanticipated delays in vaccine production led to widespread public confusion and criticism. In mid-October, Agence France-Presse reported that "long lines formed outside vaccination clinics around the United States, with many people turned away as supplies ran dry."[30] But criticism faded as the anticipated second wave of H1N1 arrived without causing a catastrophic number of deaths. In their public statements, CDC officials repeatedly emphasized their lack of knowledge about the eventual severity of the disease. As Acting Director Richard Besser said, "At the early stages of an outbreak, there's much uncertainty, and probably more than everyone would like."[31] The assertion of the unpredictability of the future course of the disease was an explicit part of U.S. health officials' strategy for communicating risk to the public.[32] Here they were following the advice of risk communication specialists: "Confidently telling us you could well be wrong inspires trust even as it alerts us to the genuine uncertainties of the situation."[33] To foster credibility, health officials performed transparency—seeking, as Besser put it, to "tell everything we knew, everything we didn't know, and what we were doing to get the answer."[34]

In Europe, when the anticipated fall flu wave finally arrived, the apparent mildness of the virus alongside public anxiety about the safety and efficacy of the vaccine led to widespread skepticism of state-led vaccination campaigns. The French government had secured an order of 94 million doses of the vaccine at a cost of nearly 900 million euros with the goal of providing two successive doses to 75 percent of the national population.[35] In the end, however, less than 10 percent of the French population received the vaccine. Similar failures of public demand for influenza vaccination occurred in other European countries. By the winter, the governments of France, Germany, and England all sought to renegotiate their advance-purchase agreements with vaccine manufacturers and to unload excess doses on poor countries in the Global South at bargain prices.[36]

A series of political controversies then erupted in Europe over national governments' intensive public health response to H1N1. In an article that appeared in *Le Monde* in January 2010, former French Red Cross president Marc Gentilini admonished the French government for its spending on the vaccination campaign, arguing that "preparing for the worst wasn't necessarily preparing correctly."[37] Critics linked government spending on the program to broader debates over government health spending. A physician and legislator for the governing conservative party decried the misallocation of resources, asserting that "the cost is more than the deficit of all France's hospitals and is three times [the amount spent] on cancer care."[38] The head of the French Socialist Party demanded a parliamentary inquiry, calling the vaccination campaign a "fiasco" and suggesting that multinational drug companies were "the big winners in this affair."[39] The French government in turn defended its actions on the grounds of precaution: "I will always prefer to be too prudent than not enough," said President Sarkozy.[40] Foreign Minister Bernard Kouchner, cofounder of Médecins Sans Frontières and no stranger to disease emergencies, was dismissive of the criticism, declaring that he was "scandalized by the fact that this is a scandal at all."

The French authorities' mistake, according to anthropologist Frédéric Keck, "was to have confused the logic of preparedness with that of precaution, and not to have taken into account the transformation this new logic requires in its communication with the public."[41] In contrast to precaution, which seeks to prevent the occurrence of a catastrophic event, preparedness implies that government officials must act as if the worst case were going to occur—while at the same time, as risk communication specialists advised, "telling us you could well be wrong."[42] In such a context, the function of an alert is not to predict the onset of a catastrophic future but rather to institute an ethos of vigilance in the face of uncertainty.

The attention of European critics then turned to the international flu specialists whose warnings had led to the mass vaccination campaigns. As Gentilini put it, "I don't blame the health minister, but the medical experts. They created an apocalyptic scenario. There was pressure from the World Health Organization, which began waving the red warning flags too early."[43] The Chair of the Council of Europe's Health Committee, German physician Wolfgang Wodarg, convoked public hearings on the matter, charging that WHO's pandemic declaration was "one of the greatest medical scandals of the century."[44] According to Wodarg and others, the swine flu pandemic had been "faked" for the benefit of international health authorities and the global pharmaceutical industry.[45]

In hearings that winter before Wodarg's Committee, witnesses argued that scarce health resources had been squandered on the response to an outbreak that turned out to be less dangerous than seasonal flu and that such resources should have been spent on "real" killers—whether heart disease in wealthy countries or infant diarrhea in poor ones. Tom Jefferson of the Cochrane Collaboration, a research group that advocates for "evidence-based health care," testified against the epidemiological basis of the pandemic countermeasures, claiming that "vaccines and antivirals have a weak or non-existent evidence base against influenza."[46] In his testimony before the Council of Europe, German epidemiologist Ulrich Keil cited data on disease mortality to criticize WHO's emphasis on managing "emerging diseases" at the expense of the actual "great killers" detected through statistical analysis: "I would like to point out," he said, "that of the 827,155 deaths in 2007 in Germany about 359,000 come from cardiovascular diseases, about 217,000 from cancer, 4968 from traffic accidents, 461 from HIV/AIDS and zero from SARS or Avian Flu."[47] Here, coming from a certain segment of public health experts, we find the public display of numbers to make the case that policies should be made on the basis of statistical risk calculation, rather than on scenarios of potential catastrophe. Of course, from the perspective of vigilance, there is no possibility that evidence of risk could be strong in epidemiological terms since vigilance is oriented precisely to events that come as a surprise.

Rather than understand the WHO emergency response as operating according to a different type of reasoned action—one concerned with anticipatory intervention in the face of an uncertain threat— critics denounced a breach of scientific ethics, arguing that hidden conflicts of interest among members of the WHO Emergency Committee must have led to the agency's pandemic declaration. One object of their suspicious attention was the removal of the measurement of severity from the official WHO pandemic preparedness guidance document several months before the appearance of the new strain of H1N1. In June 2010, to wide publicity, investigative reporters with the *British Medical Journal* revealed paid consulting relationships between leading WHO influenza experts and vaccine manufacturers. According to *BMJ*, its investigation had "identified key scientists involved in WHO pandemic planning who had declarable interests, some of who are or have been funded by pharmaceutical firms that stood to gain from the guidance they were drafting."[48] The same week, the Council of Europe released its official report, which concluded that the pandemic declaration had led to "a distortion of priorities of public health services across Europe, waste of huge sums of public money, [and the] provocation of unjustified fears among Europeans." According to the report, WHO deliberations were tainted by unstated conflicts of interest between influenza experts and the drug companies that profited from national vaccination campaigns.[49] The *Daily Mail* summarized the two reports with the headline, "The pandemic that never was: Drug firms 'encouraged world health body to exaggerate swine flu threat.'"[50]

Pandemic preparedness advocates strongly defended WHO against such accusations. Infectious disease specialist Michael Osterholm said there was not "a single shred of evidence" that scientists with ties to the vaccine industry had unduly influenced the decisions of the WHO expert committee. Meanwhile epidemiologist Marc Lipsitch commented that planning for the possibility of a severe event "is what public-health agencies should do, and what most did in this instance, and they should be commended for it."[51] An International Health Regulations (IHR) Review Committee charged with assessing the Emergency Committee's decisions later concluded that "no critic of WHO has produced any direct evidence of commercial influence on decision-making."[52] The Committee's final report strongly defended the integrity of the WHO influenza specialists: "In the Committee's view, the inference by some critics that invisible commercial influences must account for WHO's actions ignores the power of the core public health ethos to prevent disease and save lives."[53] But as we have seen, it was precisely the question of how, technically, such a "core public health ethos" should be activated that was at the center of the controversy.

The accusation of a conflict of interest was arguably the most readily available idiom of critique for those who did not accept the legitimacy of vigilance as a norm for public health intervention. The more important question to pose, however, is how vigilance as a mode of attention came to structure the devices that guided WHO decision-making in the early stages of the H1N1 pandemic. Another way to put this question is to ask: how did such a weak virus generate such a strong response? As we have seen, it was the threat posed by highly pathogenic avian influenza (H5N1) that lent urgency to the enactment of pandemic preparedness measures in North America and Europe soon after the reemergence of H5N1 in 2004. Such preparedness measures included the adoption of the revised IHR and the revision of the pandemic alert system designed to guide the interventions of decision-makers in the event of the appearance of a novel strain of influenza.[54] These measures also included efforts by Western European and North American governments to ensure that their national populations would have access to a pandemic vaccine, through the system of advance-purchase agreements. The specter of a catastrophic avian flu pandemic was thus a vehicle for the establishment of a more general form of public health preparedness, but it also provided the details of the scenario that would structure response when a different virus emerged.

Thus, when a novel subtype of influenza (H1N1) appeared in humans in spring 2009, plans that had originally been developed to prepare for H5N1 avian influenza were put into action. In her later testimony to the IHR Review Committee investigating the WHO response, Chan revised her earlier statement about the benefits of investments in preparedness: "The world was better prepared for a pandemic than at any time in history. But it was prepared for a different kind of event than what actually occurred."[55] Similarly, an official from the European Center for Disease Prevention and Control explained the intensive response in Europe: "We were all planning for the potential mutation of the avian flu over the next three to five years into a person-to-person transmittable disease."[56] In the United States, the scenario that the Congressional Budget Office had developed in 2005 to plan for a human transmissible strain of avian influenza—a vision in which 90 million people became ill and 2 million died—provided the details of what a future "severe pandemic" would look like. Given experts' concern about avian influenza, the CDC noted in retrospect, "pandemic preparedness efforts were largely based on a scenario of severe human illness caused by an H5N1 virus."[57] This problem is inherent to an apparatus of vigilance: one is responsible to plan for the worst case, but there is no guarantee that such a case will in fact occur.

It was this use of scenarios of a possible future as guides for action in the absence of statistical data about disease risk that had so exercised the WHO's critics. As Ulrich Keil said: "Governments and public health services are paying only lip service to the prevention of these great killers" like heart disease and cancer, "and are instead wasting huge amounts of money by investing in pandemic scenarios whose evidence base is weak."[58] From this perspective, public health intervention must be justified through historical evidence of future risk. According to the Council of Europe's scathing report, "It was precisely this lack of watertight evidence about the influenza phenomenon which led to the fears of the pandemic being exaggerated and the subsequent disproportionate response."[59] But for WHO officials, such an assessment could only be made in retrospect. Director-General Chan would later point to the difficulty of making informed decisions under conditions of urgency and uncertainty: "A new disease is, by definition, poorly understood as it emerges. Decisions with far-reaching consequences need to be made quickly in an atmosphere of considerable scientific uncertainty."[60] From the perspective of vigilance, as soon as a sign of the catastrophic future is detected, existing plans must be put into action.

In its final report, issued in 2011, the IHR Review Committee pointed to the difficulty WHO had faced in adjusting to the unexpected. As Chan admitted, "Managing the discrepancy between what was expected and what actually happened was problematic." The report articulated the need for mutual accommodation between techniques for managing an emerging disease and the production of knowledge about its characteristics: "Lack of certainty is an inescapable reality when it comes to influenza. One key implication is the importance of flexibility to accommodate unexpected and changing conditions."[61] In other words, health agencies must be capable of tracking and responding to transformations in real time. At the same time, the IHR Review Committee strongly defended WHO officials against the charge that they had overstated the danger posed by the virus, arguing that "reasonable criticism can be based only on what was known at the time and not on what was later learnt," and pointing to the problem of pinning down severity in the early stages of a pandemic: "the severity of the pandemic was uncertain throughout the summer of 2009, well past the time, for example, when countries would have needed to place orders for vaccine."[62] In the case of a novel pathogen, the characteristics of an encroaching pandemic cannot be determined by using accumulated data about past occurrences. At a critical moment of decision, one inevitably will suffer from a dearth of numbers.

In the 1830s and 1840s, the actuarial device in public health was invented by authorities such as William Farr and Louis-René Villermé in the broader context of an attempt to know and manage the regularly occurring risks of collective urban life. A century and a half later, sentinel devices proliferated in response to a different problem, that of the unanticipated but potentially catastrophic disease event in a globally interconnected world. These two kinds of security mechanism, one dating from the mid-nineteenth century and the other from the late twentieth, encountered one another around the question of what kind of event H1N1 2009 was to be: an alarm precipitously sounded or a bullet barely dodged.

If the framework of risk management guided national public health efforts up through the late twentieth century, the recent appearance of "emerging infections" pointed to the limit of its capacity to govern disease. An apparatus of vigilance, constructed at a global scale, now seeks to envision future disease catastrophe and to put tools in place that can avert or at least mitigate its occurrence. Among these tools are sentinel devices that alert authorities to the onset of a potential event and, just as important, trigger mechanisms that guide policy interventions in the wake of an alarm. National public health officials, once enrolled in this apparatus, cannot evade responsibility for taking preparedness measures, however costly, by citing a lack of data on disease risk.

WHO's pandemic planners might have responded to the Council of Europe's critical report with this line from philosopher Hans Jonas, writing about the principle of precaution: "The prophecy of doom is made to avert its coming, and it would be the height of injustice to later deride the 'alarmists' because 'it did not turn out to be so bad after all'—to have been wrong may be their merit."[63] And yet, despite the ubiquity among emerging disease experts of phrases like "it is not a question of if, but when," prophecy is not the right term for the field's characteristic orientation to the future, because it insistently admits its uncertainty. Rather, the figure of the sentinel, ever alert and hypersensitive, helps us to understand the particular form of anticipation at stake in the arena of global health security.

CODA: VIRUS SHARING

Although it defended the Emergency Committee's actions in response to H1N1, the IHR Review Committee framed its final report with a stark warning about the readiness of the global health system to manage future threats. "The world is ill-prepared to respond to a severe influenza pandemic or to any similarly global, sustained and threatening public-health emergency." The committee pointed in particular to global inequities in access to a pandemic vaccine. Although WHO had been able to galvanize some support from the global community for providing vaccines to poor countries, the report continued, "the unavoidable reality is that tens of millions of people would be at risk of dying in a severe pandemic."[64] The lesson the Review Committee had drawn from the H1N1 episode was not one of a tendency to overreaction in wealthy countries but rather one of the lack of response capacity in poor ones: "The fundamental gap between global need and global capacity must be closed." The committee made three recommendations on how to close this gap: first, establish a more extensive global public health reserve workforce; second, create a contingency fund for surge capacity during global public health emergencies; and finally, reach an agreement on global influenza virus sharing and access to vaccines and other benefits. This last recommendation alluded to the attempt to negotiate a settlement on virus sharing between the Indonesian government and the Global Influenza Surveillance Network (see Chapter 3). Such an agreement, urged the committee, would "lead to wider availability of vaccines and other benefits and greater equity in the face of the next pandemic."

The 2007 stalemate between the Indonesian health ministry and GISN leaders had led WHO to convene negotiations among member states around the question of whether poorer nations should be asked to share influenza virus specimens with WHO laboratories without any assurance that the eventual benefits of such sharing would be equitably distributed. As these negotiations stalled over the following two years, the international response to the 2009 H1N1 pandemic increased poor countries' distrust in the WHO influenza surveillance and response system, as vaccines against H1N1 were made available to the populations of wealthy nations through advance-purchase agreements with vaccine manufacturers, but were not shared with the countries in the Global South.

As legal scholar David Fidler noted, "Developed countries placed large advance orders for 2009-H1N1 vaccine and bought virtually all the vaccine companies could manufacture."[65] WHO and United Nations appeals for donations to purchase vaccines and other supplies for developing countries yielded some pledges from manufacturers and wealthy countries. But then, production problems limited vaccine supply in wealthy countries, reducing the prospects for donation. In the end, wealthy countries did not provide vaccine donations until it was clear that H1N1 was more mild than initially feared and that only one dose of the vaccine was necessary to immunize adults. More generally, the governments of wealthy countries did not agree on binding arrangements for more equitable vaccine access but rather sought, as Fidler put it, "to increase such access through ad hoc, reactive, and nonbinding activities that preserve national freedom of action while demonstrating some humanitarian concern."[66]

Arguing that improving access to essential medicines was "the central global governance issue of our times," WHO influenza specialist Keiji Fukuda urged international agreement on a framework that would support global responses to pandemic threats and, at the same time, ensure equitable access to vaccines for developing countries.[67] In 2011, WHO member states finally reached an agreement on rules for sharing influenza virus samples and biological information about such viruses with the influenza surveillance network. The agreement, known as the Pandemic Influenza Preparedness (PIP) Framework, sought to improve global health security "by encouraging states to share viruses and enhance equitable access to benefits." The PIP Framework had three key elements. First, a virus tracking mechanism was designed to increase the legitimacy of the WHO reference laboratories. This mechanism would monitor the global circulation of PIP Framework biological materials to create transparency in these exchanges. Second, the framework governed the exchange of biological materials through two kinds of material transfer agreements (MTAs). The first kind regulated exchange among GISN laboratories, encouraging them not to seek intellectual property rights on PIP biological materials. The second applied to transfers of viruses from WHO laboratories to entities outside the surveillance system, such as vaccine manufacturers. Here the material transfer agreement was linked to the third key element of the PIP Framework, a benefits-sharing system. To gain access to biological materials necessary for vaccine production, representatives of the multinational pharmaceutical industry agreed to pay half of the influenza surveillance and response system's annual operating costs, and to provide "equity-enhancing benefits"—presumably, access to vaccines in the event of a future pandemic. However, these latter benefits remained unspecified.

According to analysts, the PIP Framework contributed to the legitimacy of the WHO influenza surveillance system by increasing the transparency of virus transfers, and it contributed to equity in the provision of global health security through required industry contributions to the surveillance system's operating costs and through benefits provided by the second material transfer agreement. However, the framework did not solve deeper issues at the heart of the attempt to develop a functioning system of global health security that could manage future pandemic threats in an equitable manner. Although the framework was "a landmark in global governance for health," as two legal scholars commented, it reflected "compromises that could jeopardize more equitable allocation of benefits in a future pandemic."[68] Specifically, there was still no provision to guarantee that poor countries would in fact have access to affordable countermeasures in the event of the next global health emergency. And more generally, there was no mechanism to close what the IHR review committee's final report had called the "fundamental gap between global need and global capacity." As we will see in Chapter 6, this gap would become especially palpable as the 2014 Ebola epidemic spread out of control in West Africa.

5   A Fragile Assemblage

At an international influenza conference held in Malta in September 2011, Dutch virologist Ron Fouchier made a startling announcement: he had created a mutant strain of H5N1 avian influenza that spread through the air among ferrets, the closest animal model for humans. "This virus is airborne and as efficiently transmitted as the seasonal virus," Fouchier declared. Given the extremely high pathogenicity of H5N1, he later noted, this transmissible variant was "probably one of the most dangerous viruses you can make."[1]

Fouchier's research was funded by the U.S. National Institutes of Health (NIH) via a subcontract with New York City's Mount Sinai Center for Research on Influenza Pathogenesis. Working in an "enhanced" biosafety level 3 laboratory in Rotterdam, his research team began with a sample of H5N1 that had first been isolated in 2005 from an avian flu victim in Indonesia and then shared with the World Health Organization's (WHO's) Global Influenza Surveillance Network. The Dutch team initially sought to provoke respiratory transmission among the ferrets through the technique of reverse genetics—by, as Fouchier put it, "mutating the hell" out of the virus, enabling it to bind more easily to cells in the nasal and tracheal passages.[2] When this step did not lead to respiratory transmission, the scientists manipulated the virus further through the century-old technique of serial passaging—that is, passing the virus directly from ferret to ferret via nasal droplets to force its adaptation to the mammalian respiratory tract. After ten repetitions of this latter process, the virus was "airborne," spreading quickly among the laboratory's sneezing ferrets. An article by Fouchier's team, forthcoming in *Science*, promised to detail the five specific mutations necessary for the virus to become easily transmissible among mammals while maintaining its virulence. Meanwhile, the results of similar work conducted by virologist Yoshihiro Kawaoka at the University of Wisconsin–Madison, also funded by NIH, were soon to appear in *Nature*.

From the perspective of influenza virology, the experiments were significant in that they seemed to demonstrate the potential for H5N1 to naturally evolve a capacity for human-to-human transmission. This question was a long-running subject of debate among influenza scientists and public health officials. In 2005, Lee Jong-wook of the World Health Organization claimed that "it is only a matter of time before an avian flu virus—most likely H5N1—acquires the ability to be transmitted from human to human, sparking the outbreak of human pandemic influenza." In contrast, noted virologist Peter Palese of the Mount Sinai School of Medicine argued that "if H5N1 were going to become pandemic in humans, it should have happened already." Indeed, Palese continued, "probably an H5 can't make it in humans."[3] The stakes of the debate were high: the entire edifice of pandemic preparedness rested on the premise of the catastrophic potential of the appearance of a human transmissible strain of avian influenza.

The skepticism of experts such as Palese had helped motivate Fouchier's research: "There are highly respected virologists who thought until a few years ago that H5N1 could never become airborne between mammals," he said. "I wasn't convinced. To prove these guys wrong, we needed to make a virus that is transmissible."[4] For Fouchier, the significance of the experimental result extended beyond basic knowledge about avian flu viruses: it demonstrated the urgent need for ongoing research into influenza virology as an element of pandemic preparedness.

For other observers, however, there was a foreboding sense that it might not be wise to test whether a dangerous strain could emerge in the wild by creating just such a strain in the laboratory. In this spirit, a different group of actors sought to take hold of the mutant strain, or at least to stimulate broader reflection on its possible consequences. In the late summer and early fall of 2011, an internal NIH advisory board was asked to consider the biosecurity concerns raised by the *Science* and *Nature* articles in advance of their publication.[5]

The National Science Advisory Board on Biosecurity (NSABB), housed in the Office of Biotechnology within NIH, is a consultative body, made up mainly of life scientists, whose mandate is to provide guidance to federal funding agencies "regarding biosecurity oversight of dual use research."[6] Although concern over the risk of an accidental release would eventually come to the fore of the debate over flu transmission research, NSABB's official purview was limited to the question of the risk of malevolent use of scientific information. The board had been established in the context of the massive increase, after the 2001 anthrax letters, in federally sponsored research on hazardous biological agents. In the case of the experiments on influenza transmissibility, the board's task was to assess whether the published research results might "be misused to pose a biological threat to public health and/or national security." In its six years of existence, the board had never advised NIH against publication. Most prominently it had endorsed the controversial 2005 publication of the genetic sequence of the 1918 influenza virus.[7]

Thus, NSABB's recommendation in the case of the mutant H5N1 experiments, released in December 2011, was a surprising turnabout. The published articles by Fouchier and Kawaoka, the board stated, should not include "methodological and other details that could enable replication of the experiments by those who would seek to do harm." The NSABB chair, microbiologist Paul Keim, explained the board's reasoning: "Slowly, you get to the line where something shouldn't be communicated. These papers exceeded that line in our minds."[8] The board proposed to address the threat of the dissemination of dangerous knowledge through the establishment of a regulatory mechanism that would limit access to the methodological details of the experiments to a select group of scientists on a "need-to-know" basis.

But it was unclear how such a tool of selective access would function—how, as the editor of *Science* put it, "responsible scientists" making "legitimate efforts to improve public health and safety" would gain access to key experimental details that were redacted from the published articles.[9] Others pointed out that in an era of rapid circulation of scientific information, it would be difficult, if not impossible, to keep such details confined to a narrow group of authorized specialists. As a Vietnam-based influenza researcher objected, "Who chooses the 200 or 400 scientists around the world who get access? Who polices whether they immediately give it to their colleagues? It's unworkable, unpoliceable and crazy to even consider. Once it's out there, it's out there."[10] Keim acknowledged the limitations of the board's recommendation: "To say these details won't get out is unrealistic," he admitted. Rather than censor the studies' details, he explained, the board hoped to postpone publication of the two articles "so that there can be a broader discussion" of the biosecurity implications of such research.[11]

The release of NSABB's recommendation against full publication provoked a furor among influenza researchers working on viral transmission. In a January 2012 editorial in *Nature*, Palese argued, "Publishing those experiments without the details is akin to censorship, and counter to science, progress and public health."[12] Also in *Nature*, Kawaoka emphasized the urgency of conducting research on H5N1 transmission without any restriction on publication, appealing to the anticipatory rationale of global health security: "We cannot afford to lose time if we are to combat emerging pandemic threats."[13] The premise of these objections to the proposed restrictions was that viral transmission research was an urgent contribution to pandemic preparedness: it would serve as a part of a molecular sentinel device, telling virus trackers what they should be looking for in the wild.

Meanwhile, a number of external commentators excoriated the flu transmission research program for its recklessness. "The research should never have been undertaken because the potential harm is so catastrophic and the potential benefits from studying the virus so speculative," editorialized the *New York Times*.[14] As such criticism mounted, the flu virology researchers hesitantly agreed to the suggestion, made by NSABB and other sympathetic observers, that they pause their experiments until guidelines "for the safe and responsible conduct of such research" could be developed.[15] The suggestion of a research pause was a clear reference to a prior period of controversy around the potential dangers of biotechnology: the self-imposed moratorium among life scientists that preceded the famed 1975 Asilomar conference on the oversight of recombinant DNA research, which has been seen in retrospect (by life scientists, at least) as a model of successful scientific self-regulation.[16] As one of the NSABB members later put it, "Asilomar ushered in a period of cautious experimentation that was prevetted and then executed under conditions that combined biological and physical containment."[17] In this spirit, the flu transmission researchers announced their research pause as an opportunity to "clearly explain the benefits of this important research and the measures taken to minimize its possible risks."[18] As we will see, the process would turn out to be considerably more complicated than one of simply assuaging the concerns of an overly anxious public.

THE ASSEMBLAGE OF PANDEMIC PREPAREDNESS

This chapter examines the formation, and partial decomposition, of a configuration of actors and techniques assembled in response to the threat of a potential pandemic. The story it tells is initially one of opportunistic and entrepreneurial connection: a group of basic researchers in influenza virology were able to galvanize external support by connecting their enterprise to the broader project of pandemic preparedness. However, the ties binding the resulting formation proved to be weak. When a controversy erupted around the biosecurity implications of their research, the flu researchers found themselves isolated, and some voiced skepticism about the very problem that had driven support for their research. As disagreement intensified around how to understand and evaluate the risks and benefits of the research, the elements of the assemblage began to disaggregate.

The chapter uses the concept of assemblage to denote a grouping of heterogeneous elements that have been brought together contingently to address what is, at least in principle, a common scientific and governmental problem.[19] The technical and political assemblage of pandemic preparedness extends across national boundaries and includes influenza specialists, biosecurity experts, and government funding agencies, as well as virology laboratories and disease detection networks. It also includes devices, such as biosafety protocols and institutional review boards, designed to regulate the practices of the scientists.[20] The term assemblage helpfully connotes the multiple types of elements included in this configuration and indicates that these elements are not necessarily working in unison—indeed, that the grouping is an ongoing site of reflection and debate.[21] In the case I describe here, the assemblage posed the challenge of harmonization across disparate regulatory and scientific arenas. As we will see, it threatened to come apart when its central actors were enjoined to come to agreement around a common practice of technical risk assessment.

Influenza virology researchers were enrolled in governmental pandemic preparedness efforts in 2005, with the formulation of the U.S. Department of Health and Human Services' *Pandemic Influenza Preparedness and Response Plan*. The plan described the Department's assumptions, doctrine, and key actions in anticipation of the emergence of a virus with "the potential to cause more death and illness than any other public health threat."[22] An appendix to the plan outlined the scientific research activities to be funded by NIH as part of the President's requested $7.1 billion in emergency funds for avian influenza pandemic preparedness. "Basic research on influenza", it stated, "facilitates new ways of detecting and rapidly characterizing these viruses as they emerge."[23] Specifically, NIH would support research on factors contributing to the virulence of influenza viruses and on understanding "genetic changes that permit an influenza virus to suddenly acquire the ability to transmit between species." As we will see, this last clause referred to an emerging subfield of virology engaged in the laboratory creation of novel strains of influenza virus via genetic manipulation. The purpose of such investigation—which would later be termed "gain of function" research—was to study the evolution of characteristics such as virulence or transmissibility. In this early government document pledging federal support for such research, there was not yet any discussion of its potential biosafety and biosecurity implications.

The following month, Anthony Fauci, the director of the National Institute of Allergy and Infectious Disease (NIAID), testified about the pandemic threat before the House Committee on International Relations. In his written statement to the committee, "The Road to Preparedness," Fauci explained the need for government support of basic scientific research in addressing the problem of emerging infectious disease in an increasingly interdependent and vulnerable world. Fauci portrayed a future in which global health threats linked to poverty and underdevelopment could be reduced through advances in biotechnology. On the one hand, according to Fauci, "our globalized economy is exquisitely sensitive to the disruptions that would inevitably occur during a pandemic," and "many parts of the world have weak public health and health-care delivery systems, and poverty and overcrowding are widespread." On the other hand, he continued, science and medicine "have progressed dramatically, and we now have tools such as sophisticated viral surveillance techniques, effective vaccines," and antiviral drugs that could aid in responding to an emerging pandemic. For the envisioned system of pandemic preparedness to work, he argued, the U.S. government must invest in response capacity well in advance of the event's actual occurrence, given that such tools "will be of little use if we cannot bring them to bear when we need them."[24] According to Fauci, the need for disease surveillance and medical counter-measure development cemented the link between the governmental problem of pandemic preparedness and cutting-edge biological research on viral pathogens.

These technical and administrative discussions unfolded in the midst of a growth spurt in U.S. government support for basic research on influenza. NIH funding for such research, managed by NIAID, jumped from $15 million in 2001 to $212 million in 2007. A Blue Ribbon Panel on influenza research convened by NIH in 2006 identified several urgent priority research areas for government investment, including study of "the evolutionary pressures that lead to the emergence and spread of new viral subtypes—especially the factors that favor transmission from animals to humans."[25] Following the panel's recommendations, in 2007 NIAID established six new Centers of Excellence in Influenza Research and Surveillance, including one at the Mount Sinai School of Medicine that focused on influenza pathogenesis. This latter center was at the center of the controversy that arose in 2011 over federally sponsored flu virology research.[26]

NIH support of basic influenza research was critical to the enrollment of the fairly small community of flu virologists as part of the heterogeneous assemblage of pandemic preparedness. Other actors in this scientific and governmental assemblage included global public health authorities, biosecurity experts, epidemiologists, and pharmaceutical manufacturers. In principle, despite their disparate backgrounds, methods and aims, the various actors involved were all concerned with a scenario in which the H5N1 avian influenza virus evolved to be transmitted easily among humans, leading to a potentially catastrophic pandemic. However, as we will see, the assemblage proved fragile. It threatened to come apart several years later, when a public controversy erupted over the risks and benefits of the laboratory creation of a strain of H5N1 that could spread through the air between mammals. What became apparent at that point was that many, if not most, of the influenza virologists did not share a basic diagnosis of the situation with their erstwhile collaborators in public health and biosecurity.

Avian Influenza

As we saw in Chapter 2, public health officials first identified highly pathogenic avian influenza (H5N1) in 1997 in Hong Kong, where it killed six of the eighteen people who were diagnosed as infected with the virus—a startlingly high fatality rate for influenza. This outbreak presented a surprise to influenza researchers, who had until then assumed that H5 subtype influenza viruses, although deadly for birds, could not infect humans. Public health authorities warned that a zoonotic "spillover" of H5N1—the evolutionary adaptation of the avian influenza virus to the human respiratory tract—could lead to a devastating global pandemic since human populations did not have any immunity to the strain.[27]

The critical question was whether this strain of avian influenza could evolve to be transmitted easily among human populations via aerosol droplets, like seasonal influenza. All of the reported Hong Kong cases were due to close contact between humans and birds, and so widespread human-to-human transmission did not yet seem possible. Nonetheless, concerned about the possibility of viral evolution in the host reservoir that would enable such transmission, the director of Hong Kong's Department of Health, Margaret Chan, who would become the director-general of WHO in 2006, ordered a massive culling of the city's poultry population: 1.5 million chickens, ducks, geese, and quail were slaughtered, and the virus appeared to recede.[28]

In 2003, the H5N1 virus reemerged in East and Southeast Asia, detected in migratory waterfowl, and it soon spread globally along bird migration routes, rarely infecting humans, but continuing to demonstrate an alarmingly high rate of mortality when it did. According to WHO calculations, the virus killed nearly six in ten of those it infected. By comparison, the case fatality ratio for the 1918 influenza pandemic in which an estimated fifty million people died around the world was around 2.5 percent. Thus, health authorities remained on high alert for a genetic mutation or reassortment that would render the virus easily transmissible among humans and thus potentially trigger a pandemic.

Experts and officials agreed that such a transformation event was possible, but that its likelihood was impossible to calculate. As science journalist Laurie Garrett wrote, "There is no way to put a number on the probability of such natural mutational events."[29] Similarly, according to Anthony Fauci, "we cannot predict whether [a human transmissible variant of H5N1] will arise naturally, nor when or where it might appear."[30] The difficulty of calculating the risk of an H5N1 pandemic put authorities in an uncomfortable position as they sought substantial government investment in prevention and preparedness measures. If the disease never became widespread, they could be accused of overreaction and wasteful spending, but if an easily transmissible and highly virulent strain of H5N1 did emerge, only intensive advanced preparations would stave off catastrophe.

The response to this situation of uncertainty coupled with urgency was the gradual assembly of mechanisms for monitoring the disease, preventing its spread among birds, and preparing for the worst case. Biosecurity authorities ordered the culling of millions of sick or exposed chickens, epidemiologists developed molecular surveillance systems to track viral mutations across continents, health officials collected viral isolates in countries such as Vietnam and Indonesia, government agencies conducted scenario-based exercises and developed national pandemic preparedness plans, drug companies produced vaccines and antiviral drugs, and virologists analyzed the determinants of influenza virulence and transmission. The hope, shared by a range of experts and officials, was that ongoing investment in such scientific and administrative measures would mitigate the risk of a catastrophic pandemic.

Over the next few years, the H5N1 virus continued to evolve within its animal reservoirs, to be highly virulent among birds, and to fail to spread easily among humans—although it maintained its very high case fatality ratio when it did. Meanwhile, the intensive global response to the 2009 swine flu pandemic, which turned out to be less severe than many officials initially feared, arguably tempered the public sense of urgency around

H5N1 preparedness efforts (see Chapter 4). By 2011, global vigilance seemed to be waning, as years passed without the anticipated mutation or recombination event. Perhaps, as virologists such as Palese had suggested, there was something inherent to H5 viruses that necessarily limited their capacity to spread easily among humans. Only time, it seemed—and more research—would tell. Given this background, with multiple other crises demanding public attention, it was uncertain how long a condition of intensely engaged preparedness could be sustained for an event that might or might not occur.

RISK ASSESSMENT

It was in this context that the public controversy unfolded over whether and how to regulate basic scientific research on influenza transmission. In the months following NSABB's December 2011 recommendation to redact the articles by Fouchier and Kawaoka, this debate was conducted mainly in the idiom of risk assessment. NSABB defended its "unprecedented recommendation" as having been "conducted with careful consideration both of the potential benefits of publication and of the potential harm that could occur from such a precedent."[31] The flu virologists, in turn, countered with their own variant of risk analysis. As Kawaoka wrote: "I believe that the benefits of these studies—the knowledge that H5 HA-possessing viruses pose a risk and the ability to monitor them and develop countermeasures— outweigh the risks."[32] Other expert commentators, such as infectious disease specialist Thomas Inglesby of the Center for Biosecurity, weighed in using similar terms but arrived at the opposite conclusion: "The potential benefits of the research do not justify the potential dangers, so the research should be discontinued."[33]

Despite these allusions to a technical practice of risk analysis, there was no standard method for defining, measuring, and comparing the potential benefits and harms of the research. An editorial in *Nature* later noted that each side in the debate relied for its evaluation of risks and benefits on "qualitative arguments" rather than the "formal, quantitative assessment" used in the nuclear power industry that "could have helped to nail down and quantify risks" and thus better inform the debate.[34] Although risk assessment seemed to provide the only available terms for making authoritative claims about the need for regulation, as a formal technique it was ill suited to the dangers that were under discussion. It was by no means obvious how to make a quantitative assessment of the likelihood that, for example, a malevolent or disgruntled life scientist might take the published results of the study and use them to unleash a devastating global pandemic or that the accidental release of a virulent strain from a laboratory engaged in transmission research might have the same effect. The situation bore some resemblance to the case, described in Chapter 2, of the CDC vaccine advisory committee's difficulty in assessing the benefits and risks of a smallpox vaccination program without any data on the likelihood of a smallpox attack.

In a *Washington Post* editorial published just after NSABB issued its recommendation, Fauci and two other NIH leaders sought to assure readers of the experiments' safety, but nonetheless acknowledged some of the uncertainties involved: "The question is whether benefits of such research outweigh risks. The answer is not simple. A highly pathogenic bird flu virus transmissible in humans could arise in ways not predicted by laboratory studies. And it is not clear whether this laboratory virus would behave in humans as it does in ferrets."[35] Indeed, as one critical observer of the experiments later noted, it was not obvious that laboratory-induced mutations could say anything about what was likely to occur in nature. "Take dog breeding," suggested virologist Simon Wain-Hobson. "Ruthless selection of alleles over a short period has produced phenomenal phenotypic variation—dachshunds, salukis, whippets and setters."[36] Wain-Hobson's point was that Fouchier's experiment, structured by a system of artificial selection, proved nothing about the probability of such an event occurring in the wild. "Would nature have come up with the dachshund?" he pointedly asked.

Without quite being able to articulate it, the members of NSABB—mostly infectious disease biologists—found themselves in the surprising and uncomfortable position of becoming critics of the uncertain hazards generated by their colleagues' experimental research. In looking at the board's initial recommendation for redaction, it is clear that the basis of its decision was not a formal risk assessment but rather something more like the imaginative enactment of a worst-case scenario: "We found the potential risk of public harm to be of unusually high magnitude," the board stated in a published explanation of the rationale for its decision. "A pandemic, or the deliberate release of a transmissible highly pathogenic influenza A/H5N1 virus, would be an unimaginable catastrophe for which the world is currently inadequately prepared."[37] Or, as Keim put it in an interview with *Nature* in January 2012, "I don't like to scare people, but the worst-case scenarios here are just enormous."[38] The very pandemic scenario that had initially provoked the demand for basic research on influenza transmission, and thus the spike in NIH funding that supported Fouchier and Kawaoka's experiments, now provoked anxieties that had the potential to stifle this line of investigation. Although constrained in its regulatory power by the "existing institutional yardsticks" of risk assessment, the seemingly incalculable hazards involved in transmission research inclined the committee toward a precautionary approach.[39]

PRECAUTION

From the inception of NSABB, biosecurity regulators reflected on the question of how to make a risk assessment in the absence of adequate data for calculating probability. The impetus behind the board's formation dates, as noted earlier, to the period right after the 2001 anthrax letters, in the context of a massive increase in federal support for biodefense research, alongside growing concern among U.S. national security officials with the dissemination of knowledge and techniques concerning the biological manipulation of dangerous pathogens. A number of controversial biodefense-related experiments, such as the synthesis of a live poliovirus by a Department of Defense funded laboratory at SUNY Stony Brook in 2002, led security officials to ask how to regulate the production and dissemination of what came to be known as "dual use research of concern."[40] In turn, as one microbiologist later recalled, scientists working in this area began to worry that "if the community did not act to protect the integrity of science, government would overreach and there would be censorship."[41] This concern to stave off external oversight was similar to that which had animated the Asilomar discussions of the 1970s; and as we will see, the guidelines for risk management that were soon established followed the post-Asilomar model.

In October 2003, the National Academy of Sciences (NAS) convened a panel on "Biotechnology Research in the Age of Terrorism" to address the question of how to regulate "dual use" research. The NAS panel led, the following year, to the Fink Committee Report, which listed seven types of experimental research that warranted close scrutiny. The list included experiments that sought to render a vaccine ineffective or that made a pathogen more virulent.[42] Rather than create an entirely new system of oversight, the Fink Report recommended that existing Institutional Biosafety Committees, established in the wake of Asilomar-era debates over the regulation of recombinant DNA research, should serve as the setting for the review of dual use concerns. The Fink Committee also called for the creation of a national advisory board on biosecurity issues, to be managed by NIH, which was established in 2005 as NSABB.

NSABB's guiding framework built on the Fink Committee's recommendations, emphasizing local self-governance based on the existing system of institutional responsibility.[43] More generally, the board's mandate was to minimize external regulation and to maintain scientific autonomy in order to "ensure that whatever oversight measures are put in place for dual use research do not unduly burden or slow the progress of life sciences research."[44] As Fauci would later put it, in arguing against any restrictions on the publication of NIH-sponsored flu transmission research, "there cannot be any impediment to science that will ultimately be good to the general public."[45] The emphasis of NSABB's mandate on ensuring scientific autonomy rather than on close scrutiny of proposed experiments led one analyst of U.S. biosecurity policy to conclude that "the NSABB was set up not to do anything. It is just a way of pretending there is some kind of oversight when there isn't."[46]

It was this carryover from the Asilomar process that led to NSABB's adoption of the discourse of risk assessment. Following the precedent of existing NIH guidelines for biosafety oversight of recombinant DNA research, the 2007 NSABB framework recommended that biosecurity oversight also be based on a process of "risk assessment and management," both at the level of local biosafety committees and in the board's own deliberations: "Risk assessment and management should be the foundation for local oversight of dual use research of concern," the framework document instructed. "This will help minimize the potential for misuse of dual use research information while minimizing any negative impact on the conduct of science and will facilitate the responsible conduct of life sciences research."[47] The document described a series of "points to consider" in making a recommendation on the publication of potentially dangerous information. Are there reasonably anticipated risks to public health and safety from direct misapplication of this information? If a risk has been identified, in what timeframe (e.g., immediate, near future, years from now) might this information be used to pose a threat to public health and/or safety? Any such risks should then be counter-posed to potential benefits through a similar analysis. Finally, and deceptively simply, the framework document instructed the committee to address the question: "Do the benefits of communicating the information outweigh the risks?"[48]

This envisioned practice of risk assessment was based on two related assumptions: first, that it would be possible to bring potentially quite disparate types of potential benefits and risks into a common frame of evaluation; and second, that each of these various benefits and risks could be quantified so that a definitive calculation could be made. Unfortunately, as we have already seen in the case of the mutant H5N1 experiments, such a calculation was impracticable for the problems with which NSABB was concerned, given inherent uncertainties around whether the production and dissemination of "dual use" research might pose a risk.[49] As the NSABB framework document itself acknowledged, "The current inability to quantify dual use research of concern and the risk of misuse of research information raises challenges for proposing an oversight framework."[50]

The framework's provisional solution to this challenge was twofold. First, it defined NSABB's task not as one of developing static, top-down regulations but rather of ongoing adaptation to new developments in the life sciences. Here NSABB explicitly followed the model of NIH biosafety oversight of recombinant DNA research, which provided "an important historical precedent for managing risk when its magnitude is unknown," given its ability to "adapt to advancing science while nonetheless establishing a standard of practice that is embraced by public and private sectors."[51] Second, the NSABB framework retreated from a prescription of formal risk assessment, by acknowledging the need to attend to the potentially catastrophic threat posed by dual use research even in the absence of adequate quantitative data on risk. Here it implicitly invoked a principle of precaution: "Misuse of dual use research of concern is therefore a low-probability but high consequence event, and this is a significant factor in the NSABB's formulation of oversight recommendations." It was to this factor—the low-probability, high-consequence event—that NSABB had alluded in its 2011 recommendation that the methodological details of Fouchier and Kawaoka's studies be redacted, given a worst-case scenario of "unimaginable catastrophe." Thus, without quite spelling it out, NSABB was pushing against the assumptions of formal risk assessment while still depending on its function as a mode of commensuration.

DISJUNCTURE

At the critical moment in early 2012 when debate over the publication of Fouchier and Kawaoka's articles intensified, the assemblage of pandemic preparedness, composed of flu virologists, biosecurity experts, global health authorities, and others, threatened to decompose. While the debate over publication of the experiments continued to be conducted in the language of risk assessment, there was little pretense that the controversy could be resolved through a process of formal calculation. Rather, risk assessment provided an idiom through which life scientists, security experts, and other commentators articulated divergent understandings of the condition of the global pandemic preparedness system—and the possible contribution (or lack thereof) that influenza transmission research could make.

Influenza virologists continued to demand that NSABB revisit its initial recommendation of redaction, using the language of risk assessment to defend unimpeded inquiry. Potential benefits of the research, they argued, included both the capacity to track salient genetic mutations in time to alert the globe to the near-onset of a pandemic and the ability to develop effective vaccines in advance of the outbreak. As Hong Kong–based microbiologist Malik Peiris explained: "If molecular signatures for transmissibility of animal influenza viruses in humans are better defined, identifying such mutations in viruses isolated during surveillance in animals . . . might be possible and would be a further incentive to enhance animal surveillance."[52] It should be underlined that the virologists' discussion of potential benefits of transmission research was embedded within the broader assumptions of pandemic preparedness—that is, the need to engage in real-time surveillance of H5N1 evolution and to stockpile medical countermeasures in case of the emergence of a pandemic strain.

Alongside the articulation of such potential benefits, this group of influenza virologists—dubbed "the flu cabal" by journalist Laurie Garrett—made a parallel argument: that the risks of the research had been greatly overstated. First, it seemed that the actual results of the experiment in question had been misunderstood; Fouchier now reported that his team's mutant virus had not in fact spread easily through the air and that the ferrets that contracted it did not actually die at high rates. But even—and here the virologists' reasoning had the potential to undermine the very rationale for their research—the creation of a highly transmissible strain among ferrets was not necessarily a cause for concern: there was no way to be certain that the virus would behave in humans as it did for ferrets.[53]

Peter Palese, a leading investigator at the Mount Sinai influenza research center that had subcontracted to Fouchier's laboratory in Rotterdam, went further, arguing that H5N1 was not nearly as dangerous to humans as generally believed. First, he remained skeptical about H5N1's capacity, whether mutated or not, to be transmitted easily among humans. "Incidentally, I believe that the risk of future outbreaks in humans is low: H5N1 has had the opportunity to cause widespread pandemics for many, many decades, yet it has not done so."[54] Second, he argued, the catastrophic scenario of an H5N1 pandemic had been badly exaggerated by preparedness advocates. Palese and a colleague published a meta-analysis of seroprevalence studies seeking to demonstrate that H5N1 was not nearly as virulent as generally assumed. WHO's frightening case fatality rate of 59 percent, they argued, was probably "orders of magnitude too high," given the likelihood that there were thousands of undetected cases among rural populations exposed to the virus in animals. Indeed, they wrote, alluding to the epidemiological practice of WHO investigators, "the frequency and certainty with which this staggering fatality rate is reported is troubling when one considers how the numbers are generated."[55] What was striking in such claims—whatever their validity—was the suggestion that for the virologists, the catastrophic scenario that was the engine of pandemic preparedness was of lower priority than pursuing key questions about how influenza viruses evolve and their determination that basic research on the topic not be impeded.

For those observers, such as Garrett and Inglesby, who were alarmed about the risk of either an intentional or accidental release of a mutant strain of H5N1, the virologists' assessment was either disingenuous or hopelessly naive. Garrett sharply rebuked Palese and his colleagues for challenging the seriousness of the avian flu threat: "In order to reverse the NSABB fiat Fouchier, his financial supporters at Mt. Sinai School of Medicine in New York (chiefly Palese, whose lab passed NIH research money onto Dutch scientist Fouchier), and a coterie of their supporters set out to dispel *all the assumptions* that lend credence to the notion of unique H5N1 danger."[56] Health authorities' scenarios of a future avian flu pandemic, in tandem with the real world response to swine flu in 2009, had left these observers convinced that the world was far from prepared for the appearance of an easily transmissible variant of H5N1.

Critics of the flu transmission research also argued that its potential benefits were premised on a wildly unrealistic estimation of the capacities of the still-nascent global pandemic preparedness infrastructure. It would be folly, they argued, to imagine that existing disease surveillance systems, using molecular signatures gleaned from transmission research, could provide early warning of the onset of a pandemic given these systems' limited capacity. An analysis in *Nature* painted a "dire picture" of the global capacity for disease surveillance in animals, undermining the case made by Peiris and others that knowledge of a transmissible strain's "molecular signature" would make it possible to provide early warning of an emerging pandemic: "In 2010, the world's poultry population was estimated at 21 billion; yet only around 1,000 flu sequences from 400 avian virus isolates were collected—and many countries that are home to billions of farmed chickens, ducks and pigs contributed few or none."[57] Similarly, microbiologists Casadevall and Shenk wrote of data on molecular signatures that might come from gain-of-function research: "Timely surveillance efforts are remarkably patchy in their coverage and it is uncertain how this information will be immediately useful for pandemic preparedness."[58] Moreover, especially in the Global South, there was little to no possibility that an outbreak of highly transmissible avian influenza could be rapidly contained through the production and dissemination of a vaccine—a process that takes months and results in vaccines that are unaffordable to much of the world's population. Finally, as Inglesby argued, the creation of new flu strains through gain-of-function research would not actually help in vaccine development: "developing vaccines against H5N1 strains that are actually emerging in nature does not require this kind of research."[59]

Meanwhile, critics were quick to defend both the adequacy of the ferret model for modeling human transmission as well as the accuracy of WHO's estimated case fatality ratio. Palese's contention about seroprevalence "goes far beyond the evidence," argued epidemiologist Marc Lipsitch, adding in a precautionary vein that "in the situation where experts disagree, it is only responsible to plan for the possibility that the optimists are wrong."[60] More starkly, some asked: if H5N1 is not in fact a serious threat, why should the government provide so much support for research into its genetic characteristics?[61] More generally, these critics argued, external oversight of gain-of-function research was essential because the scientists involved had a vested interest in ongoing support of their research. As historian of science Susan Wright put it, alluding to the (minimal) oversight of recombinant DNA research in the wake of the Asilomar process, "Past experience shows that when bioscience foxes guard their own chicken coops, there's a tendency to overlook issues that fall outside possible benefits—like environmental, health or security dangers."[62]

In contrast to the optimism of the flu transmission researchers and their NIH patrons—that if only the virologists were left to their own devices, scientific advance would conquer the threat of a deadly virus—these critics saw scientific research itself as a risk to be managed. One proposal was that future H5N1 gain-of-function research be conducted only in biosafety level 4 (BSL-4) laboratories, a restriction that would sharply limit the amount of such research that could be performed given the expense and practical difficulty of doing basic research in such high security facilities.[63] According to U.S. biosafety guidelines, the "enhanced BSL-3" level of containment where Fouchier conducted his experiment was prescribed for work with pathogens that could cause serious disease and that spread by the respiratory route, though vaccines or treatments may be available. The features of this level of biosafety included controlled lab access, decontamination of waste and clothing, the use of biosafety cabinets, negative airflow into the lab, and dedicated power and air systems. BSL-4 laboratories, which had considerably more stringent containment standards—including the use of positive pressure suits and airlocks—were reserved for infectious agents such as Ebola and Nipah for which there were no available treatments.[64]

At the end of March 2012, three months after its initial pronouncement, NSABB reversed its position and endorsed the publication of the details of the now-revised Fouchier study.[65] This decision followed a February meeting of influenza scientists convened by WHO, which strongly endorsed the resumption of gain-of-function research.[66] Various rationales were provided for the change in NSABB's recommendation. New information had been made available to the committee about the experimental results, indicating that its risks were lower than initially thought (the new strain was not quite so deadly to ferrets) and that its potential benefits (e.g., the potential for epidemiological surveillance) were greater. But some members of the board simply noted that their initial recommendation had been toothless: redaction alongside selective access was impractical in that it was impossible to delimit who should have legitimate access to the full data, and redaction was ineffective in that the information would get out widely in any case. "Information that's not born classified can't be reborn as classified," explained one board member.[67] Others remained insistent, despite assurances from the influenza virologists, that the experiments were misguided; but like other actors in the dispute, their engagement with the multiple uncertainties involved was constrained by the idiom of risk assessment.[68] "The dust is beginning to settle on the months-long controversy," mused Nature's flu correspondent in early April 2012, while a dissatisfied NSABB member grumbled that in its final decision the board had "just kicked the can down the road to the next manuscript."[69] Meanwhile, another question loomed. As debate over how to regulate the production of dangerous knowledge continued, would the configuration of pandemic preparedness—of virologists, epidemiologists, global health authorities, biosecurity experts, and others—hold together?

ACCIDENTAL REPERCUSSIONS

In January 2013, a year after the gain-of-function researchers' self-imposed moratorium had begun, Fouchier and forty coauthors published a letter in *Nature* and *Science* triumphantly announcing the resumption of flu transmission experiments. According to the scientists, the pause had provided them with "time to explain the public-health benefits of this work, to describe the measures in place to minimize possible risks, and to enable organizations and governments around the world to review their policies."[70] Because such research was "essential for pandemic preparedness," the letter explained, scientists had a "public health responsibility to resume this important work." The authors could not have anticipated that they would soon be faced with the prospect of a new, externally imposed moratorium in a world newly attuned to the catastrophic threat of emerging disease.

In October 2014, the White House made what *Science* magazine called a "startling announcement" concerning the regulation of research in the life sciences: the federal government was immediately halting all funding of research designed to alter a pathogen to make it more virulent or more transmissible until authorities could work out a government-wide policy for evaluating the risks and benefits of such studies.[71] The White House announcement was made in the midst of the devastating Ebola epidemic in West Africa and after a series of highly publicized biosafety lapses, including the accidental release of a strain of H5N1 at CDC and NIH laboratories, had put in question the safety of experiments on dangerous pathogens.[72] It reopened a controversy that had seemed settled eighteen months earlier. The announcement urged scientists who were engaged in gain-of-function research to agree to a voluntary moratorium "while risks and benefits are being assessed," and laid out a yearlong plan for NSABB to design and carry out a risk assessment study in collaboration with the National Research Council and the Institute of Medicine. It framed the debate in narrow terms to which each side could, at least in principle, agree: formal risk assessment was the appropriate technique for adjudicating the question of whether and how the government should regulate potentially dangerous biological experimentation. NSABB awarded a contract to a private research firm, Gryphon Scientific, to engage in a risk-benefit analysis of gain-of-function research that would inform the development of new guidelines.

Soon after this deliberative process began, participants voiced skepticism as to whether the planned study would in fact settle the regulatory debate. For many participants, reported *Science*, the initial meeting hosted by the National Academies of Science in December 2014 "felt like a rehash" of the prior debate: while proponents claimed that gain-of-function studies were necessary for avian influenza surveillance and for potential vaccine development, critics argued that these studies' risks were too great, especially given their uncertain benefits. A prominent risk specialist, meanwhile, warned that a rigorous assessment could not be accomplished in such a short time frame: "Somebody may need to use the numbers for political cover," he commented, "but it will be meaningless."[73]

The problem remained that such an assessment could only be made with respect to the professed goal of the gain-of-function research—to improve pandemic preparedness. Yet the normative rationality of preparedness, concerned with potentially catastrophic events whose probability eludes calculation, seemed to preclude the formal assessment of risks and benefits. There would still be the problem of gauging the likelihood of highly uncertain hazards, such as a mutation in the wild or a laboratory accident. Meanwhile, there remained another problem, of trying to link the envisioned benefits of the research, such as improved detection of viral mutations in chickens using molecular signatures or vaccine strain selection, to the actual infrastructure of global pandemic preparedness.[74]

With the White House announcement, risk assessment had been taken out of the hands of the flu researchers as well as their critics, and was now to be enacted by an external authority: a contracted scientific research firm that sought agreed-upon means to conduct a formal risk assessment. Despite the firm's ostensible objectivity, it was unlikely that the resulting assessment would gain assent from all parties.[75] Gain-of-function research remained caught between two approaches to biological threats. The first, pandemic preparedness, provided the rationale as well as the funds for the research; the second, biosafety and biosecurity, sought to establish regulations on potentially dangerous life sciences research that would not "unduly burden or slow the progress" of such research. However, the catastrophic scenario at the heart of the former outstripped the regulatory capacities of the latter. As gain-of-function research was taken up within a more formalized biosecurity framework, the gulf widened between influenza virologists focused on continuing their research on the one hand, and health authorities concerned with the potential impact of the release of a mutated virus on the other. By demonstrating that its key actors did not agree on the basic contours of the problem to be addressed, the controversy over mutant bird flu laid bare the fragility of the pandemic preparedness assemblage and threatened to tear it apart.

6 Diagnosing Failure

In the late summer and early fall of 2014, as the Ebola epidemic spun seemingly out of control in West Africa and threatened to spread globally, multiple observers began to point to failures in the global response to the epidemic. A disease that in prior outbreaks had never caused more than a few hundred deaths had turned into a global health catastrophe. The event was already seen, as a United Nations report later put it, as "a preventable tragedy." Along with this diagnosis of failure came the assignment of blame. The international response had been "slow and feeble," wrote two leaders of Médecins sans Frontières in late August. "It can equally be defined as irresponsible."[1] World Bank president and global health advocate Jim Yong Kim pointed to multiple lapses: functioning health care systems had not been put in place in the affected region, effective monitoring was not conducted when the first cases appeared, and there was no organized response from the international community. "We were tested by Ebola and we failed," he concluded.[2] The epidemic, from this perspective, was not an unavoidable danger but a potentially manageable risk, and therefore the catastrophic outcome demanded a retrospective accounting.

Much of the blame was targeted at the World Health Organization (WHO), which was first notified of the outbreak in March 2014 but did not officially declare a global health emergency until August, and even then had difficulty galvanizing a significant international response. WHO "should be the global leader" in directing and coordinating international health efforts, argued two legal scholars, but the organization's institutional weakness and lack of control over its resources had made it incapable of guiding the global response: "Failures in leadership have allowed a preventable disease to spin out of control," they concluded, "with vast harms to social order and human dignity."[3] An editorial in the journal *Nature* shared this diagnosis: WHO had been "slow and, so far, ineffective," and its outbreak response frameworks had "failed miserably."

The *Nature* editorial focused on two administrative devices that had been put in place over the prior decade to help the international community, and WHO in particular, respond better to disease outbreaks: the revised International Health Regulations (IHR; 2005), and the more recent Emergency Response Framework (2013). Despite such attempts to improve global health security, according to the editorial, "The world is little better prepared to quickly stamp out a threatening outbreak than it was a decade ago."[4] Journalist Laurie Garrett was still more scathing, writing that "WHO's response has been abysmal. It's just shameful." At the same time, she noted in the organization's defense that it was "just a shadow of its former financial self," due to the changing priorities of its member states and resulting cutbacks in outbreak response capacity.[5] Meanwhile, WHO was also engaged in a process of critical self-scrutiny. An internal investigation found that the organization had "missed chances to prevent Ebola from spreading soon after it was first diagnosed in Liberia, Sierra Leone and Guinea last spring," due to problems such as incompetent staff and a failure to share information.[6]

This chapter offers a somewhat different interpretation of the slow response by international health officials to the 2014 Ebola outbreak. Rather than focusing blame on WHO's organizational weakness or lack of sufficient resources, its suggests that the failure was at least in part one of administrative imagination: at a crucial stage, health authorities did not conceptualize Ebola as the potential source of a catastrophic epidemic, but rather understood it as a disease that could be managed via localized humanitarian care combined with straightforward public health techniques.

EBOLA AND THE IMAGINATION

In a *New York Times* article published at the end of 2014, Centers for Disease Control and Prevention (CDC) epidemiologist and Ebola "old hand" Pierre Rollin was asked why it had taken health authorities so long to understand the seriousness of the epidemic. "It was an unprecedented outbreak," responded Rollin. "It never happened before. There were a lot of things we didn't know at that time. No one could have imagined that it would be what we have now."[7] This latter claim, that "no one could have imagined" the eventual scale of the epidemic, was perhaps surprising given the centrality of imaginative practices to the history of expert reflection about emerging infectious disease. As we have seen, beginning in the late 1980s, specialists repeatedly imagined the devastating effect a potential future outbreak might have. Indeed, their task has often been precisely to envision what preparations would be necessary to address such an emergency. And, especially in early discussions of the emerging disease threat, Ebola was the object of intensive reflection about the possibility of a catastrophic outbreak.

It was the appearance of an Ebola variant in the United States that initially helped spark widespread concern with the threat of emerging diseases. In late 1989, at a primate quarantine facility in Reston, Virginia, an outbreak of an Ebola-like virus that could be transmitted through the air among macaques caused a major scare among infectious disease and biodefense specialists. Molecular biologist and biodefense advocate Joshua Lederberg informed journalist Richard Preston about the event, resulting in a widely discussed 1992 *New Yorker* article on the "Reston virus" and then the best-selling book *The Hot Zone: The Terrifying Story of the True Origins of the Ebola Virus* (1995).[8] The Reston incident was also one of the motivations behind the influential 1992 report from the Institute of Medicine (IOM), *Emerging Infections: Microbial Threats to Health*, coedited by Lederberg. The arrival by airplane of a previously unknown virus underlined the vulnerability that accompanied a new era of global interconnection. As the IOM reported, "Infectious diseases that now affect people in other parts of the world represent potential threats to the United States because of global interdependence, modern transportation, trade, and changing social and cultural patterns."[9] Or, as Preston put it in his

1992 *New Yorker* piece, "The presence of international airports puts every virus on earth within a day's flying time of the United States." The theme of domestic vulnerability to faraway outbreaks due to global interconnection was also at the center of another event, in late 1989, focusing on the threat of an Ebola-like virus. This event was an imagined rather than an actual outbreak. At the annual meeting of the American Society of Tropical Medicine and Hygiene in Honolulu, the plenary session was devoted to an exercise simulating the rapid spread of a dangerous and unknown infectious disease. Journalist Laurie Garrett reported on the exercise in *Newsday* and devoted a chapter to the episode in her 1994 best seller, *The Coming Plague: Newly Emerging Diseases in a World Out of Balance.*[10] The "medical war-game," as Garrett called it, was led by Colonel Llewellyn J. Legters, an epidemiologist specializing in tropical diseases who was based at the Army Uniformed Services Hospital in Bethesda.[11]

Legters's exercise sought to draw attention to the lack of international public health capacity to manage the outbreak of a novel infectious disease. It was set in the near future—the spring of 1991—in the fictional African nation of Changa, a site of multiple and intersecting crises: armed conflict, population displacement, food shortages, and the collapse of public health infrastructure. As violent conflict escalated between rebel factions and Changa's ruling government, according to the script, thousands of refugees fled to neighboring countries, where they faced the threat of starvation and disease. Peace Corps volunteers, Christian aid workers, and American military personnel were working in refugee camps to provide medical care and improve hygiene. In this setting, a novel and terrifying disease appeared: at least two dozen refugees died from a mysterious ailment whose symptoms included headaches, vomiting, rash, and gastrointestinal bleeding. Several American members of an international peacekeeping force were stricken with the disease and returned to Fort Bragg. Two of them soon died of liver failure. A number of medical volunteers fell ill in the field, and anxiety intensified among civilian health workers.

The scenario continued: the State Department reported the deaths of several civilian volunteers after returning to the United States on commercial flights, on which they encountered "thousands of people who they might have exposed to the disease." An army colonel described the situation as a "global epidemiological emergency." Specialists grew increasingly worried that the cause of the disease might be a mutant, easily transmissible strain of Ebola, a disease for which there was no treatment, no vaccine, and no laboratory-based method of diagnosis. If so, Garrett noted in her *Newsday* article, health authorities faced an epidemiological nightmare: a disease that combined high virulence, high transmissibility, and the absence of effective treatments. One participant in the exercise alluded to a famed science fiction plot from the late 1960s: "You say this might be a strain of Ebola that is respiratorily transmitted. Well, if that is the case it would be very close to Andromeda"—in other words, a novel, rapidly spreading, and incurable infectious disease.

As the exercise continued, it became clear to participants that the relevant expertise and the necessary equipment to manage the outbreak were in short supply. According to a State Department official, there were only four people in the U.S. Public Health Service who had any experience with hemorrhagic fever. Field investigators urgently requested a portable biocontainment laboratory, but only one such facility could be located, and it was needed in the United States. The State Department searched for available prepackaged field hospitals to send but could not find any that were equipped for infectious disease outbreaks. The foreign quarantine branch of CDC had been, a Public Health Service official commented, "effectively emasculated by budget cuts."

Meanwhile, international organizations could not augment American capacities: "At all times the infectious disease unit at WHO is running on a shoestring," an official explained. Nor did the U.S. military have resources to manage the situation: "We have insufficient expert manpower to sustain appropriate levels of health care, and inadequate supplies," reported an Army general. The exercise ended as the disease spread unchecked: infected civilian aid workers and military peacekeepers fled the zone and brought the disease back to their home countries. Participants faced an escalating public health catastrophe with no means at their disposal to stop it.

The experience of the exercise provoked intensive discussion, among the experts assembled in Honolulu, concerning the threat posed by emerging diseases. "You never think such a thing could happen, and then it does," commented CDC physician Louisa Campbell. "And you're caught totally unprepared." William Reeves, an expert on insect-borne disease control from the University of California, noted that the lessons of the exercise were not limited to Ebola: "You could take any disease as a model—Ebola, malaria, whatever—and it would reveal the same thing. We aren't ready. Where are the people? The expertise? The equipment? Some planning needs to be done on this." Over the next two decades, health authorities began to do just that.

In the seminal 1993 volume *Emerging Viruses*, Legters and two colleagues contributed an essay on the results of the exercise, titled "Are We Prepared for a Viral Epidemic Emergency?" The essay was composed in the form of a "News Report of the Future" and included a fictional after-action report summarizing the lessons that had been learned from the experience. "To put it succinctly," the report concluded, "the outbreak has confirmed, in a very dramatic way, just how ill-prepared we are to detect global epidemic disease threats in a timely fashion, and, once detected, to respond appropriately."[12] This lack of preparedness was especially alarming, according to the report, given that the world could expect an increasing number of epidemic emergencies due to multiple factors: population growth, overcrowded cities, ecological disturbance, civil wars and refugee crises, and commercial travel that could rapidly spread diseases around the world.

It is important to emphasize the novelty, at the time, of this diagnosis of the dangers posed by emerging pathogens. The expectation that health authorities should be in a state of ongoing vigilance for the emergence of a novel pathogen was just being established in the late 1980s and early 1990s. Indeed, the "Super-Ebola" exercise in Honolulu was among the events that helped to introduce pandemic preparedness as a central problem for international health. To address the gaps in preparedness that were exposed by the exercise, Legters and his coauthors proposed the development of a global infrastructure for detecting and managing future disease outbreaks. Such an infrastructure, they wrote, would include "a surveillance system that can identify unusual disease occurrences near their point of origin; a laboratory system that can quickly characterize the causative agents; a reporting system that alerts the world health community; and a way to institute controls."[13] Among these elements, Legters and his coauthors focused in particular on the need for a disease surveillance system. They endorsed the proposal, made in the same volume by Donald A. Henderson, that CDC establish a network of research centers around the world that could serve as "'listening posts' to identify epidemiological events that might signal global epidemic disease threats."[14]

A number of public health experts proposed similar preparedness measures at this time. And over the next decade or so, many of these proposals were implemented in some fashion. A global outbreak alert and response network was set up and coordinated by the World Health Organization; tools and capacities for the laboratory identification of emerging diseases were built in a number of regional centers; incentives to address the lack of biomedical countermeasures against emerging disease threats were put in place; and a governing framework for global health emergencies was established. In a sense, then, the imaginative enactment of an Ebola-like disease outbreak provided both a motivation and a model for assembling the contemporary infrastructure of global health security.

What are we to make, then, of Pierre Rollin's claim that "no one could have imagined" the catastrophic Ebola epidemic of 2014?[15] In what sense was the event unimaginable? As we have seen, it is not that global health authorities had never contemplated an Ebola epidemic of this scale or severity. A much wider epidemic, involving a far more dangerous strain of the disease, had been envisioned in detail by international health experts twenty-five years earlier. Nor was it the prospect that an Ebola outbreak might prove especially difficult to manage in a conflict or postconflict situation. Nor, finally, was it the difficulty encountered in mobilizing trained personnel, deploying mobile infectious disease treatment units, or coordinating response through an international health agency beset by limited resources. Legters and his colleagues had anticipated all of this in designing the 1989 exercise and in assessing its results. Indeed, such considerations were among the rationales for early proposals to establish a global health security infrastructure.

Rather, it seems, what was surprising to experts like Rollin in 2014 was that "normal" Ebola, and not a strain of Super-Ebola or some other novel pathogen, could produce such a widespread epidemic given that all prior outbreaks had been limited to circumscribed areas and to relatively small numbers of cases. According to the 1989 scenario, the catastrophic outcome of the outbreak was in large part a result of the exceptional characteristics of the pathogen itself: its virulence and, in particular, its transmissibility. Given such a focus on the pathogenicity of the virus itself, the resulting emphasis on developing global disease surveillance and alert capacities seemed to be an adequate response. In 2014, however, it turned out that the devastating scale of the epidemic was due to factors that had not been the focus of the Super-Ebola exercise—factors that for the most part were not addressed by the system of global health security that was designed and built in its wake. Among these factors were the collapse of public health infrastructure in much of the region, making it difficult to isolate patients and trace contacts, the limited capacity of humanitarian organizations to contain the spread of the disease, and local communities' distrust of national and international health authorities.

MISSED OPPORTUNITY

Much of the criticism of WHO in the wake of the 2014 epidemic focused on a moment that seemed, in retrospect, like one of missed opportunity: the period in late March and early April 2014, when the outbreak was first reported to WHO. Why, a number of critics asked, did the organization not immediately declare a global health emergency and seek to galvanize international response? As the WHO's Ebola Interim Assessment Panel put it: "It is still unclear to the Panel why early warnings, approximately from May through to July 2014, did not result in an effective and adequate response."[16] Why did WHO wait until August—more than a month after Médecins Sans Frontières (MSF) declared that the outbreak was "totally out of control"—to classify the event as an emergency?

To address this question, is necessary to examine how health authorities conceptualized the outbreak in its early stages. In mid-March, MSF clinicians discovered suspected Ebola cases near the organization's malaria clinic in Guéckédou, Guinea. This was a startling event: Ebola had never before been reported in the region. Within a week, MSF had confirmed the cases and launched an emergency response, sending doctors, nurses, logisticians, and hygiene and sanitation experts to Guinea. The organization rapidly set up portable isolation units in Guéckédou and elsewhere, trained local responders, and shipped thirty-three tons of pre-packaged supplies such as personal protective equipment and palliative medicines to Guinea from warehouses in Belgium and France.[17] The outbreak, at least initially, was an event for which the organization was well prepared. As Peter Redfield has noted, MSF had lengthy experience with prior Ebola outbreaks and was the only organization with the personnel, equipment, and treatment protocols available for rapid operational response to this one.[18] However, the scale of MSF's response was limited by its capacities: the organization is well suited to provide acute care at the site of an outbreak, not to provide basic health infrastructure for a large and dispersed population nor to coordinate international response to a rapidly spreading epidemic.[19] This approach had been sufficient in prior Ebola outbreaks: until 2014, as MSF later noted, such outbreaks "took place mostly in remote villages in central and eastern Africa, where they were more easily contained."[20]

On March 25, in accordance with the International Health Regulations (IHR), the Guinean Ministry of Health officially notified WHO of the outbreak, reporting eighty-six suspected cases and sixty deaths. Such notification pointed toward the possible declaration by the WHO director-general of a "Public Health Emergency of International Concern" (PHEIC), an event that puts into motion the administrative mechanism of emergency response at the heart of IHR framework.[21] According to WHO, the IHR system has two main purposes: "to prevent the international spread of the disease" and "to prevent the application of unnecessary restrictions on travel and trade."[22] In other words, it seeks to constrain the spread of disease across borders while ensuring that goods and people continue to circulate. Within the IHR system, the declaration of a PHEIC establishes the WHO role of coordination and collaboration with presumably functioning national health systems and points toward an urgent effort to mobilize international assistance.[23] Thus, the envisioned role of WHO in the IHR system is to assist national health authorities and galvanize resources, but not to lead an operational intervention.

In any case, it is noteworthy that the Guinean authorities' notification of the outbreak of Ebola in the spring of 2014 did not immediately lead the director-general to convene an Emergency Committee or to declare a global health emergency, in contrast to the outbreak of H1N1 in 2009 (see Chapter 4). This was at least in part due to a transformation in experts' understanding of Ebola since the late 1980s, when the disease served as a paradigm for the global threat posed by "emerging viruses." Over the intervening period, Ebola had undergone a conceptual mutation: it was no longer the novel and fearsome virus that helped spark attention and resources to the phenomenon of emerging disease. By 2014, global health authorities approached its appearance with relative confidence. Its pattern of transmission was understood; methods of containment had been developed and standardized. In more than a dozen outbreaks over the prior three decades, the disease had never spread far beyond its initial site of occurrence.

There were, however, some early indications that this occurrence might be different. At the end of March, MSF described the outbreak as of "unprecedented" magnitude in Guinea, with cases also being reported in Liberia. MSF Director Bruno Jochum reported that the disease "had spread to several places and to a large city," making it "an exceptional event for an Ebola outbreak up until today."[24] Despite these worrisome signs, Jochum lamented, the international response had so far been "minimal." Meanwhile, WHO spokesman Gregory Hartl sought to assuage public concern, emphasizing that the event should not be considered an "epidemic" but was rather a "relatively small" outbreak. "Ebola already causes enough concern and we need to be very careful about how we characterize something which is up until now an outbreak with sporadic cases," he said.[25]

Alongside MSF, members of WHO's global network of infectious disease experts were soon on the ground in Guinea. After its laboratories confirmed the reported cases, the agency deployed teams to the field "to strengthen surveillance, sensitize and educate the public, manage cases and implement appropriate infection prevention and control measures in health facilities and communities affected." At an April 8 press briefing in Geneva, WHO Health Security official Keiji Fukuda provided an assessment of the situation. On the one hand, he acknowledged, this was "one of the most challenging Ebola outbreaks that we have ever faced" because of both the wide geographic distribution of cases and the level of fear and anxiety the outbreak had already generated.[26] On the other hand, Fukuda expressed confidence that it would be controlled, given experts' familiarity with the disease: "We know very well how this virus is transmitted, we know the kinds of steps that can be taken to stop the transmission of the virus." It was a straightforward matter of identifying the sick, tracing their contacts, and then taking careful prevention and control measures.

A WHO situation report posted ten days later evinced a more cautious view of the situation, pointing to the ways in which this event was in fact unlike prior Ebola outbreaks: it was occurring in a major city, a number of health workers had been infected, and there had been cross-border transmission of the virus.[27] The situation report described a WHO "surge" in West Africa of more than fifty staff members as well as members of the Global Outbreak Alert and Response Network, "in accordance with the grading of the outbreak as a Grade 2 emergency under the WHO Emergency Response Framework."[28] On the Emergency Response Framework's three-point scale, a Grade 2 emergency indicated an "event with moderate public health consequences," requiring a moderate response from health authorities.[29] The response framework sought to bring disease outbreaks into alignment with other kinds of emergencies, from natural disasters to refugee crises, so that response to these events could be coordinated across disparate bureaucratic agencies. The three-point scale was a form of technocratic triage: in a world suffused with emergencies, decision-makers must have a means for deciding how to allocate scarce resources in order to respond adequately to the most pressing situations.[30]

By early May, it seemed that Fukuda's confidence had been warranted: few new cases of Ebola had been reported in either Guinea or Liberia, although MSF "remain[ed] vigilant," and on May 14 WHO reported that "the outbreak seems to be slowing down."[31] As Pierre Rollin of CDC later recalled, "For most of May, we had no new cases showing up at the treatment centers in Guinea or Liberia, and it was possible to think it might have run its course."[32] Similarly, another international health official would later testify that "there were no cases being reported" in May, and indeed, "there was a sense that the outbreak had in fact subsided."[33] In retrospect, however, it is clear that over the next month, a second wave of the disease was unfolding outside of the view of health authorities—whether due to government reluctance to officially report disease incidence or to local communities' suspicions of foreign health workers in biocontainment suits.[34] Widespread criticism of the WHO response, and that of the global community more generally, would later focus on this period.

On June 20, an MSF director of operations appealed for assistance from international health organizations, reporting that the outbreak was "totally out of control" and that the organization could "not respond to the large number of new cases and locations alone."[35] At the same time, as MSF later reported, "Government authorities and members of the WHO in Guinea and Sierra Leone downplayed the epidemic's spread, insisting that it was under control and accusing MSF of causing unnecessary panic.[36] Three weeks later, MSF sounded an even sharper alarm, declaring that it was in a "race against time" to stop the spread of the disease in Sierra Leone. And yet the international response remained tepid and uncoordinated through end of July, when two U.S. humanitarian workers were infected with the virus and Nigeria announced its first case, a U.S. citizen who had contracted the disease in Liberia before flying to Lagos— an alarming indication, for international health authorities, that the epidemic might soon spread to new regions via air travel.[37]

The threat of global contagion finally sparked intervention at the highest levels. On August 8, WHO declared a PHEIC and established an Emergency Committee to recommend measures to manage the epidemic. "The outbreak is moving faster than we can control it," acknowledged Director-General Chan. The declaration of a global health emergency, she continued, "will galvanize the attention of leaders of countries at the top level."[38] Replying to the question of what had finally sparked the emergency declaration, Fukuda pointed to "the identification of the travel-related case, in Nigeria." Once global interconnection began to threaten other continents, the situation met the criteria for emergency. Managing the epidemic was no longer a matter to be left to charitable organizations whose mission was to assist marginalized populations and to the overwhelmed health systems of the affected countries. As MSF International President Joanne Liu put it: "The lack of international political will was no longer an option when the realization dawned that Ebola could cross the ocean."[39]

The declaration of a PHEIC was a technocratic classification that activated a system of anticipatory monitoring and response that, it was hoped, would staunch the disease's spread along the circuits of global interconnection. It did not, on its own, lead to an infusion of medical care for afflicted populations or assistance to overburdened health systems. Rather, it pointed to a series of pre-formulated recommendations designed to guide national response under the IHR. These guidelines had been envisioned for countries with functioning health systems as well as public trust in political leadership: affected states should activate their emergency management systems, authorities should engage in risk communication to improve public awareness of the disease, secure pipelines of protective medical equipment should be established, and travelers should be screened for signs of the disease. A WHO ethics committee approved the emergency use of experimental medication, insofar as any such medication could be procured.

From the perspective of relief organizations on the ground, such recommendations were largely ineffectual, given the scale of the epidemic emergency and the local incapacity to manage it. In early September, MSF described long lines of sick patients at its clinics and a desperate need for supplies and equipment, pleading that its team was "overwhelmed and cannot offer more than palliative care." Liu made an extraordinary appeal for military intervention from governments with advanced biocontainment and logistics resources, noting that the WHO's emergency declaration had "not led to decisive action, and states have essentially joined a global coalition of inaction."[40]

At a press briefing following Chan's emergency declaration, a journalist from the Associated Press questioned the director-general about WHO's belated response: "Did we not pay enough attention to this? Did we somehow fall down on the job?" Chan attributed the organization's slow response to its "stretched" resources, alluding to the Emergency Response Framework discussed earlier: WHO was "dealing with four Level Three humanitarian crises," she explained. "They are the biggest, meaning the highest level of crisis, and these are Central African Republic, South Sudan and Syria, and of course, at the same time, we are dealing with three outbreaks, Ebola, MERS-CoVirus, and H7N9." All WHO assets had been mobilized, Chan insisted.[41] And yet, as we have seen, the organization had been closely monitoring the outbreak in West Africa soon after it was first detected and had the capability at that time to coordinate a broader response, or at least to galvanize international attention to the problem.[42] A later journalistic investigation found that there had been internal debate within WHO in April 2014 about whether to declare an emergency: while a number of scientists in Africa pressed for such a declaration, the organization's leaders argued that it would not help in controlling the epidemic and could "disrupt the economic life" of the countries involved.[43] The investigation also pointed to the inappropriate application of methods of response to Ebola that had been successful in other settings to the region of the 2014 outbreak. As the Associated Press reported, "Its own experts failed to grasp that traditional infectious disease containment methods wouldn't work in a region with porous borders and broken health systems."[44]

THE POST HOC DIAGNOSIS

The period of emergency lasted roughly eighteen months, as an infusion of resources from outside along with strengthened local efforts finally slowed the spread of the disease. At the end of March 2016, Chan officially terminated the epidemic's status as a "public health emergency of international concern." This was a classificatory shift meant to signify a change in how the disease was to be managed. The announcement indicated that alongside the epidemiological end of an epidemic, there is also an administrative end. Even as cases of Ebola in West Africa continued to appear, the end of the official emergency signaled a return to normalcy, the entry into a period of reflection on the meaning of the event, in which retrospective moral judgment could be made: who is to blame? What should we have done differently?[45]

In an interview with Laurie Garrett, the Swedish statistician and WHO consultant Hans Rosling offered a deceptively simple response to this question. "If you want to blame somebody for this epidemic, blame me," he said. "It was my mistake."[46] Rosling was suggesting not a moral failure but an epistemological one. He was among those experts who, in the spring of 2014, had advised WHO against declaring the epidemic to be a global health emergency—a decision that, as we have seen, was later blamed for the slow response of international authorities to the outbreak and for its explosion into a global health catastrophe by the late summer. At the time, Rosling argued that such a declaration would divert scarce health resources in the region away from more epidemiologically significant problems such as malaria, diarrheal diseases, and bacterial infections. He shared the view of many experts that Ebola was a "small problem" compared with these less sensational but much more widespread afflictions. And, as noted, there was a solid epidemiological rationale to this position: Ebola had never before caused more than a few hundred deaths. By 2014, then, Ebola was understood to be a highly dangerous, but ultimately manageable, disease. From the perspective of traditional public health prevention, Ebola was not a high priority.

David Nabarro, a leader of the United Nations' Mission for Ebola Emergency Response, later provided some context for Rosling's view. In testimony before the British Parliament's inquiry into the response to Ebola, Nabarro pointed to a shift in health priorities at WHO, beginning in the early 1990s, toward "issues that cause the greatest suffering and death in the world—diseases of childhood, diseases around maternity, AIDS, tuberculosis and malaria." In other words, resources were shifted away from vigilant watchfulness for uncertain outbreaks and toward management of the risk of regularly occurring disease. According to Nabarro, this "very sensible governance decision" to prioritize high-mortality conditions was driven at least in part by the increasing role that donor agencies played in setting WHO budget priorities. As a result, "There has been a steady shift away from preparedness to deal with these quite rare events of outbreaks."[47]

One can point, in retrospect, to a number of reasons why the 2014 Ebola outbreak proved far worse than international health authorities like Rosling and Rollin initially imagined possible: a geographic setting of cross-border circulation, the breakdown of basic health infrastructure in afflicted areas, local distrust of health authorities in a context of recent civil conflict, poor communication and a lack of coordination among disparate response organizations, among others. Rosling's mea culpa, in the wake of the epidemic, was part of a larger process of retrospectively apportioning blame. Some of this blame was diffusely targeted at the "global community" for its slow and tepid response to the outbreak, as we saw earlier. But gradually, once the epidemic was under control, a collective effort built up among scientists and officials to find more a focused site of responsibility that would make it possible to target future reform efforts. Much of this process took the form of post hoc committee investigations.

In May 2016, the WHO released the final report of the IHR Review Committee on the organization's response to the Ebola epidemic. The report opened by pointing out that, however tragic the epidemic was, it also provided a chance to learn. "The sole consolation of the Ebola disaster is that it has galvanized the world into analyzing the failures and ensuring that it is better prepared for the next global health threat," it began. "Crisis is hardship but also opportunity."[48] In addition to the report from the IHR Review Committee, beginning in late 2015 at least five other panels of authorized experts issued official reports that diagnosed sources of failure in the international response to the outbreak and recommended reforms to prevent the occurrence of another such catastrophe. WHO issued two such reports, and other groups producing post hoc assessments included the United Nations, the World Bank, the World Economic Forum, the U.S. National Academy of Medicine, and a consortium from Harvard and the London School of Tropical Medicine and Hygiene.

Such efforts to officially allocate blame and target reform in the wake of a catastrophic outbreak are by no means new. One can date the genre of the "Commission of Inquiry" report at least back to mid-nineteenth-century investigations of cholera outbreaks in Europe. In 1854, for example, the Cholera Inquiry Commission appointed by the British Parliament found that authorities in the town of Newcastle had ignored the advice of medical experts to be especially alert as a new outbreak of the disease approached:

> "[T]he continued vigilance on the part of the authorities," which according to the report of that medical committee, has been "proved to be necessary in order to guard against a further and more destructive outbreak"—such as actually occurred last autumn—does not appear to have been exercised by those authorities.[49]

The practice of instituting a Commission of Inquiry comes into play when a collective misfortune is understood to be at least in part the result of a governmental failure—an improper action taken or a wrong decision made. The event is seen in retrospect as having been "a preventable tragedy," in the words of the United Nations report on the global response to Ebola.[50] The post hoc inquiry assumes the temporal-causal framework of risk: what might have seemed to be an external source of danger—the onset and course of an epidemic—is treated rather as the product of an internal decision: should not have authorities anticipated this outcome?[51] Like the "News Report of the Future" generated after the Super-Ebola simulation, the task of the post hoc inquiry is to pinpoint the locus of failed action in order to target future reform measures.

But alongside their consonance with this historical schema, the post hoc assessments of the international community's response to Ebola 2014 also displayed some distinctive features. One of these was the sheer number of commissions of inquiry that were established. This proliferation of commissions and reports is symptomatic of the fact that, in contrast to cholera epidemics in nineteenth-century England, in the case of the 2014 Ebola epidemic, it was not clear which governmental agency or body of authorities held jurisdiction over the management of epidemic response at a global scale. Who exactly comprised or spoke for "the global community" that, as one critical observer put it, "was sluggish in reacting to the crisis, with inadequate coordination and confused decision making"?[52] In the absence of effective national public health systems, there was not an alternative locus of responsibility for on-the-ground operational engagement: neither WHO, which had a only coordinative role, nor MSF as a nongovernmental organization designed for small-scale crises, which, as one its directors of operations put it, "does not have an Ebola army with a warehouse of personnel on standby."[53]

A second distinctive feature of the post-Ebola assessments was the type of diagnosis they sought to make. The reports from the various committees of inquiry emphasized not only a failure of response but also a failure of anticipation. As an independent panel of experts convened by Harvard and the London School of Tropical Medicine and Hygiene concluded, the epidemic exposed the global community as "altogether unprepared."[54] Similarly, the Commission on a Global Health Risk Framework for the Future, convened by the National Academy of Medicine, argued that the outbreak revealed "gaping holes in preparedness."[55] According to the UN High Panel on the Global Response to Health Crises, multiple failures had "demonstrated that the world remains ill-prepared to address the threat posed by epidemics." And the WHO's IHR Review Committee declared, "Ebola starkly revealed the fact that we still remain ill-prepared in the face of a major public health emergency."

As we have seen, this application of the norm of preparedness to the threat of infectious disease is relatively recent. The theme of "emergency preparedness" as a governmental task initially appeared in the context of economic mobilization for total war in the mid-twentieth-century United States. Mobilization preparedness asked: what kinds of anticipatory

measures—the stockpiling of scarce materials, tools to manage the allocation of resources, plans for civil defense—must be put in place *before* the
onset of the anticipated war emergency? Scenario-based exercises and
computer simulations of enemy attacks were honed during the Cold War
as methods of planning for the unprecedented catastrophe of nuclear conflict. The broader field of emergency management, oriented to a range of
crisis situations, grew out of these planning methods and came to include
techniques such as early warning systems, medical supply stockpiling, and
crisis communications.

The many of the techniques associated with emergency management were
assimilated into the field of global health security over the course of the
1990s and early 2000s. A key moment was the 2005 adoption by the World
Health Assembly of the revised International Health Regulations, officially
released in 2007 under the rubric of "global public health security." The
revised IHR instituted a view of the future of infectious disease as characterized by the unpredictable but nonetheless inexorable emergence of
novel pathogens. The problem for health authorities was to detect and contain such outbreaks before they became global catastrophes. It was at this
point that the retrospective assessment of a failed response began to pose
the now-familiar question: are we prepared for the next emergency?

To ask the question was to answer it. As the report by the IHR Review
Committee on WHO's response to the 2009 swine flu pandemic put it:
"We were lucky this time, but . . . the world is ill-prepared for a severe
pandemic or for any similarly global, sustained and threatening public
health emergency." This is the diagnostic framework of the Committee of
Inquiry report, in the era of emerging infections. In the assessment process, the outbreak of a given disease—whether H1N1, Ebola, or some other
pathogen—loses its specificity and is brought into a shared space of anticipation, inhabited by a range of diseases, some already known and some as
yet to appear.

The generic category for the anticipated event is the PHEIC, one of the
innovations of the revised IHR. As we have seen, the PHEIC is a decision
tool for use by national and international health authorities in assessing
whether a given health event should be considered a potential global
health emergency. Although it may seem like an obscure technocratic
instrument, this guide for officials in making decisions about how to

classify reported health events came to the fore in discussions of account-ability for the catastrophic scale of the 2014 Ebola epidemic.

In the various post hoc commissions of inquiry, the question was repeatedly posed: why did WHO fail to declare an official emergency early enough that the outbreak could have been contained, in late spring or early summer 2014? Given the structure of the post hoc assessment, which seeks to locate the mistaken action that led to a preventable disaster, this was a tempting moment of decision—or rather, nondecision—to focus on. One response to the question is simply that, epidemiologically speaking, as of spring 2014, Ebola was known *not* to pose the specter of global catas-trophe: as noted, experts understood it to be a relatively easily managed and small-scale disease. This assumption was the source of Hans Rosling's later expression of culpability for the catastrophe, and it was echoed in comments made by WHO officials such as Keiji Fukuda early in the out-break as well as in Pierre Rollin's claim that "no one could have imagined" the eventual extent of the epidemic. As WHO official Bruce Aylward later testified, prior Ebola outbreaks had "all been managed within a number of weeks or months at most, and they had all led to relatively small flares." In the early stages of the 2014 epidemic, he recalled, experts shared the sense that "This is Ebola. We know Ebola. This will be manageable."[56] It is in this sense that we can consider the WHO's decision against emergency classification to be a failure of administrative imagination.

TWO STATES OF EMERGENCY

We can now return to the question, suggested at the outset of the chapter, of whether WHO should be held responsible for international health authorities' failure to respond more aggressively in the immediate after-math of the outbreak. A more productive way to pose the question, argu-ably, is to ask not *whether* the initial outbreak should have been consid-ered an emergency but rather: what *kind* of emergency was it? Recall the distinction, introduced in Chapter 3, between global health security and humanitarian biomedicine. If, at the time of the outbreak, Ebola was gen-erally seen as a neglected disease that afflicted marginal populations, it called for a response from humanitarian biomedicine, concerned with the compassionate alleviation of human suffering regardless of national borders and political conflict. Alternatively, if Ebola was seen as an emerging disease that threatened global catastrophe, then it demanded the intensive, coordinated response of international and national health agencies. We can say that, sometime in late July 2014, Ebola shifted from one state of emergency to another: from humanitarian crisis to global health catastrophe. Indeed, it is possible to specify the moment of this shift: when an international air passenger traveled from Monrovia to Lagos, carrying the virus with him. Global interconnection implied global vulnerability. As Joanne Liu of MSF noted: "When Ebola became an international security threat, and no longer a humanitarian crisis affecting a handful of poor countries in West Africa, finally the world began to wake up."[57]

Accompanying this shift in the scope of response was a change in the conceptualization of the disease. What changed was not its biological meaning but rather its political and administrative significance. If, in the two decades before the 2014 outbreak, Ebola had stabilized as a dangerous but manageable virus, the public health understanding of the disease now had to take other elements into consideration, in particular, the extent to which its virulence and transmissibility—its capacity to provoke a global health emergency—depended on the condition of the public health infrastructure in which it appeared. In this sense, the new understanding of Ebola pointed attention back to the post hoc assessment of WHO's 2009 response to the H1N1 (swine flu) pandemic, which had warned that the world was ill prepared to respond to any "global, sustained and threatening public-health emergency." According to the IHR Review Committee's report, as we saw in Chapter 4, the key lesson of the 2009 pandemic was that "[t]he fundamental gap between global need and global capacity must be closed." This diagnosis would come to the center of reflections on reform of the global health system in the wake of the 2014 Ebola epidemic.

TOWARD REFORM

Although the post hoc assessment is a means of allocating blame, in retrospect, for a preventable disaster, it is not only that. Let us look again at the IHR Review Committee's final report, unveiled in May 2016. The document is a report not on the international response to Ebola in general but specifically on the "role of the International Health Regulations" in the WHO response. When providing the review committee with its official charge in August 2015, Director-General Chan instructed the committee to focus not so much on the past as on the future: "Our challenge now is to look for improvements that leave the world better prepared for the next inevitable outbreak."[58] Despite the daunting scale of the disaster it had wrought, she continued, Ebola 2014 was "not a worst-case scenario." Rather, officials must be ready for the onset of something even more potentially catastrophic—an uncontainable outbreak. "Preparedness for the future," she stated, "means preparedness for a very severe disease that spreads via the airborne route or can be transmitted during the incubation period, before an infected person shows telltale signs of illness." The image was that of an uncontainable variant of SARS or a humanly transmissible strain of H5N1—or for that matter, an airborne "Super-Ebola"—the specters that initially galvanized international health officials to design and implement a system of global health security.

In looking at the multiple post hoc assessments that were produced in the wake of the Ebola epidemic, it becomes clear that they served not only as ways to achieve closure on an epidemic narrative. They also sought to map out a future of organizational transformation. As the WHO Interim Assessment Panel put it in making its post-Ebola recommendations for reform, "The world cannot afford another period of inaction until the next health crisis."[59] There were numerous specific proposals for reform embedded in the various post hoc reports that appeared in the wake of the epidemic, many of them emphasizing the need for a total rethinking of WHO organization along with an infusion of resources for epidemic emergency preparedness. To make WHO "fit for purpose," argued David Nabarro in his testimony before the British House of Commons Committee, "the organization needs a total revamp of its work in Outbreaks and Emergencies." He summarized the administrative elements of a functional preparedness system: WHO must organize a "single programme across the six regional offices and headquarters that is centrally managed for dealing with all parts of the emergency cycle, from preparedness to alert to response to recovery and to prevention," and to accomplish this "it needs substantial increases in personnel and in finance."[60]

Once Ebola was assimilated to the more general category of "global health emergency," the retrospective critique of failure served as a framework for honing a better apparatus of detection and response to an imagined future pathogen. The IHR Review Committee's final report addressed questions such as: who will be the key organizational actors in future outbreaks? Where will the necessary funds for emergency response come from? And how will poor countries be incentivized to develop "core capacities" for managing outbreaks? The diagnosis of a failure of past preparedness, then, can only point toward a hoped-for future of better preparedness. However, insofar as health authorities cannot know what the next emerging pathogen outbreak will be, it remains possible, even likely, that they will once again have prepared for the wrong emergency.

Epilogue

The widely acknowledged failure of global health security to adequately manage the Ebola outbreak led to multiple inquiries, commission reports, and recommendations for reform, but it did not put in question the strategic logic underlying the framework. Rather, reformers raised the question of how to better meet the demand for preparedness in time for the next global health emergency. As an internal World Health Organization (WHO) report warned, the frequency and magnitude of such events was increasing but "the world is not adequately prepared to respond to the full range of emergencies with public health implications"—whether disease outbreaks, natural disasters or violent conflict. The report concluded that WHO's response to Ebola and other recent emergencies "lacked the speed, coordination, clear lines of decision making and dedicated funding to optimize implementation, reduce suffering and save lives." Given the scale and complexity of anticipated future emergencies, it advised, "WHO must substantially strengthen and modernize its emergency management capacity."[1]

According to critics, it was urgent that WHO rapidly transform its internal organization in order to maintain its role as the lead agency in managing global health crises. "The unconscionable Ebola epidemic opened a window of opportunity for fundamental reform," wrote one group of commentators, but this political window "was rapidly closing."[2] By spring 2016, WHO leaders had committed "to urgently reform the emergency work" of the organization through the establishment of a new "health emergencies" program.[3] The new program entailed three organizational reforms designed for the efficient and effective management of health emergencies. First, emergency preparedness and response would now be the responsibility of a single program within WHO, with "one budget, one set of rules and processes and one clear line of authority." Second, the new program "would be designed to address all hazards," whether disease outbreaks, natural disasters, or violent conflicts. And third, the organization's approach to emergencies would be rationalized "through one set of emergency management processes and performance metrics that will be standard across the organization."

Most significantly, the new program would involve a transformation of the organization's mission in preparing for and responding to emergencies. WHO would no longer be constrained to its traditional role of providing technical support and normative guidance but would now "give equal priority to developing and maintaining operational expertise."[4] And this operational expertise was not limited to the management of disease outbreaks but extended more broadly to the range of potential events that could cause a future emergency. Thus, the program was "designed to deliver rapid, predictable and comprehensive support to countries and communities as they prepare for, face or recover from emergencies caused by any type of hazard to human health, whether disease outbreaks, natural or man-made disasters or conflicts."[5]

But these new capacities would require significant new sources of financial support. Once again, the issue was raised of how to sustain investment in the capacity for acute response during the in-between periods of waiting for the next emergency. As the new executive director of the Health Emergencies Program, medical epidemiologist Peter Salama, noted in an interview soon after his appointment in summer 2016: "For this program to be successful, we're going to have to find a sustainable model of financing, which is not just about us going every year with a begging bowl to donors and saying, 'Look, here we are again, We're about to run out of money.'"[6] The question of where ongoing support for the emergencies program would come from soon arose in relation to the WHO response to the spread of the Zika virus in South America and beyond.

If the critical issue for global Ebola response concerned how to define the beginning of an emergency, the key question concerning Zika was: "When does an emergency end?" In November 2016, WHO Director-General Margaret Chan declared the end of the Zika virus emergency, following the recommendation of the Emergency Committee. The decision to bring the official emergency to a close came as a surprise to a number of observers. It was not made because the spread of the disease had been brought under control. In fact, as the Southern hemisphere summer approached, experts anticipated that there would be an upsurge in cases in the coming months, and that the virus would continue to spread globally. So why had WHO declared an end to the emergency? The answer to this question helps us to understand more precisely the rationale behind the new organization for governing health emergencies.

Recall that the initial declaration of a Zika emergency in February 2016 was designed to stimulate an infusion of resources for scientific research on the relation between the viral pathogen and the alarming number of microcephaly cases that were being reported among newborns in Brazil. As David Heymann, chairman of the Zika Emergency Committee, later described the situation, "There was an urgent need to know whether there was an epidemiological link between the neurological disorders and the rapidly spreading Zika epidemic."[7] One rationale for declaring the end of the emergency, then, was that this knowledge gap had been addressed through the resulting "explosion of scientific work" over the intervening months in areas such as epidemiology and virology. There was now, a WHO official reported, "a consensus that Zika is the culprit" in causing the devastating birth defects.[8] Based on the results of the scientific mobilization, concluded Salama, "we know enough about the virus to know that it will continue to spread and we know that it causes microcephaly."[9]

But despite these assurances, a number of crucial scientific questions about Zika were only beginning to be addressed. For instance, the precise causal mechanism linking the virus to neurological disorders such as microcephaly remained unknown. Moreover, there was a lingering epidemiological puzzle around the disease: why was the preponderance of reported microcephaly cases limited to particular geographic zones, even as the Zika virus traveled, with its host, to other parts of the globe?[10] Although the virus continued to circulate globally, it was not clear whether its most alarming correlates were spreading with it. Did this have something to do with the particular viral strain that was prevalent in Northeast Brazil? Or were there environmental cofactors that made adverse outcomes more likely? Such complex scientific questions could not be answered quickly.

Here is where the political-administrative category of emergency bumped up against its limits. Authorities understood that clarifying the relationship between the virus and associated neurological disorders and developing treatments or preventive measures against Zika would require lengthy scientific and public health investigation. The envisioned period of sustained attention to the disease extended well beyond the confined temporal structure of emergency. "There are many things about the virus we still don't know," said Salama, "and for that reason we'll be transforming the Zika programme from an emergency program into a medium to long-term programme of work."[11]

However, WHO would need to find significant new resources to sustain a long-term research and intervention program on Zika. This need pointed to perhaps the most salient reason why the official period of emergency was being brought to an end. Although most of the funding for the initial phase of Zika research and intervention had come from "emergency-oriented donors," explained Salama, ongoing future support for work on the virus would have to come from a different source. While the emergency donors "tend to fund us for between six and twelve months," he continued, "these research questions are clearly multi-year questions." To support the production of knowledge about Zika, it would now be necessary to engage with "the research donors that are really going to look upon this issue as a long-term development issue" rather than one of acute and urgent response.[12] Since, as Salama put it, "Zika is here to stay," it could no longer be the responsibility of the Health Emergencies Program to manage it.[13]

In its early stages in 2016, the epidemic of Zika and its connection with severe birth defects presented the now-familiar specter of a global health emergency: a previously unknown pathogen was traveling rapidly along global circuits with potentially catastrophic consequences. The disease had, it was theorized, traveled by plane from Polynesia to Brazil two years before, and it now threatened to spread further around the world as an infusion of tourists arrived in Rio for the Summer Olympic Games.

International health officials issued travel warnings and closely tracked the global spread of the virus. But by the end of the year, the disease was causing less alarm among health authorities. Outside of Northeast Brazil, where the cases of microcephaly remained concentrated, Zika was beginning to resemble other endemic mosquito-borne diseases, such as dengue and malaria. "This extraordinary event is rapidly becoming, unfortunately, an ordinary event," commented Heymann.[14]

For some observers, the Emergency Committee's decision to end the emergency was premature. "Are we going to see a resurgence in Brazil, Columbia and elsewhere?" asked Anthony Fauci, director of the National Institute of Allergy and Infectious Disease (NIAID). "If they pull back on the emergency, they'd better be able to reinstate it."[15] Just a few weeks before the committee's decision, the U.S. Congress had appropriated $152 million in emergency supplemental funding to NIAID as part of the 2017 Zika Response and Preparedness Act.[16] Others welcomed the Emergency Committee's action, suggesting that the sudden infusion of resources for the investigation of Zika had come at the expense of support for important research on other pathogens.[17] For these public health researchers, whether Zika should be classified as an emergency was as much an economic question as an epistemic one.

The difficulty of securing long-term funding for Zika response pointed to a broader problem: the disjuncture between the temporally constrained administrative structure of emergency on the one hand, and the actual course of disease on the other. In the case of Zika, the newly rationalized WHO emergency program relegated the epidemic event to the less urgent arena of "development," even as the disease continued to spread and uncertainty remained about its relationship to terrifying birth defects.

This misalignment between the normative rationality of epidemic preparedness and the experience of managing actual disease outbreaks is a recurring phenomenon, as we have seen over the course of this book. To recall the cases we have looked at: In the early 2000s, biodefense advocates presented the specter of a smallpox attack to public officials, who recommended a program of vaccination for millions of first responders; but the absence of measurable smallpox risk undermined the legitimacy of the vaccination program. Soon after that, the threat of a mutation of the H5N1 avian influenza virus led to massive investment in pandemic preparedness measures, which were later criticized when the anticipated event did not occur. These measures were then applied when a different—and far less virulent—strain of pandemic flu arrived, leading to public recrimination and accusations of corruption. The research on influenza transmission set in motion by the demand for pandemic preparedness then spawned a new biological threat, one that could not be managed according to existing regulations. In the meantime, a disease that had initially helped to focus attention on the problem of global health security, Ebola, faded from the view of preparedness planners, only to return in 2014 with calamitous effects.

These various failures and misapprehensions have not led to the abandonment of the strategy of preparedness but rather have intensified and reoriented it, as health security advocates point to ever-emerging new threats and to the need for improved, better targeted measures. We might recall the testimony of a U.S. health official in 2005: "Preparedness is a journey not a destination."[18] Another way to put it is that preparedness envisions the future not to predict what is going to happen but to generate knowledge about vulnerabilities in the present. Such knowledge directs the implementation of techniques of intervention: early warning systems, stockpiles of medical countermeasures, organizational response schemas, and so on. Once assembled, these elements not only anticipate the onset of a dangerous future event; they provide the lens through which the event may be apprehended and the tools to manage it.

However, as we have seen, the government of global health emergencies according to a rationality of preparedness faces two conundrums, one temporal and the other spatial. First, the administrative concept of "emergency" is necessarily circumscribed in time, and yet the effective management of actual outbreaks requires a sustained, long-term work of engagement. Second, the space of the "global" implies that political responsibility for addressing disease threats is simultaneously located everywhere and nowhere: efforts to construct an apparatus of emergency government with global reach consistently struggle to bind together a range of heterogeneous entities, from national health and development bureaus, to multilateral agencies, to philanthropic organizations. To point to these challenges is not to denounce the ongoing effort to become more prepared. On the contrary, the hope is that the diagnostic work of conceptual-historical analysis may make the potential pitfalls of this never-ending journey more visible along the way.

Acknowledgments

This project has relied on the support of numerous colleagues, friends, and institutions over nearly the past decade.

The project initially took form in research with Stephen Collier and Paul Rabinow on the emerging field of biosecurity. Our effort gained momentum as a number of critical interlocutors joined us, among them Carlo Caduff, Lyle Fearnley, Peter Redfield, and Dale Rose. One of the exciting directions this collaboration later took was the organization of a project with Frédéric Keck on the theme of "sentinel devices."

I was very fortunate to be hosted as a fellow by the International Center for Advanced Studies at New York University, as part of a project organized by Timothy Mitchell on "The Authority of Knowledge in a Global Age." My work in New York was greatly enriched by conversations with Stephen Collier, Eric Klinenberg, Alondra Nelson, Christopher Otter, Emily Martin, Natasha Schull, Miriam Ticktin, and Kate Zaloom. I am also grateful to Craig Calhoun, who wagered on the potential for an agenda-setting project on the social studies of risk at the Social Science Research Council. Later, SSRC also supported the formation of collaborative research group on the critical studies of global health, coorganized with Jeremy Greene, Manjari Mahajan, and Tobias Rees.

Upon my return to Southern California, friends and colleagues provided ongoing moral as well as institutional support. I am grateful to Mike Ananny, Steve Epstein, John Evans, Pierrette Hondagneu-Sotelo, Christopher Kelly, Dan Lainer-Vos, Hannah Landecker, Peter Mancall, Mike Messner, Chandra Mukerji,

170   ACKNOWLEDGMENTS

Mihir Pandya, Rebecca Plant, Ted Porter, Akos Rona-Tas, Vanessa Schwartz, John Skrentny, and Stefan Timmermans. This work has benefited greatly from exchanges with friends and colleagues in numerous other settings, both inside and outside of the academy. In particular, I would like to thank Sasha Abramsky, Miles Becker, Stefan Elbe, Nils Gilman, Mike Fischer, Ben Hurlbut, Sheila Jasanoff, Michelle Lamont, Shai Lavi, Joanna Radin, Adriana Petryna, Limor Samimian-Darash, Theresa MacPhail, and Michael Watts.

My editor at the University of California Press, Reed Malcolm, provided crucial early encouragement toward the production of this book and then remained steadfast as it gradually coalesced. Several talented editors have helped put it into much better shape: Christine Wenc, Audra Wolfe, and Alison Jacques.

As the book took on its final form, I had the good fortune to be hosted in the idyllic environment of the Center for Advanced Study in the Behavioral Sciences at Stanford University, directed by Margaret Levi.

This work was supported by a grant from the National Science Foundation Science, Technology, and Society program (Award No. 0450975). The Borchard Foundation provided a grant for an International Colloquium at the Chateau de la Bretesche. The University of Southern California's Advancing Scholarship in the Social Sciences and Humanities provided an early sabbatical award.

I am also deeply grateful for the support and inspiration that comes from my family. Thanks go to Don Arbor, Celia Bleichmar, Norberto Bleichmar, Kathleen Frumkin, George Lakoff, Robin Lakoff, Sandy Lakoff, Deb Miller, and Jill Suttie.

My daughters Natalia and Paloma came into the world as this book was being composed and made our home a place of ongoing adventure and delight. My wife, Daniela Bleichmar, has made it all possible, and more, and this book is dedicated to her.

Prior versions of some of the material presented in this book appeared in the following articles: "Preparing for the Next Emergency," *Public Culture* 19, no. 2 (2007): 247–71; "The Generic Biothreat, or How We Became Unprepared," *Cultural Anthropology* 23, no. 3 (2008): 399–428; "Two Regimes of Global Health," *Humanity* 1, no. 1 (2010): 59–79; "Real-time Biopolitics: The Actuary and the Sentinel in Global Public Health," *Economy and Society* 44, no. 1 (2015): 40–59; "A Fragile Assemblage: Mutant Bird Flu and the Limits of Risk Assessment," *Social Studies of Science* (2016).

Notes

INTRODUCTION

1. "WHO Director-General Summarizes the Outcome of the Emergency Committee Regarding Clusters of Microcephaly and Guillain-Barré Syndrome," media release, World Health Organization, February 1, 2016, http://www.who.int /mediacentre/news/statements/2016/emergency-committee-zika-microcephaly/en.

2. As Craig Calhoun writes, "Emergency is a way of grasping problematic events, a way of imagining them that emphasizes their apparent unpredictability, abnormality and brevity, and that carries the corollary that response—intervention—is necessary." Calhoun, "A World of Emergencies: Fear, Intervention, and the Limits of Cosmopolitan Order," *Canadian Review of Sociology and Anthropology* 41, no. 4 (2004): 375.

3. World Health Organization, *WHO Guidance for the Use of Annex 2 of the International Health Regulations (2005)*, WHO/HSE/IHR/2010.4 (Geneva: World Health Organization, 2008).

4. I am drawing on Alain Desrosières's definition of the act of "coding" here: "a conventional decision to construct an equivalence class between diverse objects, the 'class' being judged more 'general' than any particular object. A precondition for this is the assumption that these objects can be compared." See Desrosières, "How to Make Things Which Hold Together: Social Science, Statistics and the State," in *Discourses on Society: The Shaping of the Social Science Disciplines*, ed. Peter Wagner, Bjorn Wittrock, and Richard Whitley. Dordrecht: Kluwer, 2007.

5. For an initiation into the literature on the sovereign state of exception, see Giorgio Agamben, *State of Exception* (Chicago: University of Chicago Press, 2005).

6. Joao Biehl and Adriana Petryna, "Critical Global Health," in *When People Come First: Critical Studies in Global Health*, ed. Joao Biehl and Adriana Petryna (Princeton: Princeton University Press, 2015). For lucid discussions of the rationality underlying humanitarian approaches to global health emergencies, see Didier Fassin, *Humanitarian Reason: A Moral History of the Present* (Berkeley: University of California Press, 2012); and Peter Redfield, *Life in Crisis: The Ethical Journal of Doctors Without Borders* (Berkeley: University of California Press, 2013).

7. David L. Heymann et al., "Zika Virus and Microcephaly: Why Is This Situation a PHEIC?," *The Lancet* 387, no. 10020 (2016).

8. World Health Organization, *The World Health Report 2007: A Safer Future: Global Public Health Security in the 21st Century* (Geneva: World Health Organization, 2007).

9. For discussions of the concept of assemblage, see Paul Rabinow, *Anthropos Today: Reflections on Modern Equipment* (Princeton: Princeton University Press, 2003); and Stephen J. Collier and Aihwa Ong, "Global Assemblages, Anthropological Problems," in *Global Assemblages: Technology, Politics and Ethics as Anthropological Problems*, ed. Stephen J. Collier and Aihwa Ong (Malden, MA: Blackwell, 2005).

10. For a discussion of logics of anticipation in relation to the contemporary life sciences, see Vincanne Adams, Michelle Murphy, and Adele E. Clarke, "Anticipation: Technoscience, Life, Affect, Temporality," *Subjectivity*, no. 28 (2009): 246–65. See also Ben Anderson, "Preemption, Precaution, Preparedness: Anticipatory Action and Future Geographies," *Progress in Human Geography* 34, no. 6 (2010): 777–98.

11. Ian Hacking, *Historical Ontology* (Cambridge, MA: Harvard University Press, 2002, 11). As Michel Foucault described this approach, "it was a matter of showing by what conjunctions a whole set of practices—from the moment they became coordinated with a regime of truth—was able to make what does not exist (madness, disease, delinquency, sexuality, etc.), nonetheless become something, something however that continues not to exist." Foucault, *The Birth of Biopolitics: Lectures at the Collège de France, 1978–1979*, ed. Michel Sennelart, trans. Graham Burchell (Basingstoke, UK: Palgrave Macmillan, 1979), 19.

12. For the social inquiry into the significance of moments of critique, see Luc Boltanski and Laurent Thevenot, "The Sociology of Critical Capacity," *European Journal of Social Theory* 2, no. 3 (1999): 359–77.

13. Recent ethnographic studies of scientific practice in the field of emerging disease include Carlo Caduff, *The Pandemic Perhaps: Dramatic Events in a Public Culture of Danger* (Berkeley: University of California Press, 2015); and Theresa MacPhail, *The Viral Network: A Pathography of the H1N1 Influenza*

Pandemic (Ithaca: Cornell University Press, 2014). Hubert Dreyfus and Paul Rabinow define "serious speech acts" as "what experts say when they are speaking as experts." Dreyfus and Rabinow, *Michel Foucault: Beyond Structuralism and Hermeneutics* (Chicago: University of Chicago Press, 1982), xxiv.

14. Ian Hacking, *The Taming of Chance* (Cambridge: Cambridge University Press, 1990).

CHAPTER 1

1. U.S. Senate Democrats, "Democrats Work to Protect Americans from Avian Flu," media release, October 5, 2005, https://democrats.senate.gov/2005/10/05/democrats-work-to-protect-americans-from-avian-flu.

2. United States, Executive Office of the President, *The Federal Response to Hurricane Katrina: Lessons Learned* (Washington, DC: The White House, 2006), 52.

3. Calhoun, "A World of Emergencies: Fear, Intervention, and the Limits of Cosmopolitan Order," *Canadian Review of Sociology and Anthropology* 41, no. 4 (2004): 375.

4. François Ewald, "Insurance and Risk," in *The Foucault Effect: Studies in Governmentality*, ed. Graham Burchell, Colin Gordon, and Peter Miller (Chicago: University of Chicago Press, 1991), 199.

5. Michel Foucault, *Security, Territory, Population: Lectures at the Collège de France, 1977–1978*, ed. Arnold I. Davidson, trans. Graham Burchell (Basingstoke, UK: Palgrave Macmillan, 2007); Ian Hacking, *The Taming of Chance* (Cambridge: Cambridge University Press, 1989).

6. "The speeding up of modernization," writes Beck, "has produced a gulf between the world of quantifiable risk in which we think and act, and the world of non-quantifiable insecurities that we are creating." Beck, "The Terrorist Threat: World Risk Society Revisited," *Theory, Culture and Society* 19, no. 4 (2002): 40. See also Anthony Giddens, *Runaway World: How Globalization Is Reshaping Our Lives* (London: Profile, 2002).

7. Beck, "Terrorist Threat," 46.

8. For instance, see Lee Clarke, *Worst Cases: Terror and Catastrophe in the Popular Imagination* (Chicago: University of Chicago Press, 2005); and Cass R. Sunstein, *Worst-Case Scenarios* (Cambridge, MA: Harvard University Press, 2007).

9. Mary Douglas and Aaron Wildavsky, *Risk and Culture* (Berkeley: University of California Press, 1983); Daniel Kahneman and Amos Tversky, "Prospect Theory: An Analysis of Decision under Risk," *Econometrica* 47, no. 2 (1979): 263–92; Paul Slovic, Howard Kunreuther, and Gilbert F. White, "Decision Processes, Rationality, and Adjustment to Natural Hazards," in *Natural Hazards:*

Local, National, Global, ed. Gilbert F. White (New York: Oxford University Press, 1974).

10. Cass R. Sunstein, *Risk and Reason: Safety, Law, and the Environment* (Cambridge: Cambridge University Press, 2002); Richard A. Posner, *Catastrophe: Risk and Response* (New York: Oxford University Press, 2005).

11. Steven Epstein, *Impure Science: AIDS, Activism, and the Politics of Knowledge* (Berkeley: University of California Press, 1996); Brian Wynne, "May the Sheep Safely Graze? A Reflexive View of the Expert–Lay Knowledge Divide," in *Risk, Environment and Modernity: Towards a New Ecology,* ed. Scott Lash, Bronislaw Szerszynski, and Brian Wynne (London: Sage, 1996).

12. Michel Callon, Pierre Lascoumes, and Yannick Barthe, *Acting in an Uncertain World: An Essay on Technical Democracy* (Cambridge, MA: MIT Press, 2009); Sheila Jasanoff, *Designs on Nature: Science and Democracy in Europe and the United States* (Princeton: Princeton University Press, 2005); Langdon Winner, "On Not Hitting the Tar-Baby," in *The Whale and the Reactor: A Search for Limits in an Age of High Technology* (Chicago: University of Chicago Press, 1986).

13. Scientific claims, writes Hacking, "are candidates for truth or for falsehood only when a style of reasoning makes them so." Hacking, *Historical Ontology* (Cambridge, MA: Harvard University Press, 2003), 191.

14. Niklas Luhmann, *Observations on Modernity,* trans. William Whobrey (Stanford: Stanford University Press, 1998), 70.

15. François Ewald, "The Return of Descartes' Malicious Demon: An Outline of a Philosophy of Precaution," in *Embracing Risk: The Changing Culture of Insurance and Responsibility,* ed. Tom Baker and Jonathan Simon (Chicago: University of Chicago Press, 2002), 286.

16. "Where there are threats of serious or irreversible damage," the 1992 Rio Declaration states, "lack of full scientific certainty shall not be used as a reason for postponing cost-effective measures to prevent environmental degradation." UN General Assembly, *Report of the United Nations Conference on Environment and Development,* A/CONF.151/26, vol. 1 (Rio de Janeiro, June 3–14, 1992).

17. Ulrich Beck, "Ecological Questions in a Framework of Manufactured Uncertainties," in Steven Seidman and Jeffrey C. Alexander, eds., *The New Social Theory Reader: Contemporary Debates* (London and New York: Routledge, 2001), 271.

18. Michael Sherry, *Preparing for the Next Air War: American Plans for Postwar Defense, 1941–1945* (New Haven: Yale University Press 1977).

19. Cited in Lawrence J. Vale, *The Limits of Civil Defense in the U.S.A., Switzerland, Britain, and the Soviet Union: The Evolution of Policies since 1945* (New York: St. Martin's Press, 1987), 58. The U.S. Strategic Bombing Survey was a military-led assessment of the effects of bombing attacks during the war, with an eye toward making the case for postwar spending on the Air Force.

20. Andrew Grossman, *Neither Dead nor Red: Civil Defense and American Political Development during the Early Cold War* (New York: Routledge, 2001), 145n57.

21. Peter Galison, "War against the Center," *Grey Room*, no. 4 (2001): 6–33; Stephen J. Collier and Andrew Lakoff, "Distributed Preparedness: The Spatial Logic of Domestic Security in the United States," *Environment and Planning D: Society and Space* 26, no. 1 (2008): 7–28.

22. Cited in Grossman, *Neither Dead nor Red*, 36.

23. This definition comes from the 1946 Provost Marshal General Report, "Defense against Enemy Action Directed at Civilians." See Nehemiah Jordan, *U.S. Civil Defense before 1950: The Roots of Public Law 920*, Study S-212, Economic and Political Studies Division, Institute for Defense Analyses (Washington, DC, May 1966), 59.

24. Cited in Sharon Ghamari-Tabrizi, *The Worlds of Herman Kahn: The Intuitive Arts of Thermonuclear War* (Cambridge, MA: Harvard University Press, 2005), 231.

25. For the use of technique of the "attack narrative" to develop local response plans, see the handbook produced by the National Security Resources Board, *United States Civil Defense*, NSRB Doc. 128 (Washington, DC: Government Printing Office, 1950).

26. As historian Sharon Ghamari-Tabrizi writes, "This was Kahn's problem: how to invest hypothetical vulnerabilities, particularly unknown and undetectable ones, with urgency." *The Worlds of Herman Kahn*, 233.

27. Herman Kahn, *Thinking about the Unthinkable* (New York: Horizon, 1962), 145.

28. They abandoned their initial attempts to formalize decision making processes in crises "when it became clear that the simplification imposed in order to permit quantification made the game of doubtful value for the assessment of political strategies and tactics in the real world." Herbert Goldhamer and Hans Speier, "Some Observations on Political Gaming," *World Politics* 12, no. 1 (1959): 72.

29. As they wrote: "In political life many events are beyond the control of the most powerful actors, a fact designated in political theories by such terms as *fortuna*, 'chance,' 'God's will,' 'changes in the natural environment,' etc. We tried to simulate this by the moves of 'Nature.'" Ibid., 73.

30. Ibid., 73. As two other exercise designers put it in 1965, the referee "is, as it were, 'god,' requiring the players to live with the implications of their chosen strategies." Lincoln P. Bloomfield and Barton Whaley, "The Political-Military Exercise: A Progress Report," *Orbis* 8, winter (1965): 845–70, at 858.

31. E. L. Quarantelli, *Disaster Planning, Emergency Management and Civil Protection: The Historical Development of Organized Efforts to Plan For and to Respond to Disasters* (Newark, DE: Disaster Research Center, University of

Delaware, 2000), http://udspace.udel.edu/handle/19716/673. For the history of the field of disaster management, see Scott Gabriel Knowles, *The Disaster Experts: Mastering Risk in Modern America* (Philadelphia: University of Pennsylvania Press, 2011).

32. Such measures included prevention efforts, such as levee construction and forest management, as well as recovery mechanisms, such as the declaration of federal disasters to release assistance funds. For the history of the relation between disaster relief and social welfare in the United States, see Michelle Landis Dauber, *The Sympathetic State: Disaster Relief and the Origins of the American Welfare State* (Chicago: University of Chicago Press, 2013).

33. William L. Waugh Jr., "Terrorism, Homeland Security and the National Emergency Management Network," *Public Organization Review* 3, no. 4 (2003): 373–85. See also Knowles, *The Disaster Experts*.

34. Arthur S. Flemming, "The Impact of Disasters on Readiness for War," *Annals of the American Academy of Political and Social Science* 309, no. 1 (1957): 65–70.

35. Quarantelli, *Disaster Planning*, 17.

36. Richard T. Sylves, "Adopting Integrated Emergency Management in the United States: Political and Organizational Challenges," *International Journal of Mass Emergencies and Disasters* 9, no. 3 (1991): 421.

37. Cited in James Mann, *Rise of the Vulcans: The History of Bush's War Cabinet* (New York: Viking, 2004), 203.

38. See U.S. Department of Defense, *Quadrennial Defense Review Report* (Washington, DC, September 30, 2001), http://archive.defense.gov/pubs/qdr2001 .pdf.

39. Donald H. Rumsfeld, "Transforming the Military," *Foreign Affairs*, May/ June 2002, https://www.foreignaffairs.com/articles/2002-05-01/transforming -military. For an analysis of the relation between the "Revolution in Military Affairs" and concern, among security experts, about emerging threats such as biological weapons, see Melinda Cooper, "Pre-empting Emergence: The Biological Turn in the War on Terror," *Theory, Culture and Society* 23, no. 4 (2006): 113–35.

40. U.S. Department of Homeland Security, "Secretary Michael Chertoff, U.S. Department of Homeland Security, Second Stage Review Remarks," media release, July 13, 2005.

41. As noted earlier, many of the technical elements of the National Preparedness plans had been part of FEMA's 1984 IEMS, which operationalized all-hazards planning at the federal level.

42. Eric Lipton, "Homeland Security Chief Announces Overhaul," *New York Times*, July 14, 2005.

43. U.S. Department of Homeland Security, *Interim National Preparedness Goal* (Washington, DC, March 31, 2005), A-2.

44. Ibid., 12.

45. See Stephen J. Collier and Andrew Lakoff, "Vital Systems Security: Reflexive Biopolitics and the Government of Emergency," *Theory, Culture and Society* 32, no. 2 (2015): 19–51.

46. "Capabilities-Based Planning is defined as planning, under uncertainty, to provide capabilities suitable for a wide range of threats and hazards while working within an economic framework that necessitates prioritization and choice. Capabilities-based planning is all-hazards planning." DHS, *Interim National Preparedness Goal*, 4.

47. Eric Lipton, "U.S. Report Lists Possibilities for Terrorist Attacks and Likely Toll," *New York Times*, March 16, 2005.

48. DHS, "Secretary Michael Chertoff."

49. This tension can be seen in the 2006 controversy over the DHS Urban Area Security Initiative, which claimed to use objective risk calculation to determine the rational allocation of homeland security funds for urban security measures. For an analysis, see Andrew Lakoff and Eric Klinenberg, "Of Risk and Pork: Urban Security and the Politics of Objectivity," *Theory and Society* 39, no. 5 (2010): 503–25.

50. DHS, *Interim National Preparedness Goal*, 6.

51. Lipton, "U.S. Report Lists Possibilities."

52. Like many other preparedness techniques, the checklist of critical tasks to perform in a future emergency dates back to Cold War defense mobilization. See Harry Yoshpe, *A Case Study in Peacetime Mobilization Planning: The National Security Resources Board* (Washington, DC: Executive Office of the President, 1953), 101.

53. U.S. Department of Homeland Security, *Interim National Preparedness Guidance* (Washington, DC, April 27, 2005), 6.

54. Lipton, "Homeland Security Chief."

55. See Eric Klinenberg and Thomas Frank, "Looting Homeland Security," *Rolling Stone*, December 29, 2005, 44–54.

56. U.S. Homeland Security Council, *Planning Scenarios: Executive Summaries* (Washington, DC, July 2004). Unrelated to these scenarios, the city of New Orleans had run a hurricane exercise in 2004.

57. United States, *Federal Response to Hurricane Katrina*.

58. Calhoun, "A World of Emergencies."

CHAPTER 2

1. My account of this episode relies on Richard E. Neustadt and Harvey V. Fineberg, *The Epidemic That Never Was: Policy Making and the Swine Flu Scare* (New York: Vintage, 1983).

2. The White House, "President Outlines Pandemic Influenza Preparedness and Response," media release, November 1, 2005.

3. *Preparing for Pandemic Flu: Hearing before the Senate Special Committee on Aging*, 109th Cong. (2006) (statement of Sen. Herbert Kohl).

4. Mike Leavitt, "Remarks to the Convening of the States on Pandemic Influenza Preparedness" (speech, Pandemic Planning: Convening of the States, Washington, DC, December 5, 2005).

5. *Preparing for Pandemic Flu* (2006) (statement of Sen. Kohl).

6. *Working through an Outbreak: Pandemic Flu Planning and Continuity of Operations: Hearing before the House Committee on Government Reform*, 109th Cong. (2006) (statement of John. O. Agwunobi).

7. *Preparing for Pandemic Flu* (2006) (statement of Mike Leavitt).

8. *The Next Flu Pandemic: Evaluating U.S. Readiness: Hearing before the Committee on Government Reform*, H.R., 109th Cong. (2005) (statement of Mary C. Selecky).

9. *Enhancing Public Health and Medical Preparedness: Reauthorization of Public Health Security and Bioterrorism Preparedness and Response Act: Hearing before the Senate Committee on Health, Education, Labor, and Pensions*, 109th Cong. (2006) (statement of Richard A. Falkenrath).

10. For the history of the relation between "emerging disease" and U.S. military intervention, see Nicholas B. King, "Security, Disease, Commerce: Ideologies of Postcolonial Global Health," *Social Studies of Science* 32, no. 5–6 (2002): 763–89.

11. See Lyle Fearnley, "Epidemic Intelligence: Langmuir and the Birth of Disease Surveillance," *Behemoth: A Journal on Civilisation* 3, no. 3 (2010): 37–56.

12. For a more detailed genealogy, see Stephen J. Collier and Andrew Lakoff, "Vital Systems Security: Reflexive Biopolitics and the Government of Emergency," *Theory, Culture and Society* 32, no. 2 (2015): 19–51.

13. Michel Foucault, *Society Must Be Defended: Lectures at the Collège de France, 1975–1976*, ed. Mauro Bertani and Alessandro Fontana, trans. David Macey (New York: Picador, 1983), 242.

14. Ibid., 243.

15. George Rosen, *A History of Public Health* (Baltimore: Johns Hopkins University Press, 1993), 185.

16. Cited in Ibid., 187.

17. Ibid., 312.

18. Neustadt and Fineberg, *The Epidemic That Never Was*, 11.

19. Ibid., 14.

20. Ibid., 30. The memo would prove politically impossible to ignore, given the later possibility of a leak. A Ford advisor recalled discussing options at a meeting with the President, and thinking, "That memo's a gun to our head." Ibid., 22.

21. Ibid., 35.

22. Ibid., 46.

23. Ibid., 60.

24. Ibid., 77.

25. In their later reflections on the episode, CDC officials blamed public misunderstanding for widespread anxiety about the safety of the vaccine. "Public misperception, warranted or not, ensured that every coincidental health event that occurred in the wake of the swine flu shot would be scrutinized and attributed to the vaccine." David J. Sencer and J. Donald Millar, "Reflections on the 1976 Swine Flu Vaccination Program," *Emerging Infectious Diseases* 12, no. 1 (2006): 31.

26. Sencer and Millar write, "Had H1N1 influenza been transmitted at that time, the small apparent risk of GBS from immunization would have been eclipsed by the obvious immediate benefit of vaccine-induced protection against swine flu. However, in December 1976, with 40 million persons immunized and no evidence of H1N1 transmission, federal health officials decided that the possibility of an association of GBS with the vaccine, however small, necessitated stopping immunization, at least until the issue could be explored." Ibid.

27. Stephen J. Collier and Andrew Lakoff, "Distributed Preparedness: The Spatial Logic of Domestic Security in the United States," *Environment and Planning D: Society and Space* 26, no. 1 (2008): 7–28.

28. Collier and Lakoff, "Vital Systems Security."

29. Cited in Thomas P. Hughes, *Rescuing Prometheus* (New York: Pantheon, 1998), 141.

30. Robert H. Kupperman, Richard H. Wilcox, and Harvey Smith, "Crisis Management: Some Opportunities," *Science* 187, no. 4175 (1975): 406.

31. R. James Woolsey and Robert H. Kupperman, *America's Hidden Vulnerabilities: Crisis Management in a Society of Networks* (Washington, DC: Center for Strategic and International Studies, 1985), 2.

32. As the authors wrote, "Cooperative action during a crisis requires coordinated preparation beforehand with responsibilities clear for resolving differences concerning both the measures to be taken and the accounts to be charged." Ibid., 16.

33. Ibid.

34. Robert H. Kupperman, "Vulnerable America," in *Nuclear Arms: Ethics, Strategy, Politics*, ed. R. James Woolsey (San Francisco: Institute for Contemporary Studies Press, 1983), 202.

35. Richard Halloran, "The Game is War, and It's for Keeps." *New York Times*, June 1, 1987.

36. As Susan P. Wright (2006) argues, the very use of the term "weapons of mass destruction" to link nuclear weapons to biological weapons was a strategic act on the part of biodefense advocates. Wright, "Terrorism and Biological Weapons: Forging the Linkage in the Clinton Administration," *Politics and the Life Sciences* 25, no. 1–2 (2006): 57–115.

37. Lawrence Altman, William J. Broad, and Judith Miller, "Smallpox: The Once and Future Scourge?," *New York Times*, June 15, 1999.

38. Ibid.

39. *FEMA's Role in Managing Bioterrorist Attacks and the Impact of Public Health Concerns on Bioterrorism Preparedness: Hearing before the International Security, Proliferation, and Federal Services Subcommittee of the Senate Committee on Governmental Affairs*, 107th Cong. (2001) (statement of Tara O'Toole).

40. For the distinction between "possibilistic" and "probabilistic" approaches to threats, see Lee Clarke, *Worst Cases: Terror and Catastrophe in the Popular Imagination* (Chicago: University of Chicago Press, 2005).

41. *Bioterrorism: Our Frontline Response—Evaluating U.S. Public Health and Medical Readiness: Hearing before Public Health Subcommittee of Senate Committee on Health, Education, Labor, and Pensions*, 106th Cong. 1279 (1999) (statement of Donald A. Henderson).

42. Quoted in Tara O'Toole, Michael Mair, and Thomas V. Inglesby, "Shining Light on 'Dark Winter,'" *Clinical Infectious Diseases* 34, no. 7 (2002): 972–83.

43. Ibid., 972.

44. Ibid. For a critique, see Ronald Barrett, "Dark Winter and the Spring of 1972: Deflecting the Social Lessons of Smallpox," *Medical Anthropology* 25, no. 2 (2006): 171–91.

45. O'Toole, Mair, and Inglesby, "Shining Light," 973.

46. For quotations from the exercise, see "Dark Winter: Bioterrorism Exercise, Andrews Air Force Base" (final script, UPMC Center for Biosecurity, Washington, DC, June 22–23, 2001), http://www.upmchealthsecurity.org/our-work/events/2001_dark-winter/Dark%20Winter%20Script.pdf.

47. Ibid., 13.

48. *Combating Terrorism: Federal Response to a Biological Weapons Attack: Hearing before the House Subcommittee on National Security, Veterans Affairs, and International Relations of the Committee on Government Reform*, 107th Cong. 3 (2001). On the role of speculative practices such as simulation in the production of affect as part of the U.S. counterterrorism apparatus, see Joseph Masco, *The Theater of Operations. National Security Affect from the Cold War to the War on Terror*. Durham, NC: Duke University Press, 2014.

49. Ibid., 74.

50. Ibid., 8–9.

51. Ibid., 3–4.

52. O'Toole, Mair, and Inglesby, "Shining Light," 982.

53. Ibid., 980.

54. Ibid., 982.

55. *Combating Terrorism* (2001), 12.

56. Ibid., 54.

57. Ibid., 14.

58. Nicole Lurie, Jeffrey Wasserman, and Christopher D. Nelson, "Public Health Preparedness: Evolution or Revolution?," *Health Affairs* 25, no. 4 (2006): 935–45.

59. Cited in Dale Rose, "How Did the Smallpox Vaccination Program Come About?," in *Biosecurity Interventions: Global Health and Security in Question*, ed. Andrew Lakoff and Stephen J. Collier (New York: Columbia University Press, 2008).

60 Cited in Ibid.

61. Ibid.

62. Total U.S. government spending on civilian biodefense increased from $294.8 million in FY2001 to $7.6 billion in FY2005. See Clarence Lam, Crystal Franco, and Ari Schuler, "Billions for Biodefense: Federal Agency Biodefense Funding, FY2006–FY2007," *Biosecurity and Bioterrorism: Biodefense Strategy, Practice, and Science* 4, no. 2 (2006): 86–96.

63. Stewart Simonson, "Reflections on Preparedness: Pandemic Planning in the Bush Administration," *Saint Louis University Journal of Health Law and Policy* 4, no. 5 (2010): 13n32.

64. Ibid., 17.

65. For an analysis of this novel configuration of health and security concerns at an international scale, see Stefan Elbe, *Security and Global Health: Toward the Medicalization of Insecurity* (Cambridge, UK: Polity Press, 2010).

66. Simonson, "Reflections on Preparedness."

67. Ibid., 25.

68. Gardiner Harris, "Fear of Flu Outbreak Rattles Washington," *New York Times*, October 5, 2005.

69. Irwin Redlener, quoted in Ibid.

70. *Public Health Preparedness in the 21st Century: Hearing Before the Senate Subcommittee on Bioterrorism and Public Health Preparedness*, 109th Congress (2006).

71. *Working through an Outbreak* (2006).

72. *Enhancing Public Health* (2006) (statement of Falkenrath).

73. *The Next Flu Pandemic* (2005).

74. *Public Health Preparedness* (2006).

75. See Collier and Lakoff, "Distributed Preparedness."

76. It is worth noting that there was continued disagreement among public health and national security officials on the right prioritization of threats, and on the best means to prepare for them. See, for example, Hillel Cohen, Robert Gould, and Victor Sidel, "Bioterrorism Initiatives: Public Health in Reverse?," *American Journal of Public Health* 89, no. 11 (1999): 1629–31.

77. *The Next Flu Pandemic* (2005).

78. *Public Health Preparedness* (2006).

79. Ibid.

80. Michael Mair, Beth Maldin, and Brad Smith, "Passage of S. 3678: The Pandemic and All-Hazards Preparedness Act," *Biosecurity and Bioterrorism* 5, no. 1 (2007): 72–4.

CHAPTER 3

1. Richard Holbrooke and Laurie Garrett, "'Sovereignty' That Risks Global Health," *Washington Post*, August 8, 2008.

2. The leader of WHO's communicable diseases cluster, David Heymann, described the network as follows: GISN "identifies and tracks antigenic drift and shifts of influenza viruses to guide the annual composition of vaccines, and provides an early alert to variants that might signal the start of a pandemic." Heymann, "The International Response to the Outbreak of SARS in 2003," *Philosophical Transactions of the Royal Society B* 359, no. 1447 (2004): 1127–9.

3. Their criticism echoed U.S. Secretary of Defense Robert Gates's reaction upon hearing this accusation during a visit to Jakarta: "the nuttiest idea I've ever heard." Aubrey Belford, "Indonesia's Bird Flu Warrior Takes On the World," Agence France-Presse, October 12, 2008.

4. Lisa Schnirring, "Supari Accuses Rich Nations of Creating Viruses for Profit," CIDRAP, September 8, 2008.

5. Bryan Walsh, "Indonesia's Bird Flu Showdown," *Time*, May 10, 2007.

6. "International Health Regulations: The Challenges Ahead," *The Lancet* 369, no. 9575 (2007): 1763.

7. Maryn McKenna, "System for Global Pandemic Vaccine Development Challenged," CIDRAP, February 6, 2007.

8. Belford, "Indonesia's Bird Flu Warrior."

9. Cited in David P. Fidler, "Influenza Virus Samples, International Law, and Global Health Diplomacy," *Emerging Infectious Diseases* 14, no. 1 (2008): 92.

10. Ibid.

11. Ibid.

12. Ibid.

13. Ibid.

14. At the 2007 World Health Assembly, a group of more than twenty countries cited the CBD to claim rights to virus isolates from their territories. Maryn McKenna, "Virus Ownership Claims Could Disrupt Flu Vaccine System," CIDRAP, June 19, 2007.

15. Stephen J. Collier and Aihwa Ong, "Global Assemblages, Anthropological Problems," in *Global Assemblages: Ethics, Technology and Politics as Anthropological Problems*, ed. Aihwa Ong and Stephen J. Collier (Malden, MA: Blackwell, 2004).

16. Elizabeth Fee and Dorothy Porter, "Public Health, Preventive Medicine and Professionalization: England and America in the Nineteenth Century," in *Medicine in Society: Historical Essays*, ed. Andrew Wear (Cambridge: Cambridge University Press, 1992).

17. As Michel Foucault noted, public health experts found "phenomena that are aleatory and unpredictable when taken in themselves or individually, but which, at the collective level, display constants that are easy, or at least possible, to establish." Foucault, *Society Must Be Defended: Lectures at the Collège de France, 1975-1976*, ed. Mauro Bertani and Alessandro Fontana, trans. David Macey (New York: Picador, 1983), 243.

18. While I am focusing here on two major strands of Cold War international health, there is a complex history of pre-WWII international health efforts ranging from the Rockefeller Foundation to the League of Nations that historians of public health have recently begun to unravel. See, for example, Alison Bashford, "Global Biopolitics and the History of World Health," *History of the Human Sciences* 19, no. 1 (2006): 67–88.

19. Theodore M. Brown, Marcos Cueto, and Elizabeth Fee, "The World Health Organization and the Transition from 'International' to 'Global' Health," *American Journal of Public Health* 96, no. 1 (2006): 62–72.

20. A number of illuminating anthropological critiques of the field of humanitarian biomedicine have recently appeared. See Didier Fassin, "Humanitarianism as a Politics of Life," *Public Culture* 19, no. 3 (2007): 499–520; Miriam Ticktin, "Where Ethics and Politics Meet: The Violence of Humanitarianism in France," *American Ethnologist* 33, no. 1 (2006): 33–49; and Peter Redfield, "A Less Modest Witness: Collective Advocacy and Motivated Truth in a Medical Humanitarian Movement," *American Ethnologist* 33, no. 1 (2006): 3–26.

21. Peter Redfield, "Doctors Without Borders and the Moral Economy of Pharmaceuticals," in *Human Rights in Crisis*, ed. Alice Bullard (Aldershot, UK: Ashgate, 2008), 132.

22. Didier Fassin emphasizes the paradoxes involved in the effort by *Médecins sans Frontières* to stage what he calls a "politics of life" that deals with passive victims rather than active citizens: "humanitarian testimony establishes two forms of humanity and two sorts of life in the public space: there are those who can tell stories and those whose stories can be told only by others." Fassin, "Humanitarianism as a Politics of Life," 518.

23. Renée Fox, "Medical Humanitarianism and Human Rights: Reflections on Doctors Without Borders and Doctors of the World," *Social Science and Medicine* 41, no. 12 (1995): 1607–16.

24. Melinda French Gates, "Malaria Forum Keynote Address" (speech, Bill and Melinda Gates Foundation Malaria Forum, Seattle, October 17, 2007), http://www.gatesfoundation.org/speeches-commentary/Pages/melinda-french-gates-2007-malaria-forum.aspx.

25. For the history of modernization theory and its political context, see Nils Gilman, *Mandarins of the Future: Modernization Theory in Cold War America* (Baltimore: Johns Hopkins University Press, 2003).

26. Manjari Mahajan, "Designing Epidemics: Models, Policy-Making, and Global Foreknowledge in India's AIDS Epidemic," *Science and Public Policy* 35, no. 8 (2008): 587.

27. Vinh-Kim Nguyen, "Antiretroviral Globalism, Biopolitics, and Therapeutic Citizenship," in *Global Assemblages: Ethics, Technology and Politics as Anthropological Problems*, ed. Aihwa Ong and Stephen J. Collier (Malden, MA: Blackwell, 2004). Brazil's efforts to increase antiretroviral access serves as a model for many biomedical humanitarians. For a critique, see João Biehl, "Pharmaceutical Governance," in *Global Pharmaceuticals: Ethics, Markets, Practices*, ed. Adriana Petryna, Andrew Lakoff, and Arthur Kleinman (Durham: Duke University Press, 2006).

28. Erin Koch, "Disease as a Security Threat: Critical Reflections on the Global TB Emergency," in *Biosecurity Interventions: Global Health and Security in Question*, ed. Andrew Lakoff and Stephen Collier (New York: Columbia University Press, 2008).

29. Anne-Emanuelle Birn, "Gates' Grandest Challenge: Transcending Technology as Public Health Ideology," *The Lancet* 366, no. 9484 (2005): 514–19.

30. Redfield, "Doctors Without Borders," 140.

31. This section draws on portions of Stephen J. Collier and Andrew Lakoff, "The Problem of Securing Health," in *Biosecurity Interventions: Global Health and Security in Question*, ed. Andrew Lakoff and Stephen J. Collier (New York: Columbia University Press, 2008).

32. WHO, *The World Health Report 2007: A Safer Future: Global Public Health Security in the 21st Century* (Geneva: WHO, 2007).

33. Charles Rosenberg has contrasted this new form of "civilizational risk" with those that sparked early public health efforts, noting that anxieties about the risk of modern ways of life are here explained not in terms of the city as a pathogenic environment, but in terms of evolutionary and global ecological realities. Rosenberg, "Pathologies of Progress: The Idea of Civilization as Risk," *Bulletin of the History of Medicine* 72, no. 4 (1998): 714–30.

34. WHO, *World Health Report 2007*.

35. Nicholas King has analyzed the rise of the emerging disease framework in detail. See King, "Security, Disease, Commerce: Ideologies of Post-Colonial Global Health," *Social Studies of Science* 32, no. 5–6 (2002): 763–89.

36. Stephen S. Morse, ed., *Emerging Viruses* (New York: Oxford University Press, 1993).

37. Warwick Anderson, "Natural Histories of Infectious Disease: Ecological Vision in Twentieth Century Bioscience," *Osiris*, 2nd ser., 19 (2004): 39–61. Anderson traces its history to the mid-20th century work of disease ecologists

such as Theobald Smith, Macfarlane Burnet, and René Dubos. See also Melinda Cooper's critical analysis of the history of the concept of emergence in biological evolution, in Cooper, "Pre-empting Emergency: The Biological Turn in the War on Terror," *Theory, Culture and Society* 23, no. 4 (2006): 113–35.

38. Joshua Lederberg, Robert E. Shope, and Stanley C. Oaks Jr., eds., *Emerging Infections: Microbial Threats to Health in the United States* (Washington, DC: National Academy Press, 1992); Laurie Garrett, *The Coming Plague: Newly Emerging Diseases in a World out of Balance* (New York: Farrar, Straus and Giroux, 1994); Richard Preston, *The Cobra Event* (New York: Ballantine, 1998).

39. Stephen S. Morse, "Regulating Viral Traffic," *Issues in Science and Technology* 7, no. 1 (1990): 81–4.

40. D. A. Henderson, "Surveillance Systems and Intergovernmental Cooperation," in *Emerging Viruses*, ed. Stephen S. Morse (New York: Oxford University Press, 1993), 283.

41. The Epidemic Intelligence Service was founded in 1951 by Alexander Langmuir. For Donald A. Henderson's recollections, see Henderson, *Smallpox: The Death of a Disease* (New York: Prometheus, 2009).

42. Alexander Langmuir, "The Surveillance of Communicable Diseases of National Importance," *New England Journal of Medicine* 268, no. 4 (1963): 182–3. Langmuir pioneered a method of epidemiological surveillance designed to track each instance of a disease within a given territory—one that would serve the needs of both public health and biodefense. For an insightful historical analysis, see Lyle Fearnley, "Epidemic Intelligence: Langmuir and the Birth of Disease Surveillance," *Behemoth: A Journal on Civilisation* 3, no. 3 (2010): 37–56.

43. Stephen S. Morse, "Epidemiologic Surveillance for Investigating Chemical or Biological Warfare and for Improving Human Health," *Politics and the Life Sciences* 11, no. 1 (1992): 29.

44. Haroon Ashraf, "David Heymann—WHO's Public Health Guru," *The Lancet Infectious Diseases* 4, no. 12 (2004): 785–8.

45. Ibid., 787.

46. Heymann, "The International Response," 1127.

47. See Garrett, *The Coming Plague*.

48. Lorna Weir and Eric Mykhalovskiy, "The Geopolitics of Global Public Health Surveillance in the 21st Century," in *Medicine at the Border: Disease, Globalization, and Security, 1850–Present*, ed. Alison Bashford (Basingstoke, UK: Palgrave MacMillan, 2007).

49. Claire Hooker, "Drawing the Lines: Danger and Risk in the Age of SARS," in *Medicine at the Border: Disease, Globalization, and Security, 1850–Present*, ed. Alison Bashford (Basingstoke, UK: Palgrave MacMillan, 2007).

50. Ashraf, "David Heymann," 787.

51. Heymann, "The International Response," 1128.

52. Laurie Garrett, "The Next Pandemic?," *Foreign Affairs*, July/August 2005, https://www.foreignaffairs.com/articles/2005-07-01/next-pandemic.

53. *Avian Flu: Addressing the Global Threat: Hearing before the Committee on International Relations*, H.R., 109th Congress (2005) (statement of Michael Osterholm).

54. David Fidler, "From International Sanitary Conventions to Global Health Security: The New International Health Regulations," *Chinese Journal of International Law* 4, no. 2 (2005): 326. For an account of the significance of the revised IHR in the context of international relations, see Sara E. Davies, Adam Kamradt-Scott, and Simon Rushton. *Disease Diplomacy: International Norms and Global Health Security* (Baltimore: Johns Hopkins University Press, 2015).

55. WHO, "Revision of the International Health Regulations: Progress Report, May 2002," *Weekly Epidemiological Record* 77, no. 19 (2002): 157–60.

56. WHO, *International Health Regulations (2005): Areas of Work for Implementation*, WHO/CDS/EPR/IHR/2007.1 (Geneva: WHO, 2007), 19, http://www.who.int/ihr/finalversion9Nov07.pdf.

57. As one document suggested, "It is proposed that the revised IHR define the capacities that a national disease surveillance system will require in order for such emergencies to be detected, evaluated and responded to in a timely manner." Fidler, "From International Sanitary Conventions," 353.

58. WHO, *Global Crises–Global Solutions: Managing Public Health Emergencies of International Concern through the Revised International Health Regulations*, WHO/CDS/CSR/GAR/2002.4 (Geneva: WHO, 2002).

59. WHO, "Revision of the IHR—Progress Report, May 2002."

60. WHO Secretariat, Resolution 54.14, "Global Health Security: Epidemic Alert and Response," April 2, 2001, http://apps.who.int/gb/archive/pdf_files/WHA54/ea549.pdf.

61. WHO Resolution 54.14 (2001) reported that work was being done on developing a decision tree, which could be useful "in determining whether a public health risk is of urgent international importance, and if so, in helping decide which public health measures should be applied." See also Fidler, "From International Sanitary Conventions."

62. WHO, "Revision of the IHR—Progress Report, May 2002."

63. WHO. *WHO Guidance for the Use of Annex 2 of the International Health Regulations (2005)*, WHO/HSE/IHR/2010.4 (Geneva: WHO, 2008), 6.

64. Max Weber argued that the authority of a bureaucratic agency is grounded in its perceived objectivity—its adherence to impersonal standards of judgment: "Bureaucracy develops the more perfectly, the more it is 'dehumanized,' the more completely it succeeds in eliminating from official business love, hatred, and all purely personal, irrational, and emotional elements which escape calculation."

Weber, "Bureaucracy," in *The Essential Weber: A Reader*, ed. Sam Whimster (New York: Routledge, 2003), 249.

65. WHO. *WHO Guidance for the Use of Annex 2.*

66. Barack Obama and Richard Lugar, "Grounding a Pandemic," *New York Times*, June 6, 2005.

67. Indeed, one reason that WHO hesitated to rapidly declare an emergency in the early stages of the 2014 Ebola epidemic in West Africa was that some officials feared the economic effects of publicity around an outbreak. See Chapter 6.

68. Howard Markel, Lawrence O. Gostin, and David P. Fidler, "Extensively Drug-Resistant Tuberculosis: An Isolation Order, Public Health Powers, and Global Crisis," *JAMA* 298, no. 1 (2007): 83–6.

69. John Schwartz, "Tangle of Conflicting Accounts in TB Patient's Odyssey," *New York Times*, June 2, 2007.

70. "TB Terror," *Los Angeles Times*, June 10, 2007.

71. Janice Hopkins Tanne, "Tuberculosis Case Exposes Flaws in International Public Health Systems," *BMJ: British Medical Journal* 334, no. 7605 (2010): 1187.

72. Robert Roos, "House Panel Sees CDC Errors in Case of Traveling TB Patient," CIDRAP News, September 13, 2007.

73. U.S. House Committee on Homeland Security, *The 2007 XDR-TB Incident: A Breakdown at the Intersection of Homeland Security and Public Health*, report prepared by the majority staff (Washington, DC, September 2007), 2.

74. Quoted in Roos, "House Panel Sees CDC Errors."

75. Tanne, "Tuberculosis Case," 1187.

76. As an example, we can take the $33 million dollar initiative by the Gates Foundation, in collaboration with the Chinese Ministry of Health, to develop a quick diagnostic test for drug-resistant TB. Sandi Doughton, "Gates Foundation Launches 3rd Initiative in China," *Seattle Times*, March 31, 2009.

77. John Donnelly, "Specialists Say TB Case a Sign of Things to Come," *Boston Globe*, June 4, 2007.

78. See, for example, Paul Farmer, *Infections and Inequalities: The Modern Plagues* (Berkeley: University of California Press, 2001).

79. Fidler, "From International Sanitary Conventions," 389.

80. Philippe Calain, "From the Field Side of the Binoculars: A Different View on Global Public Health Surveillance," *Health Policy and Planning* 22, no. 1 (2007): 19.

CHAPTER 4

1. For the concept of global assemblage, see Stephen J. Collier and Aihwa Ong, "Global Assemblages, Anthropological Problems," in *Global Assemblages:*

Technology, Politics and Ethics as Anthropological Problems, eds. Aihwa Ong and Stephen J. Collier. Malden, MA: Blackwell, 2005.

2. WHO Global Influenza Programme, *Pandemic Influenza Preparedness and Response: A WHO Guidance Document* (Geneva: WHO, 2009).

3. Ibid., 26.

4. WHO, *Influenza Pandemic Plan: The Role of WHO and Guidelines for National and Regional Planning*, WHO/CDS/CSR/EDC/99.1 (Geneva: WHO, 1999).

5. WHO, "Influenza A(H1N1): Statement by WHO Director-General Dr. Margaret Chan," media release, April 29, 2009, http://www.who.int/mediacentre /news/statements/2009/h1n1_20090429/en.

6. Ibid.

7. WHO Director-General, *Implementation of the International Health Regulations (2005): Report of the Review Committee on the Functioning of the International Health Regulations (2005) in relation to Pandemic (H1N1) 2009*, 64th World Health Assembly, WHO A64/10 (Geneva, May 5, 2011), 97.

8. Ibid., 98.

9. Harvey V. Fineberg and Mary Elizabeth Wilson, "Epidemic Science in Real Time," *Science*, May 22, 2009, 987.

10. Michel Foucault, *Security, Territory, Population: Lectures at the Collège de France, 1977–1978*, ed. Arnold I. Davidson, trans. Graham Burchell (Basingstoke, UK: Palgrave Macmillan, 2007), 60.

11. Ian Hacking describes this process as an "avalanche of printed numbers." Hacking, "Biopower and the Avalanche of Printed Numbers," *Humanities in Society* 5 (1982): 279–95.

12. Niklas Luhmann has described this relation between present decision and future responsibility: "the present can calculate a future that can always turn out otherwise; so the present can assure itself that it calculated correctly, even if things turn out differently." Luhmann, *Observations on Modernity*, trans. William Whobrey (Stanford: Stanford University Press, 1998), 70.

13. "These are phenomena that are aleatory and unpredictable when taken in themselves or individually, but which, at the collective level, display constants that are easy, or at least possible, to establish." Foucault, *Society Must Be Defended: Lectures at the Collège de France, 1975–1976*, ed. Mauro Bertani and Alessandro Fontana, trans. David Macey (New York: Picador, 2003), 243.

14. John M. Eyler, *Victorian Social Medicine: The Ideas and Methods of William Farr* (Baltimore: Johns Hopkins University Press, 1979).

15. Cited in Ibid., 73.

16. William Coleman, *Death Is a Social Disease: Public Health and Political Economy in Early Industrial France* (Madison: University of Wisconsin Press, 1982).

17. Francis Chateauraynaud and Didier Torny, "Mobiliser autour d'un risque: Des lanceurs aux porteurs d'alerte," in *Risques et crises alimentaires*, ed. Cécile Lahellec (Paris: Lavoisier, 2005).

18. Andrew Lakoff, "The Indicator Species: Tracking Ecosystem Collapse in Arid California," *Public Culture* 28, no. 2 (2016): 237–59; Chloe Silverman, "How Do You Spot a Healthy Honey Bee?," *Limn* 3 (2013), http://limn.it/how-do-you-spot-a-healthy-honey-bee.

19. Frédéric Keck, *Un monde grippé* (Paris: Flammarion, 2010).

20. Guillaume Lachenal, "Lessons in Medical Nihilism: Virus Hunters, Neoliberalism and the AIDS Crisis in Cameroon," in *Para-States and Medical Science: Making African Global Health*, ed. Paul Wenzel Geissler (Durham: Duke University Press, 2015); Lyle Fearnley, "Redesigning Syndromic Surveillance for Biosecurity," in *Biosecurity Interventions: Global Health and Security in Question*, ed. Andrew Lakoff and Stephen J. Collier (New York: Columbia University Press, 2008).

21. For an analysis of the ambiguity of the WHO pandemic classification system, see Sudeepa Abeysinghe, "When the Spread of Disease Becomes a Global Event: The Classification of Pandemics," *Social Studies of Science* 43, no. 6 (2013): 905–26.

22. Jeanne Whalen, "Rich Nations Lock in Flu Vaccine as Poor Ones Fret," *Wall Street Journal*, May 16, 2009.

23. David Brown, "Vaccine Would Be Spoken For," *Washington Post*, May 7, 2009.

24. Ibid.

25. WHO, "World Now at the Start of 2009 Influenza Pandemic: Statement to the Press by WHO Director-General Dr. Margaret Chan," media release, June 11, 2009, http://www.who.int/mediacentre/news/statements/2009/h1n1_pandemic_phase6_20090611/en.

26. Marc Lipsitch et al., "Managing and Reducing Uncertainty in an Emerging Influenza Pandemic," *New England Journal of Medicine* 361, no. 2 (2009): 112–15.

27. WHO Director-General, report of the IHR Review Committee (2011), 100.

28. Rob Stein, "Millions of H1N1 Vaccine Doses May Have to Be Discarded," *Washington Post*, April 1, 2010.

29. For a discussion of the formulation of this prioritization scheme, which focused on ensuring the continuing operation of critical infrastructures during an envisioned health emergency, see Carlo Caduff, "Public Prophylaxis: Pandemic Influenza, Pharmaceutical Prevention and Participatory Governance," *BioSocieties* 5, no. 2 (2010): 199–218.

30. Agence France-Presse, "Americans First before US Donates H1N1 Flu Vaccine: Official," October 28, 2009.

31. Brendan Maher, "Crisis Communicator," *Nature* 463, no. 14 (2010): 150.

32. Anthropologist Theresa MacPhail calls this approach "strategic uncertainty." MacPhail, *The Viral Network: A Pathography of the H1N1 Influenza Pandemic* (Ithaca: Cornell University Press, 2014).

33. Peter M. Sandman, "Acknowledging Uncertainty." Available at: http://www.psandman.com/col/uncertin.htm

34. Cited in Ibid., 144.

35. Michael Schwarzinger et al., "Low Acceptability of A/H1N1 Pandemic Vaccination in French Adult Population: Did Public Health Policy Fuel Public Dissonance?," *PLoS ONE* 5, no. 4 (2010), http://dx.doi.org/10.1371/journal.pone.0010199.

36. "EU Governments Seek to Offload Flu Vaccines," EurActiv.com, January 5, 2010.

37. Anne Chaon, "France Joins Europe Flu Vaccine Sell-Off," Agence France-Presse, January 3, 2010. In addition to public skepticism about the vaccination campaign, national governments held excess doses of the vaccine because it had been determined that only one dose, rather than two, would be required for immunization.

38. Scheherazade Daneshkhu and Andrew Jack, "Sarkozy Under Fire on Flu Vaccine 'Fiasco,'" *Financial Times*, January 5, 2010.

39. Ibid.

40. Jeanne Whalen and David Gauthier-Villars, "European Governments Cancel Vaccine Orders," *Wall Street Journal*, January 10, 2010.

41. "Expertise et choix politique: reflexions a partir de la grippe aviaire: entretien avec Frédéric Keck," interview by Olivier Mongin and Marc-Olivier Padis, *Esprit* 3 (March/April 2011): 168–77.

42. Sandman, "Acknowledging Uncertainty."

43. "Flu Vaccine Overstock," *The World*, Public Radio International (PRI), January 11, 2010, http://www.pri.org/stories/2010-01-11/flu-vaccine-overstock.

44. Fiona Macrae, "The 'False' Pandemic: Drug Firms Cashed In on Scare over Swine Flu, Claims Euro Health Chief," *Daily Mail*, January 17, 2010.

45. Wolfgang Wodarg, "Faked Pandemics—A Threat to Health." Motion of a Recommendation by the Parliamentary Assembly of the Council of Europe, Doc. 122110 (Strasbourg: Council of Europe, 2009).

46. Cited in Sudeepa Abeysinghe, "Vaccine Narratives and Public Health: Investigating Criticisms of H1N1 Pandemic Vaccination," *PLoS Currents* 7 (February 25, 2015).

47. Parliamentary Assembly of the Council of Europe, Committee of Social, Health, and Family Affairs, *The Handling of the H1N1 Pandemic: More Transparency Needed*, public hearing (Strasbourg, January 26, 2010) (statement of Ulrich Keil).

48. Deborah Cohen and Philip Carter, "WHO and the Pandemic Flu 'Conspiracies,'" *BMJ: British Medical Journal* 340, no. c2912 (2010): 1274–9.

49. PACE, Resolution 1749(1), *The Handling of the H1N1 Pandemic: More Transparency Needed: Report by the Social Health and Family Affairs Committee* (2010).

50. Fiona Macrae, "The Pandemic That Never Was: Drug Firms 'Encouraged World Health Body to Exaggerate Swine Flu Threat,'" *Daily Mail*, June 4, 2010.

51. Declan Butler, "Flu Experts Rebut Conflict Claims," *Nature* 465 (2010): 672–3.

52. WHO Director-General, report of the IHR Review Committee (2011), 133. The IHR Review Committee was chaired by Harvey Fineberg, who had been coauthor of the report on the Ford administration's response to the 1976 swine flu outbreak. That report had emphasized the importance of flexibility in response to changing conditions. See Chapter 2.

53. WHO Director-General, report of the IHR Review Committee (2011), 17.

54. It should be noted that the alert system was specific to pandemic influenza and did not apply to other IHR events. And although all IHR signatories were bound to respond to a WHO PHEIC, not all member states had adopted the pandemic alert system.

55. Margaret Chan, "Director-General Responds to Assessment of WHO's Handling of the Influenza Pandemic" (remarks at the fourth meeting of the Review Committee of the International Health Regulations, WHO, Geneva, March 28, 2011).

56. The IHR Review Committee agreed with this assessment: "The response to the emergence of pandemic influenza A (H1N1) was the result of a decade of pandemic planning, largely centered on the threat of an influenza A (H5N1) pandemic." WHO Director-General, report of the IHR Review Committee (2011).

57. "Despite differences in planning scenarios and the actual 2009 H1N1 pandemic, many of the systems established through pandemic planning were used and useful for the 2009 H1N1 pandemic response." CDC, "2009 H1N1 Pandemic: Summary Highlights, April 2009–April 2010," last updated June 16, 2010, http://www.cdc.gov/h1n1flu/cdcresponse.htm.

58. PACE, *Handling of the H1N1 Pandemic*, public hearing (statement of Keil), 3.

59. PACE, Resolution 1749(1), *Handling of the H1N1 Pandemic*.

60. Laura MacInnis, "WHO Chief Defends Her Agency's Pandemic Response," Reuters, September 28, 2010.

61. Intriguingly, this was the same conclusion that the Review Committee chair, Harvey Fineberg, had reached in his book evaluating the much-criticized U.S. CDC response to swine flu in 1976, coauthored with Richard E. Neustadt: *The Epidemic That Never Was: Policy Making and the Swine Flu Scare* (New York: Vintage, 1983).

62. WHO Director-General, report of the IHR Review Committee (2011).

63. Hans Jonas, *The Imperative of Responsibility: In Search of an Ethics for the Technological Age* (Chicago: University of Chicago Press, 1985).

64. "WHO Director-General, report of the IHR Review Committee (2011), 20."

65. David P. Fidler, "Negotiating Equitable Access: Global Health Diplomacy and the Controversies surrounding Avian Influenza H5N1 and Pandemic Influenza H1N1," *PLOS Medicine* (May 4, 2010), http://dx.doi.org/10.1371/journal.pmed.1000247.

66. Ibid.

67. Ibid.

68. David P. Fidler and Lawrence O. Gostin, "The WHO Pandemic Influenza Preparedness Framework: A Milestone in Global Governance for Health." *Journal of the American Medical Association* 306, no. 2 (2011), 200–201.

CHAPTER 5

1. Martin Enserink, "Scientists Brace for Media Storm around Controversial Flu Studies," *Science*, November 23, 2011.

2. Anthropologist Carlo Caduff has described Peter Palese's pioneering work in reverse genetics at New York's Mount Sinai influenza research center. The technique enabled Palese's laboratory to reconstruct the 1918 Spanish influenza virus. Caduff, "Pandemic Prophecy, or How to Have Faith in Reason," *Current Anthropology* 55, no. 3 (2014): 296–315.

3. Michael Fumento, "The Threat of an Avian Flu Pandemic Is Over-Hyped," *Virtual Mentor* 8, no. 4 (2006): 265–70.

4. Denise Grady and Donald G. McNeil Jr., "Debate Persists on Deadly Flu Made Airborne," *New York Times*, December 26, 2011.

5. Martin Enserink and David Malakoff write, "NSABB itself was first alerted to the studies by NIAID staff late last summer and received copies of the papers in mid-October." Enserink and Malakoff, "Will Flu Papers Lead to New Research Oversight?," *Science*, January 6, 2012. Based on fieldwork with US biosecurity authorities, anthropologist Limor Samimian-Darash reports that the editor of *Science* first alerted NIH to the potential issues raised by the article. Personal communication, November 2014.

6. U.S. Department of Health and Human Services, Secretary, *Charter of National Science Advisory Board for Biosecurity* (Washington, DC, March 15, 2016), http://osp.od.nih.gov/sites/default/files/NSABB_Charter_2016.pdf.

7. For a discussion, see "Special Report: The 1918 Flu Virus Is Resurrected," *Nature* 437 (October 6, 2005): 794–95.

8. Enserink and Malakoff, "New Research Oversight," 22

9. Quoted in Daniel Patrone, David Resnik, and Lisa Chin, "Biosecurity and the Review and Publication of Dual-Use Research of Concern," *Biosecurity and Bioterrorism* 10, no. 3 (2012): 2090–8.

10. Ian Sample, "Bird Flu: How Two Mutant Strains Led to an International Controversy," *Guardian*, March 28, 2012.

11. Robert Roos, "US Government Urges Journals to Omit Details of Two H5N1 Studies," CIDRAP News, December 20, 2011.

12. Peter Palese, "Don't Censor Life-Saving Science," World View, *Nature* 481, no. 7380 (2012): 115.

13. Yoshihiro Kawaoka, "H5N1: Flu Transmission Work Is Urgent," Comment, *Nature* 482, no. 7384 (2012): 155.

14. "An Engineered Doomsday," editorial, *New York Times*, January 8, 2012.

15. Kenneth I. Berns et al., "Adaptations of Avian Flu Virus Are a Cause for Concern," *Science*, February 10, 2012.

16. "There are many parallels with the situation in the 1970s and recombinant DNA technologies." Ibid. For a trenchant analysis of the continual invocation of Asilomar in contemporary debates over biotechnology, see J. Benjamin Hurlbut, "Remembering the Future: Science, Law and the Legacy of Asilomar," in *Dreamscapes of Modernity: Sociotechnical Imaginaries and the Fabrication of Power*, ed. Sheila Jasanoff and Sang-Hyun Kim (Chicago: University of Chicago Press, 2015).

17. Arturo Casadevall and Thomas Shenk, "The H5N1 Moratorium Controversy and Debate," *mBio* 3, no. 5 (2012): 1–2. A central element of the post-Asilomar guidelines for regulation of recombinant DNA research is the NIH-based system of institutional biosafety committees that gauges experiments according to levels of risk. Some critics have argued that in establishing these guidelines NIH was more concerned with defending scientists from external oversight than with protecting the public against potential biological hazards. See Susan Wright, *Molecular Politics: Developing American and British Regulatory Policy for Genetic Engineering, 1972–1982* (Chicago: University of Chicago Press, 1994).

18. Ron A. M. Fouchier et al., "Pause on Avian Flu Transmission Studies," Correspondence, *Nature* 481, no. 7382 (2012): 443.

19. In this case, the concept of technopolitical assemblage is preferable to scientific network because the latter—at least in the way it is used by the actors involved (e.g., the "Global Influenza Surveillance Network")—presupposes more harmonization of standards, less heterogeneity of actors, and more stability over time than an assemblage.

20. Stephen J. Collier and Aihwa Ong describe such assemblages as domains "in which the forms and values of individual and collective existence are problematized or at stake." Collier and Ong, "Global Assemblages, Anthropological Problems," in *Global Assemblages: Technology, Politics and Ethics as Anthropological Problems*, ed. Aihwa Ong and Stephen J. Collier (Malden, MA: Blackwell, 2005).

21. Paul Rabinow suggests that contemporary assemblages are composed of "a distinctive matrix of heterogeneous elements, techniques, and concepts" that "are comparatively effervescent, disappearing in years, decades, rather tha

centuries." Rabinow, *Anthropos Today: Reflections on Modern Equipment* (Princeton: Princeton University Press, 2003), 56. For an emphasis on understanding the processes through which heterogeneous assemblages are composed and stabilized, see Bruno Latour, *Reassembling the Social: An Introduction to Actor-Network Theory* (Oxford: Clarendon, 2005). G. E. Marcus and E. Saka point out that recent uses of the concept of assemblage are in large part inspired by the work of Deleuze and Guatteri, and in particular their "understanding of states of temporality as emergence, combined with the heterogeneous as a productive property of open systems." Marcus and Saka, "Assemblage," *Theory, Culture and Society* 23, no. 2–3 (2006): 103.

22. U.S. Department of Health and Human Services, *HHS Pandemic Influenza Plan* (Washington, DC, November 2005), 4, https://www.cdc.gov/flu/pandemic-resources/pdf/hhspandemicinfluenzaplan.pdf.

23. Ibid., G-44. Eventually Congress allocated $3.3 billion of this request to the Department of Health and Human Services. U.S. Dept. of Health and Human Services, "Pandemic Planning Update: Report from Secretary Michael O. Leavitt," March 13, 2006, https://www.hsdl.org/?view&did=462040.

24. Anthony S. Fauci, "Testimony to Committee on International Relations, U.S. House of Representative[s]," OLPA website, December 7, 2005, https://olpa.od.nih.gov/hearings/109/session1/testimonies/pandemic5.asp.

25. National Institute for Allergy and Infectious Disease, *Report of the Blue Ribbon Panel on Influenza Research* (Bethesda: NIAID, 2006).

26. Brendan Maher, "Bird Flu Research: The Biosecurity Oversight," *Nature* 485, no. 7399 (2012). The press release announcing the establishment of the Mount Sinai Center for Research on Influenza Pathogenesis stated: "Mount Sinai researchers Adolfo García-Sastre and Peter Palese, in collaboration with Daniel Perez, at University of Maryland, and Ron Fouchier, at Erasmus Medical Center in Rotterdam, will continue to conduct molecular studies to identify influenza virus genes associated with the development of disease, the adaptability of flu viruses in birds and mammals, and the transmission of flu viruses between different hosts." Mount Sinai Hospital, "NIH Establishes Center of Excellence for Influenza Research at Mount Sinai," media release, April 2, 2007, http://www.infectioncontroltoday.com/news/2007/04/nih-establishes-center-of-excellence-for-influenz.aspx.

27. See David Quammen, *Spillover: Animal Infections and the Next Human Pandemic* (New York: W. W. Norton, 2012).

28. Frédéric Keck, *Un Monde Grippé* (Paris: Flammarion, 2010).

29. Laurie Garrett, "The Bioterrorist Next Door," *Foreign Policy*, December 15, 2011.

30. Anthony S. Fauci, Gary J. Nabel, and Francis S. Collins, "A Flu Virus Risk Worth Taking," *Washington Post*, December 30, 2011.

31. Berns et al., "Adaptations of Avian Flu Virus," 154.

32. Kawaoka, "H5N1: Flu Transmission Work."

33. Tom Inglesby, "Sunday Dialogue: Bird Flu Experiments," Letters, *New York Times*, January 28, 2012.

34. "Vigilance Needed," Editorial, *Nature* 493, no. 7433 (2013): 451–2.

35. Fauci, Nabel, and Collins, "A Flu Virus Risk."

36. Simon Wain-Hobson, "H5N1 Viral-Engineering Dangers Will Not Go Away," World View, *Nature* 495, no. 7442 (2013): 411.

37. Berns et al., "Adaptations of Avian Flu Virus."

38. Heidi Ledford, "Call to Censor Flu Studies Draws Fire," News in Focus, *Nature* 481, no. 7379 (2012): 9.

39. Ulrich Beck, *World at Risk* (Cambridge: Polity, 2009).

40. Kathleen M. Vogel, "Biodefense: Considering the Socio-Technical Dimension," in *Biosecurity Interventions: Global Health and Security in Question*, ed. Andrew Lakoff and Stephen J. Collier (New York: Columbia University Press, 2008).

41. Ledford, "Call to Censor Flu Studies."

42. National Research Council, *Biotechnology Research in an Age of Terrorism* (Washington, DC: National Academies Press, 2004).

43. Maher, "Biosecurity Oversight." As the 2007 NSABB framework document stated, "The foundation of oversight of dual use research includes investigator awareness, peer review, and local institutional responsibility." National Science Advisory Board for Biosecurity, *Proposed Framework for the Oversight of Dual Use Life Sciences Research: Strategies for Minimizing the Potential Misuse of Research Information* (Bethesda, MD, 2007). It is worth noting that the system of biosafety classification (BSL-1, BSL-2, BSL-3, and BSL-4) that became a significant topic of debate during the mutant H5N1 controversy also dates from post-Asilomar regulation.

44. NSABB, *Proposed Framework*, 4.

45. Sample, "Bird Flu: Two Mutant Strains."

46. Steinbrunner, quoted in Ledford, "Call to Censor Flu Studies," 9.

47. NSABB, *Proposed Framework*, 10.

48. Ibid., Appendix 4, p. 50.

49. In a critical assessment of US biosecurity policy, Ori Lev and Limor Samimian-Darash note that a "DURC assessment is essentially a biosecurity assessment," but that "the scientific community is not equipped with the knowledge, expertise, and capabilities to conduct a security assessment." Lev and Samimian-Darash, "Biosecurity Policy in the US: A Critical Assessment," *Frontiers in Public Health* 2 (2014): 110.

50. NSABB, *Proposed Framework*.

51. Ibid.

52. J.S.M. Peiris, L.L.M. Poon, and Y. Guan, "Surveillance of Animal Influenza for Pandemic Preparedness," *Science*, March 9, 2012.

53. Peter Palese and Taia T. Wang, "H5N1 Influenza Viruses: Facts, Not Fear," *Proceedings of the National Academy of Sciences* 109, no. 7 (2012): 2211–3.

54. Palese, "Don't Censor Life-Saving Science."

55. Palese and Wang, "H5N1 Influenza Viruses."

56. Laurie Garrett, "Much Ado about What? The H5N1 Story Gets Murkier Every Day," author's blog, March 7, 2012, http://lauriegarrett.com/blog/2012/3/7/much-ado-about-what-the-h5n1-story-gets-murkier-every-day.

57. Declan Butler, "Flu Surveillance Lacking," *Nature* 483, no. 7391 (2012): 520.

58. Casadevall and Shenk, "The H5N1 Moratorium Controversy."

59. Inglesby, "Bird Flu Experiments."

60. Lisa Schnirring, "Debate on H5N1 Death Rate and Missed Cases Continues," CIDRAP News, February 24, 2012.

61. As Laurie Garrett wrote, "In 2002 the NIH research budget for all influenza research was $17 million. Since H5N1 reemerged in 2003 the NIH has spent $1.9 billion, some of it directed to Fouchier, Palese, Kawaoka, and several of the scientists now decrying the NSABB decision. Should [politicians] not cut off that money on the grounds that H5N1 is not dangerous and therefore poses no unique threat to the American people?" Garrett, "Much Ado about What?"

62. Susan Wright, "Sunday Dialogue: Bird Flu Experiments," Letters, *New York Times*, January 28, 2012.

63. W. Ian Lipkin, "Biocontainment in Gain-of-Function Infectious Disease Research," *mBio* 3, no. 5 (2012). According to the Federation of American Scientists, as of 2016 there were only 13 BSL-4 laboratories in operation in the United States. Of these, most were government rather than university-based. See FAS, "BSL-4 Laboratories in the United States," n.d., http://fas.org/programs/bio/research.html.

64. Robert Roos, "Research on Contagious H5N1 viruses: Space suits needed?," CIDRAP News, March 6, 2012.

65. Declan Butler and Heidi Ledford, "US Biosecurity Board Revises Stance on Mutant-Flu Studies," *Nature News*, March 30, 2012.

66. The report of this February 2012 "technical consultation," meeting convened by the WHO, echoed the flu researchers' articulation of potential benefits: "If disseminated to the public health and scientific community, the results would offer significant benefits to global health. Specifically, the findings could be used to improve the sensitivity of public health surveillance, facilitate the early detection of potentially pandemic H5N1 strains, and might aid the development of vaccines and the assessment of the potential value of other countermeasures." WHO, *Report on Technical Consultation on H5N1 Research Issues* (Geneva: WHO, February 16–17, 2012), http://www.who.int/influenza/human_animal_interface/mtg_report_h5n1.pdf.

67. Butler and Ledford, "US Biosecurity Board Revises Stance."

68. A minority report, signed by six board members, pronounced: "While there may be benefits to the dissemination of the mutation data in the Fouchier manuscript and global cooperation is essential for pandemic influenza preparedness, it is unlikely that the benefits will be realized in the near-term." Berns et al., "Adaptations of Avian Flu Virus."

69. Butler, "Flu Surveillance Lacking"; Jon Cohen, "A Flawed Flu Papers Process?," *Science*, April 13, 2012.

70. Ron A. M. Fouchier et al., "Transmission Studies Resume for Avian Flu," *Nature* 493, no. 7434 (2013): 609.

71. Jocelyn Kaiser and David Malakoff, "U.S. Halts Funding for New Risky Virus Studies, Calls for Voluntary Moratorium," *Science*, October 17, 2014.

72. An increasingly prominent group of scientists had been challenging the claims made by the flu researchers that their work did not present biosafety concerns. Harvard epidemiologist Marc Lipsitch, for example, used data on biosafety accidents in Federal research labs to estimate the risk posed by an escape of a modified strain of H5N1. Lipsitch, "Anthrax? That's Not the Real Worry," *New York Times*, June 29, 2014.

73. Jocelyn Kaiser, "Academy Meeting on Risky Virus Studies Struggles to Find Common Ground," *Science*, December 17, 2014.

74. Gaymon Bennett criticizes the use of "older regimes of calculation and control" to manage the risks and uncertainties of transmission research: "This has taken the form of trying to institute regimes of prior review and post hoc redaction—technologies of prevention that rationalize decision making." The problem, he continues, is "potential dangers can rarely be calculated and are never fully controlled." Bennett, "The Malicious and the Uncertain," in *Modes of Uncertainty: Anthropological Cases*, ed. Paul Rabinow and Limor Samimian-Darash (Chicago: University of Chicago Press, 2015), 142.

75. As Fouchier said, in anticipation of the release of the report: "I have always said that the quantitative risk-benefit analysis is a dead-end street. Even if they could be quantified, the weighing of risks and benefits will be a personal (subjective) issue." Sara Reardon, "US Plan to Assess Risky Disease Research Shapes Up," *Nature News*, October 1, 2015.

CHAPTER 6

1. Thomas Nierle and Bruno Jochum, "Ebola: the failures of the international outbreak response," Editorial, *Le Temps*, August 29, 2014.

2. Larry Elliott, "Ebola Crisis: Global Response Has 'Failed Miserably,' Says World Bank Chief," *Guardian*, October 9, 2014.

3. Lawrence O. Gostin and Eric A. Friedman, "Ebola: A Crisis in Global Health Leadership," *The Lancet* 384, no. 9951 (2014): 1323–5.

4. The editorial continued: "This massive deployment of the US military and the combined resources of the UN is a damning indictment of the World Health Organization (WHO), the UN's health arm charged with tackling outbreaks of potential international concern." "First Response, Revisited," Editorial, *Nature* 513, no. 7519 (2014): 459.

5. "The WHO's legislative body, the World Health Assembly, has consistently voted to downgrade the institution's capacity to deal with outbreaks and infectious disease in favor of increasing commitment to noncommunicable disease programs such as cancer and heart disease." Laurie Garrett, "Epic Failures Feeding Ebola Crisis," interview by Danielle Renwick, Council on Foreign Relations, September 18, 2014, http://www.cfr.org/public-health-threats-and-pandemics/epic-failures-feeding-ebola-crisis/p33465.

6. Maria Cheng and Adam Geller, "Report Finds Global Agency Missed Chance to Halt Ebola as Obama Names Leader of US Response," Associated Press, August 17, 2014.

7. Kevin Sack, Sheri Fink, Pam Belluck, and Adam Nossiter, "How Ebola Roared Back," *New York Times*, December 29, 2014.

8. Richard Preston, "Crisis in the Hot Zone," *New Yorker*, October 26, 1992. For Lederberg's role in alerting Preston to the story, see Priscilla Wald, *Contagion: Cultures, Carriers, and the Outbreak Narrative* (Durham: Duke University Press, 2008), 31.

9. Institute of Medicine, *Emerging Infections: Microbial Threats to Health*, ed. Joshua Lederberg, Robert E. Shope, and Stanley C. Oaks Jr. (Washington, DC: National Academies Press, 1992).

10. Laurie Garrett, "A Medical War Game," *Newsday*, January 23, 1990. The narrative here is based on Garrett's account.

11. Legters had served as a U.S. Army Special Forces doctor in Vietnam, where he treated the first reported case of drug-resistant malaria in 1964. Two years later he founded the Field Epidemiological Survey Team to track this strain of malaria in the midst of the war. See Norma Mohr, *Malaria: Evolution of a Killer* (Seattle: Serif and Pixel, 2001).

12. Llewellyn J. Legters, Linda H. Brink, and Ernest T. Takafuji, "Are We Prepared for a Viral Epidemic Emergency?," in *Emerging Viruses*, ed. Stephen S. Morse (New York: Oxford University Press, 1993), 277.

13. Ibid., 279.

14. Ibid., 280.

15. The analysis of this exercise first appeared as part of the introduction to a special issue of *Limn* magazine, titled "Ebola's Ecologies" (2015) and was coauthored with Stephen J. Collier and Christopher Kelty. See http://limn.it/introduction-ebolas-ecologies.

16. "Although WHO has considerable numbers of policies and procedures in place, notably the International Health Regulations (2005) and the Emergency Response Framework, these were activated late." WHO, *Report of the Ebola Interim Assessment Panel* (Geneva, May 8, 2015).

17. MSF's 2015 report, *Pushed to the Limit and Beyond*, described the initial response: "The team immediately set up the priority activities for an Ebola outbreak: caring for the sick in Gueckedou hospital, training local health staff on how to protect themselves, raising awareness of the virus in the community, conducting safe burials, and running ambulances."

18. Peter Redfield, "Medical Vulnerability, or Where There Is No Kit," *Limn* 5 (2015). limn.it/medical-vulnerability-or-where-there-is-no-kit.

19. Redfield remarks: "Like an emergency physician, MSF primarily seeks to stabilize patients, deferring responsibility for their future well-being to existing authorities"—an approach that "presumes the existence of a political, as well as technical health infrastructure." Ibid.

20. MSF, *Pushed to the Limit*, 6.

21. A "Public Health Emergency of International Concern" is defined in the 2005 IHR as an "extraordinary event which is determined . . . (i) to constitute a public health risk to other States through the international spread of disease and (ii) to potentially require a coordinated international response."

22. International Development Committee, "Oral Evidence: Responses to the Ebola Crisis: Follow-Up, HC 338," House of Commons, November 25, 2015 (testimony of Bruce Aylward). For a cogent analysis of IHR as a system of regulation, see Sven Opitz, "Regulating Epidemic Space: The *Nomos* of Global Circulation," *Journal of International Relations and Development* 19, no. 2 (201): 263–84.

23. IHR (2005) states: "If WHO . . . declares that a public health emergency of international concern is occurring, it may offer. . . . further assistance to the State Party, including an assessment of the severity of the international risk and the adequacy of control measures. Such collaboration may include the offer to mobilize international assistance in order to support the national authorities in conducting and coordinating on-site assessments." WHO, *International Health Regulations (2005)*, 2nd ed. (Geneva, WHO, 2008), 15. For an analysis of how this coordinative rather than operational role impeded WHO response to the 2014 epidemic, see Adam Kamradt-Scott, "WHO's to Blame? The World Health Organization and the 2014 Ebola Outbreak in West Africa," *Third World Quarterly* 37, no. 3 (2016): 401–18.

24. Saliou Samb, "WHO Says Guinea Outbreak Small as MSF Slams International Response," Reuters, April 1, 2014.

25. Ibid.

26. WHO, "Ebola Outbreak Guinea Presser," transcript, April 8, 2014.

27. WHO, African Region, "SITREP 2 Ebola Virus Disease, West Africa," April 17, 2014.

28. Deployments included fifty-two WHO staff members and twenty-two experts from among its global outbreak and response network (GOARN) partners. Ibid.

29. WHO, *ERF: Emergency Response Framework* (Geneva: WHO, 2013), 19.

30. As WHO noted in its description of the response framework, the first decade of the twenty-first century had seen "an average of more than 700 natural and technological emergencies occurred globally every year, affecting approximately 270 million people and causing over 130,000 deaths annually." Ibid., 9.

31. MSF, "'We Cannot Say That the Outbreak Is Over,'" media release, May 2, 2014, http://reliefweb.int/report/guinea/we-cannot-say-ebola-outbreak-over; WHO, "Epidemiological Update: Outbreak of Ebola Virus Disease in West Africa," European Centre for Disease Prevention and Control website, May 14, 2014.

32. Brad Wieners and Makiko Kitamura, "Ebola: Doctors Without Borders Shows How to Manage a Plague," *Businessweek*, November 13, 2014.

33. IDC, "Oral Evidence: Responses to the Ebola Crisis: Follow-Up, HC 338," House of Commons, November 25, 2015 (testimony of David Nabarro).

34. MSF later reported, "After a short period of raised hopes in May as cases appeared to be declining in Guinea and Liberia, the hidden outbreak in Sierra Leone mushroomed and reignited the outbreak for its neighbors." MSF, *Pushed to the Limit*, 7.

35. Kashmira Gander, "Ebola Outbreak: Virus Is 'Totally Out of Control' Warns Doctors Without Borders Medic," *Independent*, June 20, 2014; MSF, *Pushed to the Limit*, 7.

36. MSF, *Pushed to the Limit*, 7. David Nabarro later reflected on why MSF was not listened to more seriously: "I believe that sometimes the open mind is not maintained when information comes from sources that tend to be the providers of alert on a lot of occasions. You get a kind of discounting capacity in your head." IDC, "Oral Evidence."

37. At this point WHO increased its Emergency Response Framework Grade to Level 3.

38. WHO, "WHO Virtual Press Conference following the Meeting of the International Health Regulations Emergency Committee regarding the 2014 Ebola Outbreak in West Africa," transcript, August 8, 2014.

39. Quoted in MSF, *Pushed to the Limit*, 11.

40. MSF, "Global Bio-Disaster Response Urgently Needed in Ebola Fight," September 2, 2014.

41. WHO, "WHO Virtual Press Conference."

42. Another reason WHO may have been hesitant to immediately declare a PHEIC is that in 2009, the agency was accused of rashly declaring an emergency very soon after the appearance of H1N1 (swine flu).

43. According to a memo from Sylvie Briand and Keiji Fukuda from June 10, 2014, declaring an emergency or convening an emergency committee "could be

seen as a hostile act" by national governments. Maria Cheng and Raphael Satter, "Emails Show the World Health Organization Intentionally Delayed Calling Ebola a Public Health Emergency," Associated Press, March 20, 2015.

44. Maria Cheng and Adam Geller, "Report Finds Global Agency Missed Chance to Halt Ebola as Obama Names Leader of US Response," Associated Press, August 17, 2014.

45. Charles E. Rosenberg, "What Is an Epidemic? AIDS in Historical Perspective," *Daedalus* 118, no. 2 (1989): 1–17.

46. Quoted in Laurie Garrett, "Ebola's Lessons: How the WHO Mishandled the Crisis," *Foreign Affairs*, August 18, 2015.

47. International Development Committee, "Oral Evidence" (testimony by David Nabarro).

48. WHO Director-General, *Implementation of the International Health Regulations: Report of the Review Committee on the Role of the International Health Regulations (2005) in the Ebola Outbreak and Response*, 69th World Health Assembly, WHO A69/21 (May 13, 2016), 6.

49. Cholera Inquiry Commission, *Report to the Queen's Most Excellent Majesty*, part 1 (1854), http://www.genuki.bpears.org.uk/NBL/Cholera/Pt1.html.

50. United Nations, *Protecting Humanity from Future Health Crises: Report of the High-level Panel on the Global Response to Health Crises* (Geneva, January 25, 2016), 21.

51. Niklas Luhmann, *Risk: A Sociological Theory* (Berlin: Walter de Gruyter, 1993).

52. Jeremy Farrar, "Preparing the WHO for the Next Global Health Crisis," *Wall Street Journal*, May 24, 2016.

53. MSF "couldn't be everywhere at once, nor should it be our role to single-handedly respond." *Pushed to the Limit*, 9. As Peter Redfield (2015) wrote of the situation in mid-2014, "Who, after all, was in charge? This core concern of security thinking grew increasingly unclear in the absence of effective national health care."

54. Suerie Moon et al., "Will Ebola Change the Game? Ten Essential Reforms before the Next Pandemic: The Report of the Harvard-LSHTM Independent Panel on the Global Response to Ebola," *The Lancet* 386, no. 10009 (2015): 2205.

55. GHRF Commission (Commission on a Global Health Risk Framework for the Future), *The Neglected Dimension of Global Security: A Framework to Counter Infectious Disease Crises* (Washington, DC: National Academy of Medicine, 2016).

56. IDC, "Oral Evidence," (testimony by Aylward).

57. Quoted in MSF, *Pushed to the Limit*, 11.

58. Margaret Chan, "WHO Director-General Addresses the Review Committee of the International Health Regulations Focused on the Ebola Response" (opening remarks at the Review Committee, Geneva, August 24, 2015), http:/www.who.int/dg/speeches/2015/review-committee-ihr-ebola/en.

59. WHO, *Report of the Ebola Interim Assessment Panel.*

60. International Development Committee, "Oral Evidence" (testimony by David Nabarro).

EPILOGUE

1. WHO. Report by the Secretariat. "Ensuring WHO's capacity to prepare for and respond to future large-scale and sustained outbreaks and emergencies." EB136/49 (Geneva: World Health Organization, January 9, 2015).

2. Lawrence O. Gostin, Mary C. DeBartolo, and Eric A. Friedman. "The International Health Regulations 10 Years On: The Governing Framework for Global Health Security." *The Lancet* 386 no. 10009 (2015): 2225.

3. WHO. "Progress Report on the Development of the WHO Health Emergencies Program" (Geneva: World Health Organization, March 30, 2016).

4. WHO. Report by the Secretariat. "Ensuring WHO's capacity to prepare for and respond to future large-scale and sustained outbreaks and emergencies."

5. WHO. "WHO Announces Head of New Health Emergencies Programme" (Geneva: World Health Organization, June 28, 2016).

6. Helen Branswell, "The WHO Has Stumbled in Its Response to Emergencies. Can This Man Get the Next One Right?" *Stat News.* November 15, 2016, https://www.statnews.com/2016/11/15/who-health-emergencies-peter-salama.

7. "The Zika virus public health emergency: 6 months on," *The Lancet* vol. 388, July 30, 2016, p. 449.

8. Bruce Aylward, quoted in "The Zika Virus Public Health Emergency: 6 Months On," *The Lancet* 388 no. 10043 (2016): 449.

9. WHO PIP Review Group transcript, November 22, 2016, http://who.int /mediacentre/multimedia/Zika-virus-update-presser-22NOV2016.pdf?ua=1.

10. "There is a huge variability" in the incidence of complications from Zika, pointed out David Heymann, asking: "Is that simply because the virus has gone through the population at a different time, or is it really because there are other factors at play that make one part of the world more likely to result in complications than another?" WHO RUSH Zika 4th Emergency Committee Presser, September 2, 2016, http://www.who.int/mediacentre/ec-transcript-1-september-2016.pdf.

11. WHO PIP Review Group transcript.

12. Ibid.

13. Donald G. McNeil, Jr., "'Zika Is No Longer a Global Emergency,' W.H.O. Says," *New York Times*, November 19, 2016.

14. "The Zika Virus Public Health Emergency: 6 Months On," 449.

15. Quoted in McNeil, "Zika Is No Longer a Global Emergency."

16. The bill provided a total of $1.1 billion in supplemental emergency funding to combat Zika. The support for NIAID was for "research on the virology, natural history, and pathogenesis of the Zika virus infection and preclinical and clinical development of vaccines and other medical countermeasures for the Zika virus and other vector-borne diseases, domestically and internationally." American Society for Microbiology, "September 29, 2016—Congress Passes Short-Term Continuing Resolution and Funds Zika Response," https://www.asm.org /index.php/cvs-2017-program/137-policy/documents/statements-and-testimony /94609-zika-cr-9-29-16.

17. As one specialist in emerging viruses reported, "A lot of people said that diseases like dengue have been a problem for years, and perhaps the money should be more equally allocated." Jessica Hamzelou, "Zika Is No Longer an Emergency—It's Worse Than That, Says WHO," *New Scientist*, November 22, 2016, https://www.newscientist.com/article/2113718-zika-is-no-longer-an-emergency-its-worse-than-that-says-who.

18. See Chapter 2.

Bibliography

Abeysinghe, Sudeepa. "Vaccine Narratives and Public Health: Investigating Criticisms of H1N1 Pandemic Vaccination." *PLoS Currents* 7 (February 25, 2015).

Abeysinghe, Sudeepa. "When the Spread of Disease Becomes a Global Event: The Classification of Pandemics." *Social Studies of Science* 43, no. 6 (2013): 905–26.

Adams, Vincanne, Michelle Murphy, and Adele E. Clarke. "Anticipation: Technoscience, Life, Affect, Temporality." *Subjectivity*, no. 28 (2009): 246–65.

Agamben, Giorgio. *State of Exception*. Chicago: University of Chicago, 2005.

Anderson, Ben. "Preemption, Precaution, Preparedness: Anticipatory Action and Future Geographies." *Progress in Human Geography* 34, no. 6 (2010): 777–98.

Anderson, Warwick. "Natural Histories of Infectious Disease: Ecological Vision in Twentieth Century Bioscience." *Osiris*, 2nd ser., 19 (2004): 39–61.

Ashraf, Haroon. "David Heymann—WHO's Public Health Guru." *The Lancet Infectious Diseases* 4, no. 12 (2004): 785–8.

Barrett, Ronald. "Dark Winter and the Spring of 1972: Deflecting the Social Lessons of Smallpox." *Medical Anthropology* 25, no. 2 (2006): 171–91.

Bashford, Alison. "Global Biopolitics and the History of World Health." *History of the Human Sciences* 19, no. 1 (2006): 67–88.

Beck, Ulrich. "Ecological Questions in a Framework of Manufactured Uncertainties." In *The New Social Theory Reader: Contemporary Debates*, edited by Steven Seidman and Jeffrey C. Alexander, 267–275. London and New York: Routledge: 2001.

Beck, Ulrich. "The Terrorist Threat: World Risk Society Revisited." *Theory, Culture and Society* 19, no. 4 (2002): 39–55.

Beck, Ulrich. *World at Risk.* Cambridge: Polity, 2009.

Bennett, Gaymon. "The Malicious and the Uncertain." In *Modes of Uncertainty: Anthropological Cases*, edited by Paul Rabinow and Limor Samimian-Darash, 123–44. Chicago: University of Chicago Press, 2015.

Berns, Kenneth I., Arturo Casadevall, Murray L. Cohen, Susan A. Ehrlich, Lynn W. Enquist, J. Patrick Fitch, David R. Franz, Claire M. Fraser-Liggett, Christine M. Grant, Michael J. Imperiale, et al. "Adaptations of Avian Flu Virus Are a Cause for Concern." *Science* 482 no. 7384 (2012): 660–1.

Biehl, João. "Pharmaceutical Governance." In *Global Pharmaceuticals: Ethics, Markets, Practices*, edited by Adriana Petryna, Andrew Lakoff, and Arthur Kleinman, 206–39. Durham: Duke University Press, 2006.

Biehl, João, and Adriana Petryna. "Critical Global Health." In *When People Come First: Critical Studies in Global Health*, edited by João Biehl and Adriana Petryna, 1–20. Princeton: Princeton University Press, 2015.

Birn, Anne-Emanuelle. "Gates' Grandest Challenge: Transcending Technology as Public Health Ideology." *The Lancet* 366, no. 9484 (2005): 514–19.

Bloomfield, Lincoln P., and Barton Whaley. "The Political-Military Exercise: A Progress Report." *Orbis* 8 (1965): 854–70.

Boltanski, Luc, and Laurent Thevenot. "The Sociology of Critical Capacity." *European Journal of Social Theory* 2, no. 3 (1999): 359–77.

Brown, Theodore M., Marcos Cueto, and Elizabeth Fee. "The World Health Organization and the Transition from 'International' to 'Global' Health." *American Journal of Public Health* 96, no. 1 (2006): 62–72.

Butler, Declan. "Flu Experts Rebut Conflict Claims." *Nature News*, June 8, 2010, 672–3.

Butler, Declan. "Flu Surveillance Lacking." *Nature* 483, no. 7391 (2012): 520–2.

Butler, Declan, and Heidi Ledford. "US Biosecurity Board Revises Stance on Mutant-Flu Studies." *Nature News*, March 30, 2012. doi:10.1038/nature.2012 .10369.http://www.nature.com/news/us-biosecurity-board-revises-stance-on-mutant-flu-studies-1.10369

Caduff, Carlo. *The Pandemic Perhaps: Dramatic Events in a Public Culture of Danger.* Berkeley: University of California Press, 2015.

Caduff, Carlo. "Pandemic Prophecy, or How to Have Faith in Reason." *Current Anthropology* 55, no. 3 (2014): 296–315.

Caduff, Carlo. "Public Prophylaxis: Pandemic Influenza, Pharmaceutical Prevention and Participatory Governance." *BioSocieties* 5, no. 2 (2010): 199–218.

Calain, Philippe. "From the Field Side of the Binoculars: A Different View on Global Public Health Surveillance." *Health Policy and Planning* 22, no. 1 (2007): 13–20.

Calhoun, Craig. "A World of Emergencies: Fear, Intervention, and the Limits of Cosmopolitan Order." *Canadian Review of Sociology and Anthropology* 41, no. 4 (2004): 373–95.

Callon, Michel, Pierre Lascoumes, and Yannick Barthe. *Acting in an Uncertain World: An Essay on Technical Democracy.* Cambridge, MA: MIT Press, 2009.

Casadevall, Arturo, and Thomas Shenk. "The H5N1 Moratorium Controversy and Debate." *mBio* 3, no. 5 (2012).

Chateauraynaud, Francis and Didier Torny. "Mobiliser autour d'un risque: Des lanceurs aux porteurs d'alerte." In *Risques et crises alimentaires,* edited by Cécile Lahellec, 329–39. Paris: Lavoisier, 2005.

Cholera Inquiry Commission, *Report to the Queen's Most Excellent Majesty,* part 1 (1854). http://www.genuki.bpears.org.uk/NBL/Cholera/Pt1.html.

Clarke, Lee. *Worst Cases: Terror and Catastrophe in the Popular Imagination.* Chicago: University of Chicago Press, 2005.

Cohen, Deborah, and Philip Carter. "WHO and the Pandemic Flu 'Conspiracies.'" *BMJ: British Medical Journal* 340, no. c2912 (2010): 1274–9.

Cohen, Hillel, Robert Gould, and Victor Sidel. "Bioterrorism Initiatives: Public Health in Reverse?" *American Journal of Public Health* 89, no. 11 (1999): 1629–31.

Cohen, Jon. "A Flawed Flu Papers Process?" *Science,* April 13, 2012. http://www.sciencemag.org/news/2012/04/flawed-flu-papers-process.

Coleman, William. *Death Is a Social Disease: Public Health and Political Economy in Early Industrial France.* Madison: University of Wisconsin Press, 1982.

Collier, Stephen J., and Andrew Lakoff. "Distributed Preparedness: The Spatial Logic of Domestic Security in the United States." *Environment and Planning D: Society and Space* 26, no. 1 (2008): 7–28.

Collier, Stephen J., and Andrew Lakoff. "The Problem of Securing Health." In Lakoff and Collier, *Biosecurity Interventions,* 7–32.

Collier, Stephen J., and Andrew Lakoff. "Vital Systems Security: Reflexive Biopolitics and the Government of Emergency." *Theory, Culture and Soc* 32, no. 2 (2015): 19–51.

Collier, Stephen J., and Aihwa Ong. "Global Assemblages, Anthropological Problems." In *Global Assemblages: Technology, Politics and Ethics as Anthropological Problems,* edited by Aihwa Ong and Stephen J. Collier, Malden, MA: Blackwell, 2005.

Commission on a Global Health Risk Framework for the Future (GHRF Commission). *The Neglected Dimension of Global Security: A Framewor Counter Infectious Disease Crises.* Washington, DC: National Academy Medicine, 2016.

Cooper, Melinda. "Pre-empting Emergence: The Biological Turn in the War on Terror." *Theory, Culture and Society* 23, no. 4 (2006): 113–35.

Dauber, Michelle Landis. *The Sympathetic State: Disaster Relief and the Origins of the American Welfare State.* Chicago: University of Chicago Press, 2013.

Davies, Sara E., Adam Kamradt-Scott, and Simon Rushton. *Disease Diplomacy: International Norms and Global Health Security.* Baltimore: Johns Hopkins University Press, 2015.

Desrosières, Alain. "How to Make Things Which Hold Together: Social Science, Statistics and the State." In *Discourses on Society*, edited by Peter Wagner, Björn Wittrock, Richard P. Whitley, 195–218. Dordrecht: Kluwer, 2007.

Douglas, Mary, and Aaron Wildavsky. *Risk and Culture.* Berkeley: University of California Press, 1983.

Dreyfus, Hubert, and Paul Rabinow. *Michel Foucault: Beyond Structuralism and Hermeneutics.* Chicago: University of Chicago Press, 1982.

Elbe, Stefan. *Security and Global Health: Toward the Medicalization of Insecurity.* Cambridge: Polity Press, 2010.

Enserink, Martin. "Scientists Brace for Media Storm around Controversial Flu Studies." *Science*, November 23, 2011. http://www.sciencemag.org /news/2011/11/scientists-brace-media-storm-around-controversial-flu -studies.

Enserink, Martin, and David Malakoff. "Will Flu Papers Lead to New Research Oversight?" *Science*, January 6, 2012.

Epstein, Steven. *Impure Science: AIDS, Activism, and the Politics of Knowledge.* Berkeley: University of California Press, 1996.

Ewald, François. "Insurance and Risk." In *The Foucault Effect: Studies in Governmentality*, edited by Graham Burchell, Colin Gordon, and Peter Miller, 197–210. Chicago: University of Chicago Press, 1991.

Ewald, François. "The Return of Descartes' Malicious Demon: An Outline of a Philosophy of Precaution." In *Embracing Risk: The Changing Culture of Insurance and Responsibility*, edited by Tom Baker and Jonathan Simon, 273–302. Chicago: University of Chicago Press, 2002.

Eyler, John M. *Victorian Social Medicine: The Ideas and Methods of William Farr.* Baltimore: Johns Hopkins University Press, 1979.

Farmer, Paul. *Infections and Inequalities: The Modern Plagues.* Berkeley: University of California Press, 2001.

Fassin, Didier. "Humanitarianism as a Politics of Life." *Public Culture* 19, no. 3 (2007): 499–520.

Fassin, Didier. *Humanitarian Reason: A Moral History of the Present.* Berkeley: University of California Press, 2012.

Fearnley, Lyle. "Epidemic Intelligence: Langmuir and the Birth of Disease Surveillance." *Behemoth: A Journal on Civilisation* 3, no. 3 (2010): 37–56.

Fearnley, Lyle. "Redesigning Syndromic Surveillance for Biosecurity." In Lakoff and Collier, *Biosecurity Interventions*, 61–88.

Fee, Elizabeth, and Dorothy Porter. "Public Health, Preventive Medicine and Professionalization: England and America in the Nineteenth Century." In *Medicine in Society: Historical Essays*, edited by Andrew Wear, 249–75. Cambridge: Cambridge University Press, 1992.

Fidler, David P. "Influenza Virus Samples, International Law, and Global Health Diplomacy." *Emerging Infectious Diseases* 14, no. 1 (2008): 88–94.

Fidler, David P. "From International Sanitary Conventions to Global Health Security: The New International Health Regulations." *Chinese Journal of International Law* 4, no. 2 (2005): 325–92.

Fidler, David P. "Negotiating Equitable Access: Global Health Diplomacy and the Controversies surrounding Avian Influenza H5N1 and Pandemic Influenza H1N1." *PLOS Medicine* (May 4, 2010). http://dx.doi.org/10.1371/journal.pmed.1000247.

Fidler, David P., and Lawrence O. Gostin. "The WHO Pandemic Influenza Preparedness Framework: A Milestone in Global Governance for Health." *Journal of the American Medical Association* 306, no. 2 (2011): 200–1.

Fineberg, Harvey V., and Mary Elizabeth Wilson. "Epidemic Science in Real Time." *Science* 324 no. 5930 (2009): 987.

Flemming, Arthur S. "The Impact of Disasters on Readiness for War." *Annals of the American Academy of Political and Social Science* 309, no. 1 (1957): 65–70.

Foucault, Michel. *The Birth of Biopolitics: Lectures at the Collège de France, 1978–1979*, edited by Michel Sennelart, translated by Graham Burchell. Basingstoke, UK: Palgrave Macmillan, 1979.

Foucault, Michel. *Security, Territory, Population: Lectures at the Collège de France, 1977–1978*, edited by Arnold I. Davidson, translated by Graham Burchell. Basingstoke, UK: Palgrave Macmillan, 2007.

Foucault, Michel. *Society Must Be Defended: Lectures at the Collège de France, 1975–1976*, edited by Mauro Bertani and Alessandro Fontana, translated by David Macey. New York: Picador, 2003.

Fouchier, Ron A. M., Adolfo García-Sastre, Yoshihiro Kawaoka, Wendy S. Barclay, Nicole M. Bouvier, Ian H. Brown, Ilaria Capua, Hualan Chen, Richard W. Compans, Robert B. Couch, et al. "Transmission Studies Resume for Avian Flu." *Nature* 493, no. 7434 (2013): 609.

Fox, Renée. "Medical Humanitarianism and Human Rights: Reflections on Doctors Without Borders and Doctors of the World." *Social Science and Medicine* 41, no. 12 (1995): 1607–16.

Fumento, Michael. "The Threat of an Avian Flu Pandemic Is Over-Hyped." *Virtual Mentor* 8, no. 4 (2006): 265–70.

Galison, Peter. "War against the Center." *Grey Room*, no. 4 (2001): 6–33.

Garrett, Laurie. "The Bioterrorist Next Door." *Foreign Policy*, December 15, 2011.

Garrett, Laurie. "Ebola's Lessons: How the WHO Mishandled the Crisis." *Foreign Affairs*, August 18, 2015. https://www.foreignaffairs.com/articles /west-africa/2015-08-18/ebolas-lessons.

Garrett, Laurie. "The Next Pandemic?" *Foreign Affairs*, July/August 2005. https://www.foreignaffairs.com/articles/2005-07-01/next-pandemic.

Garrett, Laurie. *The Coming Plague: Newly Emerging Diseases in a World out of Balance*. New York: Farrar, Straus and Giroux, 1994.

Ghamari-Tabrizi, Sharon. *The Worlds of Herman Kahn: The Intuitive Arts of Thermonuclear War*. Cambridge, MA: Harvard University Press, 2005.

Giddens, Anthony. *Runaway World: How Globalization Is Reshaping Our Lives*. London: Profile, 2002.

Gilman, Nils. *Mandarins of the Future: Modernization Theory in Cold War America*. Baltimore: Johns Hopkins University Press, 2003.

Goldhamer, Herbert, and Hans Speier. "Some Observations on Political Gaming." *World Politics* 12, no. 1 (1959): 71–83.

Gostin, Lawrence O., and Eric A. Friedman. "Ebola: A Crisis in Global Health Leadership." *The Lancet* 384, no. 9951 (2014): 1323–5.

Gostin, Lawrence O., Mary C. DeBartolo, and Eric A. Friedman. "The International Health Regulations 10 Years On: The Governing Framework for Global Health Security." *The Lancet* 2015; 386: 2222–6.

Grossman, Andrew. *Neither Dead nor Red: Civil Defense and American Political Development during the Early Cold War*. New York: Routledge, 2001.

Hacking, Ian. "Biopower and the Avalanche of Printed Numbers." *Humanities in Society* 5 (1982): 279–95.

Hacking, Ian. *Historical Ontology*. Cambridge, MA: Harvard University Press, 2003.

Hacking, Ian. *The Taming of Chance*. Cambridge: Cambridge University Press, 1990.

Hamzelou, Jessica. "Zika Is No Longer an Emergency—It's Worse Than That, Says WHO." *New Scientist*, November 22, 2016. https://www.newscientist.com /article/2113718-zika-is-no-longer-an-emergency-its-worse-than-that-says-who.

Henderson, D. A. *Smallpox: The Death of a Disease*. New York: Prometheus, 2009.

Henderson, D. A. "Surveillance Systems and Intergovernmental Cooperation." In Morse, *Emerging Viruses*, 283–9.

Heymann, David L. "The International Response to the Outbreak of SARS in 2003." *Philosophical Transactions of the Royal Society B* 359, no. 1447 (2004): 1127–9.

Heymann, David L., Abraham Hodgson, Amadou Alpha Sall, David O. Freed-
man, J. Erin Staples, Fernando Althabe, Kalpana Baruah, Ghazala Mahmud,
Nyoman Kandun, Pedro F. C. Vasconcelos, et al. "Zika Virus and Microcephaly: Why Is this Situation a PHEIC?" *The Lancet* 384, no. 10020 (2016):
719–21.

Hooker, Claire. "Drawing the Lines: Danger and Risk in the Age of SARS." In
Medicine at the Border: Disease, Globalization, and Security, 1850–Present,
edited by Alison Bashford, 179–95. Basingstoke, UK: Palgrave MacMillan,
2007.

Hughes, Thomas. *Rescuing Prometheus*. New York: Pantheon, 1998.

Hurlbut, J. Benjamin. "Remembering the Future: Science, Law and the Legacy
of Asilomar." In *Dreamscapes of Modernity: Sociotechnical Imaginaries and
the Fabrication of Power*, edited by Sheila Jasanoff and Sang-Hyun Kim,
126–51. Chicago: University of Chicago Press, 2015.

Institute of Medicine. *Emerging Infections: Microbial Threats to Health in the
United States*, edited by Joshua Lederberg, Robert E. Shope, and Stanley C.
Oaks Jr. Washington, DC: National Academy Press, 1992.

"International Health Regulations: The Challenges Ahead." *The Lancet*, 369,
no. 9575 (2007): 1763.

Jasanoff, Sheila. *Designs on Nature: Science and Democracy in Europe and the
United States*. Princeton: Princeton University Press, 2005.

Jonas, Hans. *The Imperative of Responsibility: In Search of an Ethics for the
Technological Age*. Chicago: University of Chicago Press, 1985.

Jordan, Nehemiah. *U.S. Civil Defense before 1950: The Roots of Public Law 920*.
Study S-212. Washington, DC: Economic and Political Studies Division,
Institute for Defense Analyses, May 1966.

Kahn, Herman. *Thinking about the Unthinkable*. New York: Horizon,
1962.

Kahneman, Daniel, and Amos Tversky. "Prospect Theory: An Analysis of
Decision under Risk." *Econometrica* 47, no. 2 (1979): 263–92.

Kaiser, Jocelyn. "Academy Meeting on Risky Virus Studies Struggles to Find
Common Ground." *Science*, December 17, 2014.

Kaiser, Jocelyn, and David Malakoff. "U.S. Halts Funding for New Risky Virus
Studies, Calls for Voluntary Moratorium." *Science*, October 17, 2014.

Kamradt-Scott, Adam. "WHO's to Blame? The World Health Organization and
the 2014 Ebola Outbreak in West Africa." *Third World Quarterly* 37, no. 3
(2016): 401–18.

Kawaoka, Yoshihiro. "H5N1: Flu Transmission Work Is Urgent." Comment.
Nature 482, no. 7384 (2012): 155.

Keck, Frédéric. "Expertise et choix politique: reflexions a partir de la grippe
aviaire: entretien avec Frédéric Keck." Interview by Olivier Mongin and
Marc-Olivier Padis. *Esprit* 3 (March/April 2011): 168–77.

Keck, Frédéric. *Un Monde Grippé*. Paris: Flammarion, 2010.

King, Nicholas. "Security, Disease, Commerce: Ideologies of Postcolonial Global Health." *Social Studies of Science* 32, no. 5–6 (2002): 763–89.

Knowles, Scott Gabriel. *The Disaster Experts: Mastering Risk in Modern America*. Philadelphia: University of Pennsylvania Press, 2011.

Koch, Erin. "Disease as a Security Threat: Critical Reflections on the Global TB Emergency." In Lakoff and Collier, *Biosecurity Interventions*, 121–46.

Kupperman, Robert. "Vulnerable America." In *Nuclear Arms: Ethics, Strategy, Politics*, edited by James Woolsey, 570–80. San Francisco: Institute for Contemporary Studies Press, 1983.

Kupperman, Robert H., Richard H. Wilcox, and Harvey Smith. "Crisis Management: Some Opportunities," *Science*, February 7, 1975, 404–10.

Lachenal, Guillaume. "Lessons in Medical Nihilism: Virus Hunters, Neoliberalism and the AIDS Crisis in Cameroon." In *Para-States and Medical Science: Making African Global Health*, edited by Paul Wenzel Geissler, 103–41. Durham: Duke University Press, 2015.

Lakoff, Andrew, Stephen J. Collier, and Christopher Kelty. "Introduction: Ebola's Ecologies." *Limn* 5 (2015). http://limn.it/introduction-ebolas-ecologies.

Lakoff, Andrew. "The Indicator Species: Tracking Ecosystem Collapse in Arid California." *Public Culture* 28, no. 2 (2016): 237–59.

Lakoff, Andrew, and Stephen J. Collier, eds. *Biosecurity Interventions: Global Health and Security in Question*. New York: Columbia University Press, 2008.

Lakoff, Andrew, and Eric Klinenberg. "Of Risk and Pork: Urban Security and the Politics of Objectivity." *Theory and Society* 39, no. 5 (2010): 503–25.

Lam, Clarence, Crystal Franco, and Ari Schuler. "Billions for Biodefense: Federal Agency Biodefense Funding, FY2006–FY2007." *Biosecurity and Bioterrorism: Biodefense Strategy, Practice, and Science* 4, no. 2 (2006): 86–96.

Langmuir, Alexander. "The Surveillance of Communicable Diseases of National Importance." *New England Journal of Medicine* 268, no. 4 (1963): 182–92.

Latour, Bruno. *Reassembling the Social: An Introduction to Actor-Network Theory*. Oxford: Clarendon, 2005.

Ledford, Heidi. "Call to Censor Flu Studies Draws Fire." News in Focus. *Nature* 481, no. 7379 (2012): 9–10.

Legters, Llewellyn J., Linda H. Brink, and Ernest T. Takafuji. "Are We Prepared for a Viral Epidemic Emergency?" In Morse, *Emerging Viruses*, 269–82.

Lev, Ori, and Limor Samimian-Darash. "Biosecurity Policy in the US: A Critical Assessment." *Frontiers in Public Health* 2 (2014): 110.

Lipkin, W. Ian. "Biocontainment in Gain-of-Function Infectious Disease Research." *mBio* 3, no. 5 (2012). doi: 10.1128/mBio.00290-12

Lipsitch, Marc, Steven Riley, Simon Cauchemez, Azra C. Ghani, and Neil M. Ferguson. "Managing and Reducing Uncertainty in an Emerging Influenza Pandemic." *New England Journal of Medicine* 361, no. 2 (2009): 112–15.

Luhmann, Niklas. *Observations on Modernity*. Translated by William Whobrey. Stanford: Stanford University Press, 1998.

Luhmann, Niklas. *Risk: A Sociological Theory*. Berlin: Walter de Gruyter, 1993.

Lurie, Nicole, Jeffrey Wasserman, and Chistopher D. Nelson. "Public Health Preparedness: Evolution or Revolution?" *Health Affairs* 25, no. 4 (2006): 935–45.

MacPhail, Theresa. *The Viral Network: A Pathography of the H1N1 Influenza Pandemic*. Ithaca: Cornell University Press, 2014.

Mahajan, Manjari. "Designing Epidemics: Models, Policy-Making, and Global Foreknowledge in India's AIDS Epidemic." *Science and Public Policy* 35, no. 8 (2008): 585–96.

Maher, Brendan. "Bird Flu Research: The Biosecurity Oversight." *Nature* 485, no. 7399 (2012): 431–4.

Maher, Brendan. "Crisis Communicator." *Nature* 463, no. 14 (2010): 150–2.

Mair, Michael, Beth Maldin, and Brad Smith. "Passage of S. 3678: The Pandemic and All-Hazards Preparedness Act." *Biosecurity and Bioterrorism* 5, no. 1 (2007): 72–4.

Mann, James. *Rise of the Vulcans: The History of Bush's War Cabinet*. New York: Viking, 2004.

Marcus, George Marcus and Erkan Saka. "Assemblage." *Theory, Culture and Society* 23, no. 2–3 (2006): 101–6.

Markel, Howard, Lawrence O. Gostin, and David P. Fidler. "Extensively Drug-Resistant Tuberculosis: An Isolation Order, Public Health Powers, and Global Crisis." *JAMA* 298, no. 1 (2007): 83–6.

Masco, Joseph. *The Theater of Operations. National Security Affect from the Cold War to the War on Terror*. Durham: Duke University Press, 2014.

McNeil, Donald G., Jr. "'Zika Is No Longer a Global Emergency,' W.H.O. Says," *New York Times*, November 19, 2016.

Médecins Sans Frontières. *Pushed to the Limit and Beyond: A Year into the Largest Ever Ebola Outbreak*. Geneva: Médecins Sans Frontières, 2015.

Mohr, Norma. *Malaria: Evolution of a Killer*. Seattle: Serif and Pixel, 2001.

Moon, Suerie, Devi Sridhar, Muhammad A Pate, Ashish K Jha, Chelsea Clinton, Sophie Delaunay, Valnora Edwin, Mosoka Fallah, David P Fidler, Laurie Garrett, et al. "Will Ebola Change the Game? Ten Essential Reforms before the Next Pandemic. The Report of the Harvard-LSHTM Independent Panel on the Global Response to Ebola." *The Lancet* 386, no. 10009 (2015): 2204–21.

Morse, Stephen S., ed. *Emerging Viruses*. New York: Oxford University Press, 1993.

Morse, Stephen S. "Epidemiologic Surveillance for Investigating Chemical or Biological Warfare and for Improving Human Health." *Politics and the Life Sciences* 11, no. 1 (1992): 28–9.

Morse, Stephen S. "Regulating Viral Traffic." *Issues in Science and Technology* 7, no. 1 (1990): 81–4.

National Institute for Allergy and Infectious Disease. *Report of the Blue Ribbon Panel on Influenza Research*. Bethesda, MD, 2006.

National Research Council. *Biotechnology Research in an Age of Terrorism*. Washington, DC: National Academies Press, 2004.

National Science Advisory Board for Biosecurity. *Proposed Framework for the Oversight of Dual Use Life Sciences Research: Strategies for Minimizing the Potential Misuse of Research Information*. Bethesda, MD, 2007.

National Security Resources Board. *United States Civil Defense*. NSRB Doc. 128. Washington, DC: Government Printing Office, 1950.

Neustadt, Richard E., and Harvey V. Fineberg. *The Epidemic That Never Was: Policy Making and the Swine Flu Scare*. New York: Vintage, 1983.

Nguyen, Vinh-Kim. "Antiretroviral Globalism, Biopolitics, and Therapeutic Citizenship." In *Global Assemblages: Ethics, Technology and Politics as Anthropological Problems*, edited by Aihwa Ong and Stephen J. Collier, 124–44. Malden, MA: Blackwell, 2004.

O'Toole, Tara, Michael Mair, and Thomas V. Inglesby. "Shining Light on 'Dark Winter.'" *Clinical Infectious Diseases* 34, no. 7 (2002): 972–83.

Opitz, Sven. "Regulating Epidemic Space: The *Nomos* of Global Circulation." *Journal of International Relations and Development* 19, no. 2 (201): 263–84.

Palese, Peter. "Don't Censor Life-Saving Science." World View. *Nature* 481, no. 7380 (2012): 115.

Palese, Peter, and Taia T. Wang. "H5N1 Influenza Viruses: Facts, not Fear." *Proceedings of the National Academy of Sciences* 109, no. 7 (2012): 2211–3.

Patrone, Daniel, David Resnik, and Lisa Chin. "Biosecurity and the Review and Publication of Dual-Use Research of Concern." *Biosecurity and Bioterrorism* 10, no. 3 (2012): 2090–8.

Peiris, J. S. M., L. L. M. Poon, and Y. Guan. "Surveillance of Animal Influenza for Pandemic Preparedness." *Science*, March 9, 2012, 1173–4.

Posner, Richard A. *Catastrophe: Risk and Response*. New York: Oxford University Press, 2005.

Preston, Richard. *The Cobra Event*. New York: Ballantine, 1998.

Quammen, David. *Spillover: Animal Infections and the Next Human Pandemic*. New York: W. W. Norton, 2012.

Quarantelli, E. L. *Disaster Planning, Emergency Management and Civil Protection: The Historical Development of Organized Efforts to Plan For and to Respond to Disasters*. Newark, DE: Disaster Research Center, University of Delaware, 2000. http://udspace.udel.edu/handle/19716/673.

Rabinow, Paul. *Anthropos Today: Reflections on Modern Equipment*. Princeton: Princeton University Press, 2003.

Reardon, Sara. "US Plan to Assess Risky Disease Research Shapes Up." *Nature News*, October 1, 2015.

Redfield, Peter. "Doctors Without Borders and the Moral Economy of Pharmaceuticals." In *Human Rights in Crisis*, edited by Alice Bullard, 129–44. Aldershot, UK: Ashgate, 2008.

Redfield, Peter. "A Less Modest Witness: Collective Advocacy and Motivated Truth in a Medical Humanitarian Movement." *American Ethnologist* 33, no. 1 (2006): 3–26.

Redfield, Peter. *Life in Crisis: The Ethical Journal of Doctors Without Borders*. Berkeley: University of California Press, 2013.

Redfield, Peter. "Medical Vulnerability, or Where There Is No Kit." *Limn* 5 (2015). limn.it/medical-vulnerability-or-where-there-is-no-kit.

Rose, Dale. "How Did the Smallpox Vaccination Program Come About?" In Lakoff and Collier, *Biosecurity Interventions*, 89–120.

Rosen, George. *A History of Public Health*. Baltimore: Johns Hopkins University Press, 1993.

Rosenberg, Charles E. "Pathologies of Progress: The Idea of Civilization as Risk." *Bulletin of the History of Medicine* 72, no. 4 (1998): 714–30.

Rosenberg, Charles E. "What Is an Epidemic? AIDS in Historical Perspective." *Daedalus* 118, no. 2 (1989): 1–17.

Rumsfeld, Donald H. "Transforming the Military." *Foreign Affairs*, May/June 2002. https://www.foreignaffairs.com/articles/2002-05-01/transforming-military.

Sandman, Peter M. "Acknowledging Uncertainty." http://www.psandman.com/col/uncertin.htm

Schwarzinger, Michael, Rémi Flicoteaux, Sébastien Cortarenoda, Yolande Obadia, and Jean-Paul Moatti. "Low Acceptability of A/H1N1 Pandemic Vaccination in French Adult Population: Did Public Health Policy Fuel Public Dissonance?" *PLoS ONE* 5, no. 4 (2010). http://dx.doi.org/10.1371/journal.pone.0010199.

Sencer, David J., and J. Donald Millar. "Reflections on the 1976 Swine Flu Vaccination Program." *Emerging Infectious Diseases* 12, no. 1 (2006): 29–33.

Sherry, Michael. *Preparing for the Next Air War: American Plans for Postwar Defense, 1941–1945*. New Haven: Yale University Press, 1977.

Silverman, Chloe. "How Do You Spot a Healthy Honey Bee?" *Limn* 3 (2013). http://limn.it/how-do-you-spot-a-healthy-honey-bee.

Simonson, Stewart. "Reflections on Preparedness." *Saint Louis University Journal of Health Law and Policy* 4, no. 5 (2010): 5–33.

Slovic, Paul, Howard Kunreuther, and Gilbert F. White. "Decision Processes, Rationality, and Adjustment to Natural Hazards." In *Natural Hazards:*

Local, National, Global, edited by Gilbert F. White, 187–205. New York: Oxford, 1974.

"Special Report: The 1918 Flu Virus Is Resurrected." *Nature* 437 (October 6, 2005): 794–95.

Sunstein, Cass R. *Risk and Reason: Safety, Law, and the Environment.* Cambridge: Cambridge University Press, 2002.

Sunstein, Cass R. *Worst-Case Scenarios.* Cambridge, MA: Harvard University Press, 2007.

Sylves, Richard T. "Adopting Integrated Emergency Management in the United States: Political and Organizational Challenges." *International Journal of Mass Emergencies and Disasters* 9, no. 3 (1991): 413–24.

Tanne, Janice Hopkins. "Tuberculosis Case Exposes Flows in International Public Health Systems." *BMJ: British Medical Journal* 334, no. 7605 (2007): 1187.

Ticktin, Miriam. "Where Ethics and Politics Meet: The Violence of Humanitarianism in France." *American Ethnologist* 33, no. 1 (2006): 33–49.

United Nations. *Protecting Humanity from Future Health Crises: Report of the High-level Panel on the Global Response to Health Crises.* Geneva, January 25, 2016.

United Nations General Assembly. *Report of the United Nations Conference on Environment and Development.* A/CONF.151/26, vol. 1. Rio de Janeiro, June 3–14, 1992.

U.S. Department of Defense. *Quadrennial Defense Review Report.* Washington, DC, September 30, 2001. http://archive.defense.gov/pubs/qdr2001.pdf.

U.S. Department of Health and Human Services. *HHS Pandemic Influenza Plan.* Washington, DC, November 2005. https://www.cdc.gov/flu/pandemic-resources/pdf/hhspandemicinfluenzaplan.pdf.

U.S. Department of Health and Human Services. "Pandemic Planning Update: Report from Secretary Michael O. Leavitt." Washington, DC, March 13, 2006. https://www.hsdl.org/?view&did=462040.

U.S. Department of Health and Human Services, Secretary. *Charter of National Science Advisory Board for Biosecurity.* Washington, DC, March 15, 2016. http://osp.od.nih.gov/sites/default/files/NSABB_Charter_2016.pdf.

U.S. Department of Homeland Security. *Interim National Preparedness Goal.* Washington, DC, March 31, 2005.

U.S. Department of Homeland Security. *Interim National Preparedness Guidance.* Washington, DC, April 27, 2005.

U.S. Executive Office of the President. *The Federal Response to Hurricane Katrina: Lessons Learned.* Washington, DC: The White House, 2006.

U.S. Homeland Security Council. *Planning Scenarios: Executive Summaries.* Washington, DC, July 2004.

U.S. House Committee on Homeland Security. *The 2007 XDR-TB Incident: A Breakdown at the Intersection of Homeland Security and Public Health.* Report prepared by the majority staff. Washington, DC, September 2007.

Vale, Lawrence J. *The Limits of Civil Defense in the U.S.A., Switzerland, Britain, and the Soviet Union: The Evolution of Policies since 1945.* New York: St. Martin's Press, 1987.

Vogel, Kathleen M. "Biodefense: Considering the Socio-Technical Dimension." In Lakoff and Collier, *Biosecurity Interventions,* 227–55.

Wain-Hobson, Simon. "H5N1 Viral-Engineering Dangers Will Not Go Away." World View. *Nature* 495, no. 7442 (2013): 411.

Wald, Priscilla. *Contagion: Cultures, Carriers, and the Outbreak Narrative.* Durham: Duke University Press, 2008.

Waugh, William L., Jr. "Terrorism, Homeland Security and the National Emergency Management Network." *Public Organization Review* 3, no. 4 (2003): 373–85.

Weber, Max. "Bureaucracy." In *The Essential Weber: A Reader,* edited by Sam Whimster, 245–9. New York: Routledge, 2003.

Weir, Lorna, and Eric Mykhalovskiy. "The Geopolitics of Global Public Health Surveillance in the 21st Century." In *Medicine at the Border: Disease, Globalization, and Security, 1850–Present,* edited by Alison Bashford, 240–63. Basingstoke, UK: Palgrave MacMillan, 2007.

Winner, Langdon. "On Not Hitting the Tar-Baby." In *The Whale and the Reactor: A Search for Limits in an Age of High Technology,* 138–54. Chicago: University of Chicago Press, 1986.

Woolsey, R. James, and Robert H. Kupperman. *America's Hidden Vulnerabilities: Crisis Management in a Society of Networks.* Washington, DC: Center for Strategic and International Studies, 1985.

World Health Organization. *ERF: Emergency Response Framework.* Geneva: World Health Organization, 2013.

World Health Organization. *Global Crises—Global Solutions: Managing Public Health Emergencies of International Concern through the Revised International Health Regulations.* WHO/CDS/CSR/GAR/2002.4. Geneva: World Health Organization, 2002.

World Health Organization. *Guidance for the Use of Annex 2 of the International Health Regulations (2005).* Geneva: World Health Organization, 2010.

World Health Organization. *Implementation of the International Health Regulations (2005),* 64th World Health Assembly, WHO A64/10. Geneva, May 5, 2011.

World Health Organization. *Influenza Pandemic Plan: The Role of WHO and Guidelines for National and Regional Planning.* WHO/CDS/CSR/EDC/99.1. Geneva: World Health Organization, 1999.

World Health Organization. *International Health Regulations (2005)*. 2nd ed. Geneva: World Health Organization, 2008.

World Health Organization. *International Health Regulations (2005): Areas of Work for Implementation*. WHO/CDS/EPR/IHR/2007.1. Geneva: World Health Organization, 2007. http://www.who.int/ihr/finalversion9Nov07.pdf.

World Health Organization. *Progress Report on the Development of the WHO Health Emergencies Program*. March 30. Geneva: World Health Organization, 2016.

World Health Organization. Report by the Secretariat. *Ensuring WHO's capacity to prepare for and respond to future large-scale and sustained outbreaks and emergencies*. EB136/49. January 9. Geneva: World Health Organization, 2015.

World Health Organization. *Report of the Ebola Interim Assessment Panel*. A68/25. Geneva: World Health Organization, 2015.

World Health Organization. *Report on Technical Consultation on H5N1 Research Issues*. Geneva, February 16–17, 2012. http://www.who.int/influenza/human_animal_interface/mtg_report_h5n1.pdf.

World Health Organization. "Revision of the International Health Regulations: Progress Report, May 2002." *Weekly Epidemiological Record* 77, no. 19 (2002): 157–60.

World Health Organization. *WHO Guidance for the Use of Annex 2 of the International Health Regulations (2005)*. WHO/HSE/IHR/2010.4. Geneva: World Health Organization, 2008.

World Health Organization. *The World Health Report 2007: A Safer Future: Global Public Health Security in the 21st Century*. Geneva: World Health Organization, 2007.

World Health Organization. African Region. "Situation Report 2 Ebola Virus Disease, West Africa." Brazzaville, Congo, April 17, 2014.

World Health Organization Director-General. *Implementation of the International Health Regulations: Report of the Review Committee on the Role of the International Health Regulations (2005) in the Ebola Outbreak and Response*. 69th World Health Assembly, WHO A69/21. Geneva, May 13, 2016.

World Health Organization Global Influenza Programme. *Pandemic Influenza Preparedness and Response: A WHO Guidance Document*. Geneva: World Health Organization, 2009.

Wright, Susan P. "Terrorism and Biological Weapons: Forging the Linkage in the Clinton Administration." *Politics and the Life Sciences* 25, no. 1–2 (2006): 57–115.

Wright, Susan. *Molecular Politics: Developing American and British Regulatory Policy for Genetic Engineering, 1972–1982*. Chicago: University of Chicago Press, 1994.

Wynne, Brian. "May the Sheep Safely Graze? A Reflexive View of the Expert–Lay Knowledge Divide." In *Risk, Environment and Modernity: Towards a New Ecology*, edited by Scott Lash, Bronislaw Szerszynski, and Brian Wynne, 44–83. London: Sage, 1996.

Yoshpe, Harry. *A Case Study in Peacetime Mobilization Planning: The National Security Resources Board*. Washington, DC: Executive Office of the President, 1953.

"The Zika Virus Public Health Emergency: 6 Months On." *The Lancet*, 388 no. 10003, (2016): 449.

Index

actuarial devices: accumulation of vital statistics, 102; invention of, 103, 113
advance-purchase agreements, 105, 108, 115
Advisory Committee on Immunization Practices (ACIP), 42, 57, 58
African bush meat, 104
Agence France-Presse, 70, 108, 189n30
alert and response, 104–14; access to pandemic vaccine, 105; actuarial device, 113; advance-purchase agreements with pharmaceutical companies, 105, 108; Chan, Margaret, 106; criticism of, 108–9; in Europe, 108–9; in France, 108–9; H1N1 virus, 106, 107, 108; measurement of severity, 104, 107, 108, 110, 189n21; national treatment protocols, 107; novel subtype of influenza (H1N1), 112; pandemic 2009 (H1N1) virus, 106; Pandemic Evaluation Group, 107; problem of the denominator, 106; question of how to define a pandemic, 105; rates of hospitalization, 107; sentinel devices, 113–14; serological surveys, 106; in the U.S., 107–8, 112; vaccine prioritization scheme, 107; WHO pandemic declaration, 104–6; WHO pandemic declaration, criticism of, 109–11

Alexander, Russell, 42–43, 44
Alibek, Ken, 50
all-hazards planning, 28, 62
American College of Emergency Physicians, 64
American Society of Tropical Medicine and Hygiene, 143
America's Forgotten Pandemic: The Influenza of 1918 (Crosby), 59
America's Hidden Vulnerabilities (Kupperman and Woolsey), 47–48, 179n32
ANSER Institute for Homeland Security, 52
"Are We Prepared for a Viral Epidemic Emergency?" (report), 145
Asilomar conference (1975), 121–22, 129, 193nn16,17
assemblage: concept of, 122, 172n9, 187n1, 193n19; of disparate elements, 7, 12; of pandemic preparedness, 122–25; term assemblage, 122–23, 193n21
Associated Press, 152, 153
avian influenza, 67
avian influenza pandemic, 10
avian influenza pandemic (2005), 35–36
Aylward, Bruce, 158

Beck, Ulrich, 16, 19
Besser, Richard, 108